7/11

The Complete Guide to

# Helping Your Baby Sleep Through the Night So You Can Too:

## 101 Tips and Tricks Every Parent Needs to Know

By Jessica Linnell

THE COMPLETE GUIDE TO HELPING YOUR BABY SLEEP THROUGH THE NIGHT SO YOU CAN TOO: 101 TIPS AND TRICKS EVERY PARENT NEEDS TO KNOW


1405 SW 6th Avenue • Ocala, Florida 34471 • Phone 800-814-1132 • Fax 352-622-1875
Web site: www.atlantic-pub.com • E-mail: sales@atlantic-pub.com
SAN Number: 268-1250



Library of Congress Cataloging-in-Publication Data

Linnell, Jessica, 1979-
The complete guide to helping your baby sleep through the night so you can too : 101 tips and tricks every parent needs to know / by Jessica Linnell.
p. cm.
Includes bibliographical references and index.
ISBN-13: 978-1-60138-392-1 (alk. paper)
ISBN-10: 1-60138-392-4 (alk. paper)
1. Infants--Sleep. 2. Parent and infant. 3. Infants--Development. I. Title.
BF720.S53L56 2010
649'.122--dc22

2009054426



PROJECT MANAGER: Melissa Peterson • mpeterson@atlantic-pub.com
PEER REVIWER: Marilee Griffin • PRE-PRESS & PRODUCTION DESIGN: Holly Marie Gibbs
INTERIOR DESIGN: Samantha Martin

Printed on Recycled Paper

Printed in the United States

**We recently lost our beloved pet "Bear," who was not only our best and dearest friend but also the "Vice President of Sunshine" here at Atlantic Publishing. He did not receive a salary but worked tirelessly 24 hours a day to please his parents. Bear was a rescue dog that turned around and showered myself, my wife, Sherri, his grandparents Jean, Bob, and Nancy, and every person and animal he met (maybe not rabbits) with friendship and love. He made a lot of people smile every day.**

**We wanted you to know that a portion of the profits of this book will be donated to The Humane Society of the United States.** ***–Douglas & Sherri Brown***

---

The human-animal bond is as old as human history. We cherish our animal companions for their unconditional affection and acceptance. We feel a thrill when we glimpse wild creatures in their natural habitat or in our own backyard.

Unfortunately, the human-animal bond has at times been weakened. Humans have exploited some animal species to the point of extinction.

The Humane Society of the United States makes a difference in the lives of animals here at home and worldwide. The HSUS is dedicated to creating a world where our relationship with animals is guided by compassion. We seek a truly humane society in which animals are respected for their intrinsic value, and where the human-animal bond is strong.

Want to help animals? We have plenty of suggestions. Adopt a pet from a local shelter, join The Humane Society and be a part of our work to help companion animals and wildlife. You will be funding our educational, legislative, investigative and outreach projects in the U.S. and across the globe.

Or perhaps you'd like to make a memorial donation in honor of a pet, friend or relative? You can through our Kindred Spirits program. And if you'd like to contribute in a more structured way, our Planned Giving Office has suggestions about estate planning, annuities, and even gifts of stock that avoid capital gains taxes.

Maybe you have land that you would like to preserve as a lasting habitat for wildlife. Our Wildlife Land Trust can help you. Perhaps the land you want to share is a backyard—that's enough. Our Urban Wildlife Sanctuary Program will show you how to create a habitat for your wild neighbors.

So you see, it's easy to help animals. And The HSUS is here to help.

**2100 L Street NW • Washington, DC 20037 • 202-452-1100**
**www.hsus.org**

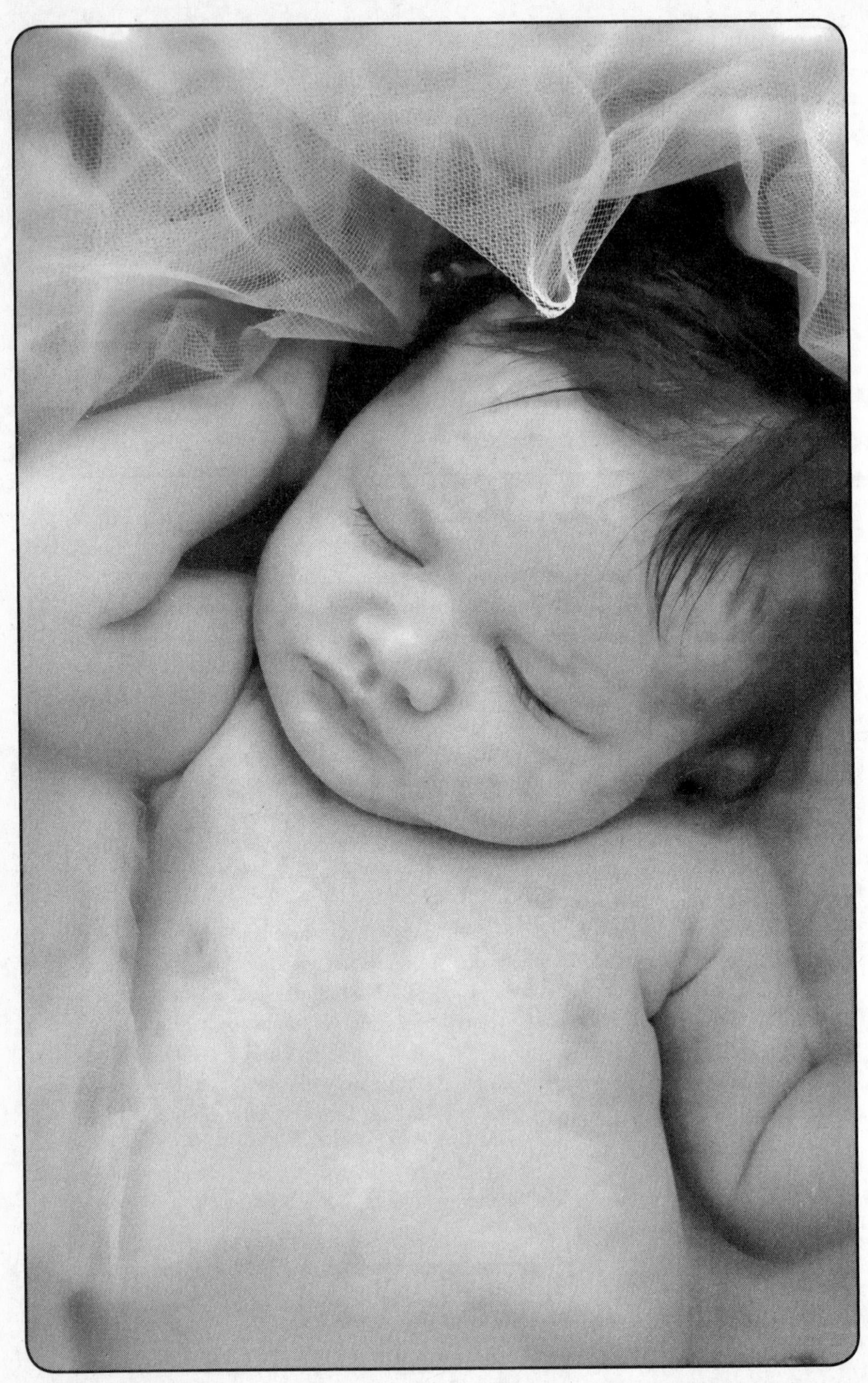

*Photo courtesy of Sivan Grosman, founder of Sivan Photography (**http://sivanphotography.com**)*

# trademarks



# acknowledgments

*Special thanks to Sivan Grosman for contributing such beautiful photographs.*

***http://sivanphotography.com***

# table of contents


## Preface 15

## Introduction 19

## Chapter 1: Baby Sleeping Facts 25

Understand Basic Sleep Facts....26

Understand Your Baby's Sleep Needs....28

Set Realistic Expectations....31

Sleep Patterns Will Change as Your Baby Grows....36

Do Not Expect Too Much Too Soon....37

Healthy Sleep Habits are Taught, Not Naturally Acquired....41

Healthy Sleep Habits are Vital to Good Daytime Functioning....43

Babies Need Practice to Develop Healthy Sleep Habits....44

Crashing is Not a Healthy Sleep Habit....45

Remember Safety When Sleep Training Your Baby....47

## Chapter 2: Current Sleep Habits 51

Create a Sleep Log....51

Analyze Your Completed Sleep Log....53

Use Your Sleep Log to Determine the Best Plan for Your Child and Family....56

Use Sleep Logs to Analyze the Success of the New Sleep Plan....57

## Chapter 3: Causes of Sleep Problems 63

Identify Whether Medical Issues are Affecting Your Baby's Sleep....64

Identify if Anxiety or Psychological Disorders are Affecting Your Baby's Sleep....67

Identify Trained Behaviors that are Affecting Your Baby's Sleep....71

Identify Other Factors that Affect Your Baby's Sleep....72

Some Babies will Take Longer to Learn to Sleep Well Than Others....73

Starting Sleep Training Early Can Prevent Problems From Arising....74

Parents Can Contribute to a Child's Sleep Problems....76

Understand Nighttime Behavior, and Deal with it Appropriately....78

Remember: Almost Every Baby has the Ability to Sleep Well....79

## Chapter 4: Strategies for Getting Your Baby to Sleep 85

Recognize Your Baby's Drowsy Signs....105

Do Not Give Up on Sleep Training if the First Strategy Does Not Work ....106

Decide if Co-sleeping or the Family Bed is Right for You ....107

Know When Your Baby Needs You ....115

Avoid Strategy Jumping ....116

Gradual Approaches are More Prone to Cause Relapses ....117

Parental Inconsistency Often Leads to Bad Sleep Habits ....118

Combat Stalling Tactics Before Your Child Tries Them ....121

Pick a Sleep Strategy that Both Parents are Comfortable With ....123

Do Not Make Decisions About Sleep Strategies or Change Sleep Strategies in the Middle of the Night ....124

## Chapter 5: Setting the Mood for Sleep 127

Understand that a Baby's Environment Can Enhance or Detract From Her Sleep ....128

Pick the Right Room and Furniture ....130

Pick the Right Bed ....132

Pick the Sound ....134

Pick the Right Sleepwear ....135

Pick the Right Crib Accessories ....136

Pick the Right Bedtime Story ....139

Pick the Right Lighting ....140

Pick the Right Temperature ....141

Pick the Right Smell ....142

Pick the Right Position ....143

Pick the Right Feeding Times ....144

## Chapter 6: Establishing a Routine 151

Plan Your Baby's Bedtime Routine Before Bedtime....................151

Maintain Your Routine Even When Life Gets in the Way ........153

Make Sure Your Baby Knows She is Safe,
Cared for, and Loved Before Bed........................................156

Establish a Realistic Bedtime................................................160

Establish a Realistic Wake-up Time......................................161

Getting Your Baby to Sleep Well
Starts First-thing in the Morning..........................................162

Establish Appropriate and Consistent Naptimes....................163

Do Not Stimulate Your Baby Before Bed ..............................167

Remember: Routines Will Change as Your Baby Ages............168

Do Not Give in to Pleading ...................................................169

## Chapter 7: Breaking Bad Habits 171

Recognize Your Child's Sleep Associations...........................172

It is Not Too Late to Change Sleep Associations ....................173

Replace Bad Sleep Associations with Good Ones ...................175

Taper Off Nighttime Feedings as Your Child Ages..................176

You Baby Should Fall Asleep in the Same Place
He Will Sleep Throughout the Night ....................................177

Your Willpower Must be Greater Than Your Baby's................178

Ask for Help..........................................................................179

Put Yourself in Your Baby's Shoes .......................................181

Do Not Take Frustration Out on Your Baby ...........................181

Exercise Your Child or Stimulate
Your Baby During the Day ...................................................182

## Chapter 8: Napping 187

Know How Long Your Baby Should Nap for His Age..............187

Identify Your Baby's Naptime Associations..............................189

Remember: Almost all Babies and Children Need Naps ..........189

Keep Naptimes and Lengths Consistent –
Even When Nighttime Sleep is Not.............................................191

Put Your Baby to Sleep for Naptime Using
the Same Method You Use for Bedtime ......................................192

Do Not Let Your Baby Nap Too Late in the Day .......................193

Do Not Rush to Comfort Your Baby
if He Stirs During Naptime..........................................................195

Not All Children are Impacted the
Same by Naptime Discrepancies ................................................196

Do Not Skip Naps in Order For
Your Baby to Sleep Better at Night.............................................197

If Your Baby Refuses to Nap, Insist on a Rest Time Instead .....198

## Chapter 9: Older Siblings and Multiple Births 203

Pick Appropriate Bed Times for Each Child Separately...........203

Do Not be Afraid of Waking Older Children.............................204

Involve Older Children in the Process .......................................205

Ensure Healthy Sleep Habits of Older
Children Before the Baby's Arrival.............................................206

Mold Older Children in to "Heavy" Sleepers ...........................212

Separate Children During Bedtime if Necessary ......................214

Teach Twins to Fall Asleep Separately ........................................218

Consider Using Separate Cribs or Rooms for Twins ................219

## Chapter 10: Changes in Routine 221

Milestones will Impact Your Child's Sleep Schedule ............... 221

Stress Can Impact Your Baby's Sleep ............... 222

After a Temporary Routine Change or Illness, Resume the Normal Schedule ASAP ............... 223

Do Not Disrupt Your Baby's Sleep Schedule to Accommodate Visiting Family or Friends ............... 224

Do Not be Discouraged if Old Techniques Stop Working ............... 225

Be Patient and Know that Temporary Periods of Disrupted Sleep are Normal ............... 226

## Chapter 11: Sleepless Parents 231

Identify Root Causes of Sleepless Nights ............... 231

Create Order and Structure in Your Own Life ............... 233

De-stress Before Your Bedtime and Create a Bedtime Routine for Yourself ............... 234

Give Yourself Time to Relearn How to Sleep Through the Night ............... 236

Exercise Daily ............... 237

Avoid Caffeine or Other Stimulants Late in the Day ............... 238

Eat Healthy During the Day and Avoid Big Meals Before Bedtime ............... 239

Create a Relaxing Environment Conducive to Sleep ............... 240

## Chapter 12: When All Else Fails 243

Take a Break ............... 243

Do Not Play the Blame Game ............... 244

Remind Yourself that Sleep Training is Worth the Effort ............... 245

Get More Help ............... 245

## Conclusion 251

## Appendix A: Checklists, Sleep Logs, and Charts 255

Average Sleep Needs of Babies and Toddlers....255

Weekly Sleep Log....256

Weekly Daytime Sleep Log....257

Weekly Daytime Feeding Log....258

Weekly Diaper Log....259

Setting the Mood Checklist....260

## Appendix B: Expert Biographies and Contact Information 263

## Appendix C: Additional Resources 273

Books on Babies....273

Books on Adult Sleep....274

Books on Baby/Toddler Sleep....275

Books on Co-Sleeping....276

Web Sites....276

Helpful Organizations....279

Other SIDS Web Sites/Articles....280

## Bibliography 281

## Author Biography 283

## Index 285

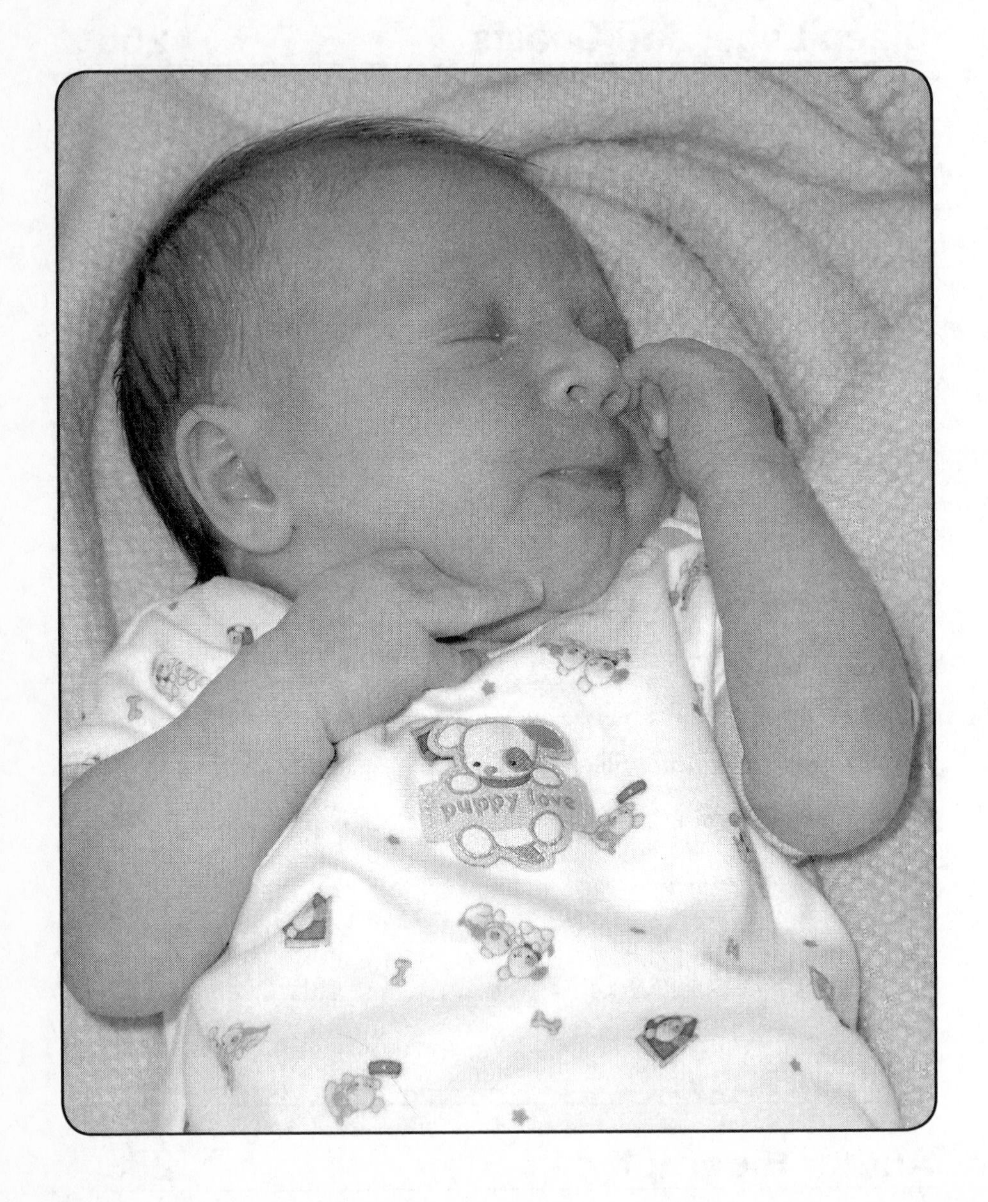
puppy love

# preface

New parents often ask friends, pediatricians, and maybe even the woman behind the counter at the supermarket the question that this book sets out to answer: How can I get my baby to sleep through the night? No matter how many people these parents ask, chances are they get a different answer each time. Countless books have been written about the subject. Some claim letting a baby cry it out is the only way to move toward a full night's sleep. Other books tout no-cry methods as a guaranteed method that works.

After hours of research and countless interviews with experts, it may seem there is no one solve-all method, technique, tip, or trick to get your baby to sleep through the night. This does not mean getting your baby to sleep at night is impossible. On the contrary, many ways exist. Though not all methods will work for all babies or for all families, almost all babies, barring serious medical conditions, have the ability to sleep well.

This book was written to educate you, whether you are a new parent or have three children already, about how to effectively get your baby to sleep through the night, now and in the future. This book will teach you the basic sleep needs and habits of babies, how to objectively analyze the different strategies for getting babies to sleep through the night, and help you decide the best method for your family. Experts in childcare and sleep, pediatricians, and parents were interviewed for this book and will offer their advice. Whether you are struggling with getting your baby to sleep or are reading this book to prevent problems before they arise, you will find tips, techniques, strategies, and tricks to help your whole family enjoy a restful night.

Unlike many other books written on this subject, in this book, no one method or technique is favored over another. Each technique will be presented objectively with advantages and disadvantages listed for each technique or method described. Ultimately, as a parent, you must decide the method that is right for your baby and your family. You must also come to an agreement with your partner about which strategy you will employ before a problem presents itself. Teaching a baby to sleep can be stressful to even the most stable relationships. And yes, a baby can be – and, many argue, *needs* to be – taught how to sleep.

Because no one correct answer exists, and because opinions vary so widely regarding the best method, some opinions or expert advice contained in this book may seem contradictory. Even the experts do not completely agree on a best or worst sleep strategy. When the advice or opinions of experts are presented, many different viewpoints will be offered. You should read all the advice and opinions with an open mind. Once you have read through the whole book, decide which strategies might be best for your family. Sit down with your partner and discuss your top picks. Weigh the pros and cons of each option, and be sure you and your partner agree (and are comfortable with) your selection.

Remember: Sleep is important for you, your partner, and your baby. Although it might take some dedication to develop a routine that works for everyone involved, it will be well worth the work. Sleep deprivation might not be completely avoidable with a new baby, but with the tips in this book and the advice from experts, sleep deprivation should be short lived. Soon, you, your partner, and your baby will be enjoying the rest you need. Do not be tempted to give up sleep training just because it does not seem to work immediately. Teaching your baby to sleep well takes time, but if plans are followed consistently and no medical issues are involved, it will come sooner than you might expect.

Please note that this book is not a substitute for medical advice. The experts in this book have varying opinions on many parenting issues, from the best sleep training method to when to quit overnight feedings. Only you and your child's pediatrician can decide what strategies are best for your child. If you have concerns about your baby's sleeping or eating cycle, consult your child's pediatrician.

Enjoy your reading, and happy sleeping.

SUPER PUPPY
TO THE RESCU

# introduction

If you are reading this book as a new parent, you are likely already overwhelmed by all the changes in your life. A lack of sleep can exaggerate this feeling and cause you to question your sanity at times. Maybe you are an expectant parent who is already worried about losing sleep once your baby arrives. Maybe you are reading this book because while your first two children were "perfect" sleepers, your newest member of the family will not sleep more than two hours a night. Whatever your situation, this book will offer valuable advice so you, your family, and your baby can enjoy a full night's sleep.

Sleep deprivation is a sleeping disorder characterized by having too little sleep. New parents experience sleep deprivation at alarming rates. Many new parents try to follow the popular saying "sleep when your baby sleeps," but are often too anxious about leaving the baby along long enough to accomplish this, or they find their time is better spent catching up on other household duties they have let slide. Even parents of older babies often experience sleep deprivation due to childcare responsibilities — especially if they have older children to care for as well. By the time everyone is home from work and after-school activities, dinner is made, and the kids are in bed, parents must find time to clean, pay bills, and give their personal relationships some attention. Parents often must make the decision of sleeping or letting these responsibilities slide.

According to the National Sleep Foundation (**www.sleepfoundation.org**), newborns sleep a total of 10.5 to 18 hours a day on an irregular schedule, with periods of one to three hours spent awake. Though this may seem like a long time, these periods of sleep often do not last more than a few hours. Newborns typically eat every two to four hours, and in the beginning must be awaken to be fed. Even if a new parent sleeps during these short periods, it is impossible to sleep deeply enough to get the rest you need when you must feed your baby every few hours.

Sleep deprivation can cause a series of physical issues, ranging from mild to extremely problematic including irritability, dizziness and nausea, headaches, memory lapses, increased blood pressure, obesity, and in new mothers, postpartum depression. The National Commission on Sleep Disorders Research found that infant abuse may be more likely for sleep-deprived parents. These parents may be more likely to be aggressive to a crying baby. Even more, the National Sleep Foundation found that more than 1,500 people die each year due to fatigue-related vehicle crashes.

As you can see, ensuring your baby sleeps through the night is not only healthy for him or her, it is just as important for you and all those who live in your home, including other children.

This book contains advice from mothers, fathers, sleep experts, child experts, and many others with experience on how to (and how not to) get your baby to sleep through the night. Do no be fooled: Getting an adequate amount of sleep is not just a luxury, but a necessity for productive and loving daytime parenting and functioning. No matter what your situation — stay-at-home mom, working mother, or single mother or father — regular sleep is important. Your baby needs restful sleep as well. As you will read in Chapter 1, good sleep is vital to your baby's daytime functions, growth, and health.

This book offers 101 tips and tricks for teaching your baby to sleep through the night, while providing the facts necessary for you to make the best decisions for your family. While reading this book, keep in mind that teaching a baby to sleep, much like teaching a child anything, will take time and practice. You may have to try a technique for days or even weeks before you see results. You might also find certain techniques do not work for your parenting philosophy, your lifestyle, or your baby's temperament. This book will guide you through choosing the right strategy for your family.

Chapter 4 discusses different strategies for getting babies to sleep through the night. As mentioned in the preface, not all strategies are the same, and some strategies (and experts for that matter) will present contradictory techniques. The best way to decide which method will work for you, your baby, and your family is to be open-minded while reading the strategies. Talk about the options with your pediatrician and partner, and find one that fits best with your baby's personality and your family's lifestyle.

Other chapters describe reasons why your baby may not be sleeping to their potential, including medical factors, behavioral issues, and bad habits or sleep associations you might be encouraging or allowing your baby to develop. Though experts vary on their ideas of the best method for getting a baby to sleep, most agree sleeping through the night is possible in almost every situation and for every family. Rarely, medical issues are the cause of sleep troubles. This means almost all issues can be resolved with behavioral or parenting changes.

A note about gender references throughout the book: In order to avoid repetitive language when referencing babies, the book will use "him" or "her," "he" or "she," and "his" or "hers" interchangeably throughout the book. The strategies used in the book are not particular toward male or female babies, and all strategies can be utilized whether male or female pronouns are used.

Remember: One day your baby will grow into a toddler, a child, and then a teenager. When that day comes, you will drag him out of bed wishing he would sleep less. As with most childhood issues, your baby should outgrow sleep problems. In the meantime, be patient. Read through the advice included in this book. Stay calm when making decisions about sleep strategies. Enjoy the time you have with your baby, and remember that these hard times will pass. Sleep tight!

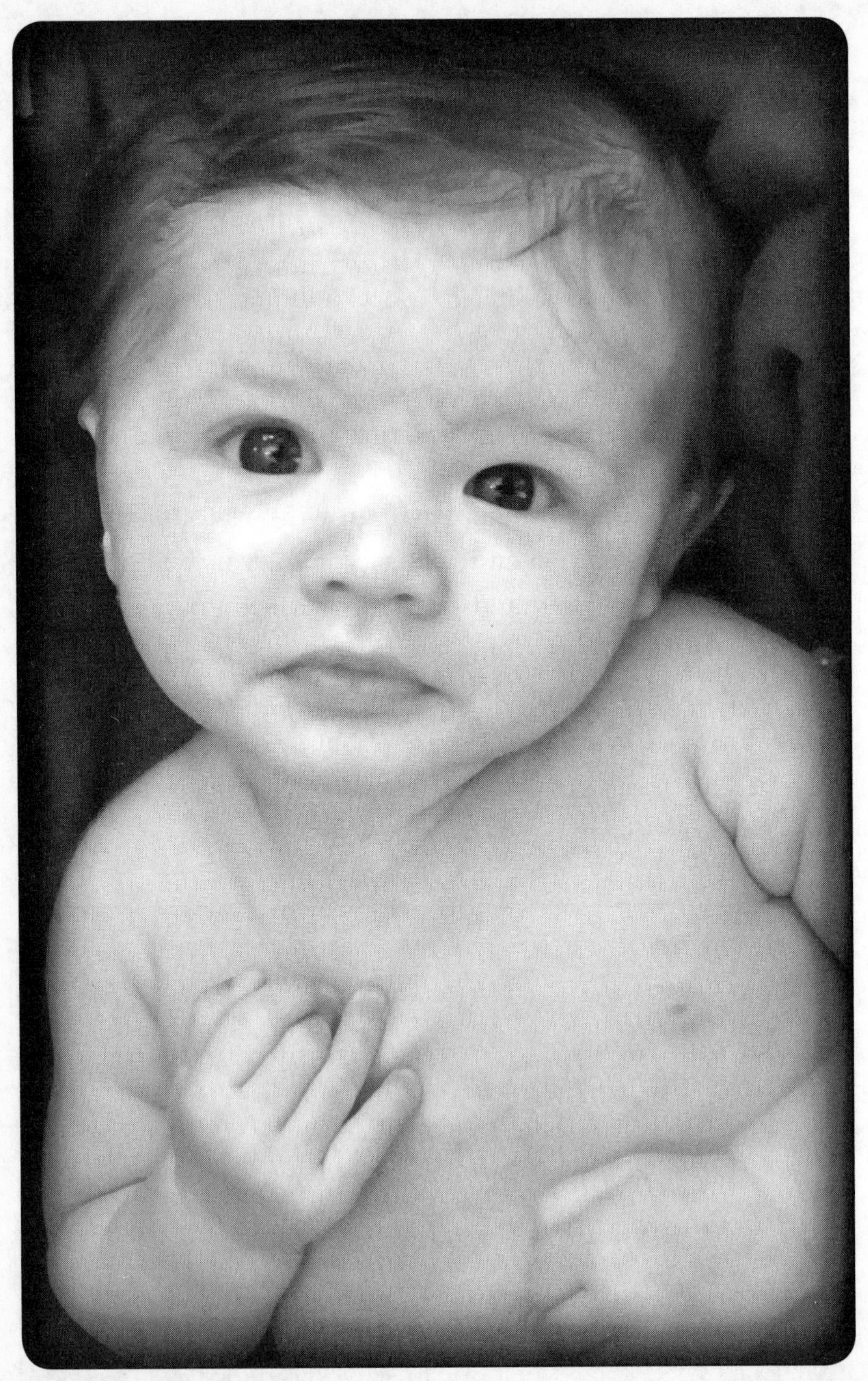

*Photo courtesy of Sivan Grosman, founder of Sivan Photography (**http://sivanphotography.com**)*

# chapter 1

## Baby Sleeping Facts

To teach your baby or child to sleep, you must first understand what he needs to successfully accomplish this task. You must also know what you can realistically expect from him at a particular age and how best to teach him good sleep habits. As Kim West, "The Sleep Lady," described in her book *Good Night, Sleep Tight*, you should think of yourself as a coach when teaching and encouraging your baby to sleep through the night. Just as a football coach would do, you can teach your baby the skills needed, give advice and encouragement, and offer tips when your baby or child "loses" the game. And, just as a coach, you cannot "play" for your baby. Your baby must learn to sleep on his own; he performs the act of sleeping on his own. A coach does not play for his team any more than you can sleep for your baby. The first step in becoming a good sleep coach is to know what your baby needs.

# • TIP #1 •

## Understand Basic Sleep Facts

Before you can teach your baby to sleep through the night, you must first understand basic facts about sleep needs. By knowing the basics regarding sleep and sleep cycles, you can better understand how best to teach your baby to sleep. You also will be able to diagnose sleep issues more thoroughly and effectively if you possess the necessary underlying knowledge.

Though the need to sleep is instinctual, how and when we sleep is a learned behavior, and it is a skill babies must be taught. A baby can, and will, fall asleep on her own when she feels the need to sleep. A newborn's sleep timing system, also known as circadian rhythm, is not fully established. Because this system is still developing, newborns will exhibit irregular sleep schedules. Circadian rhythm is a cyclical period of human activity and rest, which lasts approximately 24 hours. This biological clock regulates all aspects of survival, including sleeping, eating, activity, digesting, and hormonal levels. Circadian rhythm is a cycle of behaviors that all living things exhibit. Although this system and rhythm is instinctively based, it can be altered by external or environmental factors. For instance, daylight can affect one's circadian rhythm. Shift workers can alter their circadian rhythm through artificial light and darkness to adjust their schedule to sleeping during the day and waking to work at night.

Every person's circadian rhythm varies. This phenomenon accounts for why some people are considered night owls and others early birds. Knowing that this instinctual rhythm exists and working within your baby's individual rhythm will help make sleep training easier. If you go against your baby's natural timing, you might encounter more issues with training, but it does not make training impossible. Just as a shift worker can train himself to sleep and wake at different times, you can train your baby to sleep and wake at times different from his natural system. Using external stimulus and environmental cues, you can create a new circadian rhythm for your baby or for yourself, if needed.

Another important aspect of sleep to understand is the different cycles of sleep that occur within the night. Sleep is divided into two types. The first type is rapid eye movement (REM) sleep. During REM sleep, most dreams occur, and our body's systems are much more active than in the second type of sleep. During the second type of sleep, known as non-REM sleep, our heart rate and breathing are regular, and our body is much less "active" than during REM sleep. Throughout the night, we cycle back and forth between REM and non-REM sleep. In between these cycles, we often wake slightly. Many times, we will not remember these slight periods of wakefulness because sleep returns quickly. If for some reason we wake more fully, perhaps due to a change in our environment, falling back asleep may be more challenging.

These sleep cycles are true for both adults and babies (although babies experience more REM sleep than adults). Consequently, babies too will experience these intermittent wakings during the night. Though as adults we know how to fall asleep by ourselves, newborn babies have not yet learned this skill. This situation accounts for why babies wake during the night and cry for their parents. Once a baby has learned to fall asleep on his own, he will also be able to put himself to back to sleep during the night. As a parent, it is important to understand your baby will indefinitely wake during the night. Your job is not to prevent him from waking, but to teach him how to fall back asleep without your assistance.

# • TIP #2 •

## Understand Your Baby's Sleep Needs

Newborns, toddlers, young children, teenagers, and adults have different sleep needs. Although exact sleep patterns and amounts vary from child to child, most newborns sleep approximately 16 hours a day. The problem is, newborns usually do not sleep more than six hours at a time, and sometimes snooze for as few as 20 minutes in a cycle. *See Appendix A for a comprehensive, age-specific sleep chart.*

A newborn often has no distinct pattern of sleep cycles from day to day and can go through seven separate sleep cycles within one day's time. At this young age, your baby will not know the difference between day and night. His sleep patterns will not be consistent from day to day or from nighttime to daytime. Part of good sleep training will consist of teaching your baby the difference between day and night, including that he should sleep more at night than during the day. A newborn will not know this fact, and though you will eventually need to encourage longer sleep periods at night than during the day, your newborn baby is too young to "force" such sleep patterns. At this age, most experts recommend parents hold on for dear life and do whatever they need to do to get through this period of time (including such methods as sleeping when the baby sleeps). You can begin teaching the difference between night and day without enforcing any patterns at this age. *See Chapter 3, Tip #20 for more information about starting sleep training at an early age.*

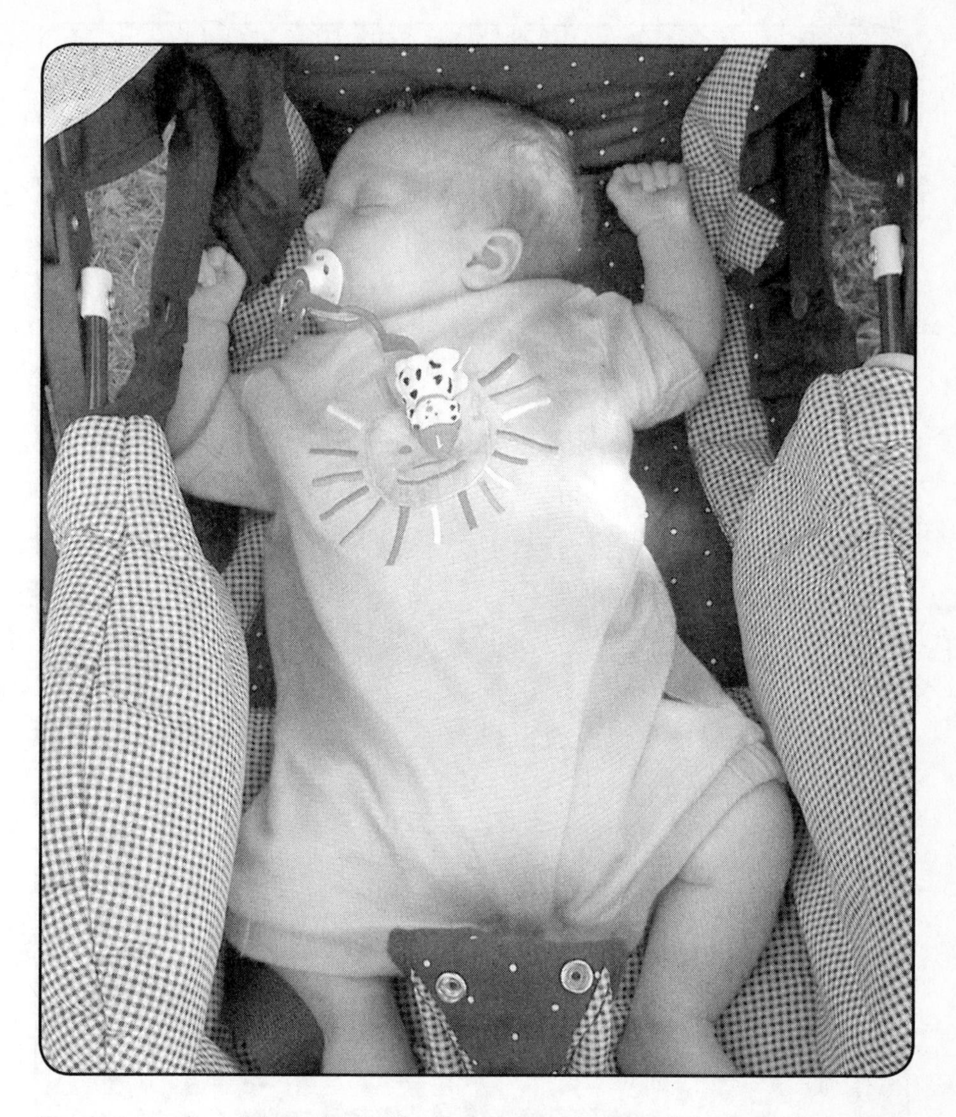

By 3 months old, babies need approximately 13 hours of sleep within a 24-hour period. You may start to notice routine patterns developing in your baby and might see three daytime nap periods begin. Naps will usually be in mid-morning, mid-afternoon, and early evening, the last of which should be the shortest of the three naptimes. Many experts also say babies should be sleeping through the night by this age. *See Tip #3 in this chapter for the definition of sleeping through the night.*

A 6-month-old baby should exhibit more developed sleep patterns, perhaps sleeping nine to 11 hours during the night with two daytime naps (midmorning and mid-afternoon). At this age, your baby will require between 12 and 13 hours of sleep during a day's time.

Your 1-year-old baby will need approximately ten to 12 hours of sleep per day, with one or two naps and usually nine to ten hours of sleep at night. You should find putting your baby to sleep at this age is easier because she is awake for longer spans of time than before.

At 2 years old, your child's sleep needs decrease to only approximately 11 ½ hours per day. He should still nap once after lunch and should sleep nine to ten hours at night.

• Tip #3 •

## Set Realistic Expectations

The first step to setting realistic expectations for your baby is knowing the general parameters that define sleep at each age or stage of development. *Review Tip #2 in this chapter for age-specific guidelines for sleep.* If your baby was born premature, adjust her actual age to meet what her age would be if she had been born on the scheduled due date. Studies have shown developmental stages are based more on how old your baby is according to the conception date more than the birth date. For instance, if your baby is 3 weeks old, but was born one week early, consider him 2 weeks old when trying to apply the guidelines listed in this book (or other general guidelines based on the age of a baby).

The second step to setting realistic expectations is knowing what is considered "sleeping through the night" regarding babies of a specific age. Though most parents would define sleeping through the night as having a baby who sleeps eight to ten continual hours of sleeps, experts disagree. Most studies and experts define sleeping through the night as a baby who sleeps five to six continual hours. This variance in opinions or definitions can create frustration for parents. If your goal is to have your baby sleep eight to ten hours a night, you might have to set your expectations lower until your baby is capable of such long sleep periods. Remember: Most pediatricians recommend newborns eat every two to four hours, depending on whether you are breastfeeding or bottlefeeding your baby. Breastfed babies must be fed more often because mother's milk is digested more quickly. "Sleeping through the night," as defined by most new parents, may not only be impossible, but it may be unhealthy. New parents should consult their pediatrician on how often their newborn should eat and how to this correlates to sleeping through the night, and realize that waking up every few hours for the first month or so is typical.

If your baby is sleeping five to six hours a night, be thankful. Many parents experience situations where their baby will not sleep more than two hours at a time. Remember that your situation is temporary, and be patient. Your baby will soon be able to sleep for longer periods and will adjust to a sleep schedule that more closely matches your own.

Set your expectations based on your own baby and your own situation, not on someone else's experience. You might have a neighbor or relative who brags that her son slept 12 hours a day since birth with never a tear shed at night or a fight to go to bed. Understand that while this situation may exist, it is not the norm. Decide what schedule works best for your baby and your family.

Do not set expectations for your child simply based on what your family or friends think is appropriate, or how long you would like your baby to sleep based on your own schedule.

Pay attention to your baby's natural schedule and his circadian rhythm. Disruption of the cycle — caused by going to bed at an unnatural time or having to get up before our body is "ready" to — causes poor daytime functioning and a general sense of tiredness and irritability. Your baby's biological rhythms begin developing before birth. Working with, not against, your baby's natural rhythm will make sleep time easier for you and your baby.

## CASE STUDY: WORD FROM THE EXPERTS: DEFINITION OF SLEEPING THROUGH THE NIGHT

When it comes to babies, "Sleeping through the night refers to five continual hours of sleep, which usually occurs from 12 a.m. to 5 a.m."

**– Judy Arnall, co-founder of Parenting Canada; owner of Professional Parenting Canada**

Barb Dehn defined sleeping through the night as, "a baby sleeping for more than eight hours in a row." Her son slept through the night when he was about 3 ½ months old, which is when she believes babies are first able to sleep through the night. She said, "By the time a baby weighs 12 pounds or is at least 12 weeks old, she will have the stomach capacity to 'tank up' before bedtime. Research has shown that by this age, babies will start cycling into deeper sleep and are less likely to awake fully by outside noise or stimulus during the night."

**– Barb Dehn, RN, MS, NP**

Laura Heinsohn considered sleeping through the night for a baby as "three to four hours of continuous sleep."

**– Laura Heinsohn, director of Family Bureau of Investigation Parenting Workshops**

"Before a baby is 6 months old, sleeping six hours a night should be considered sleeping through the night. Because babies are growing so fast during this time, it is unreasonable to expect them to sleep more than six hours in a night. Between 6 months and 1 year old, parents can expect their baby to start sleeping eight hours or more. Although babies are still growing rapidly from 6 months to 1 year old, babies are starting to eat heartier meals, which allows them to sleep for longer stretches."

**– Bette Levy Alkazian, MA, licensed marriage and family therapist**

"Sleeping through the night means a baby sleeps for a six-hour stretch," said Linda Kerr. She said she too could sleep during this time and be able to function the next day on that amount of sleep. Though she would have loved her baby to sleep from 10 p.m. to 6 a.m., Kerr was elated to have her baby sleep from 11 p.m. to 5 a.m. Her Baby-Bunching business partner, Cara Fox, agreed. Fox said, "For newborns, a six-hour stretch of uninterrupted sleep is considered sleeping through the night. By the time a baby is 1 year old, she considers ten to 12 hours of uninterrupted sleep as sleeping through the night."

**– Baby Bunching experts Linda Kerr and Cara Fox**

"Before 4 to 6 months old, a baby should not be expected to sleep through the night because he cannot sleep that long without feeding. After a baby has reached 6 months old, sleeping through the night means no longer than eight hours at time (such as from 9 p.m. to 5 a.m.)," said Claudia Heilbrunn. She cautions that a baby should not be required to sleep longer than eight hours.

**– Claudia Heilbrunn, parenting expert, author, and certified life coach**

"Eight to 12 hours' uninterrupted sleep is considered sleeping through the night."

**– Karen Pollak, founder, Babies2Sleep**

"Sleeping through the night is a six- to eight-hour stretch."

**– Stephanie Smith, mother of twins**

"Sleep habits of infants less than 1 year old vary greatly between one baby and another, and with regard to each baby as he or she matures. During the first few weeks of life, the part of the brain that has our "internal clock" (the suprachiasmatic nucleus [SCN] of the hypothalamus) is immature and not synchronized with the day/night cycle. During that period, the baby has short periods of wake and sleep distributed in a random fashion. At around 4 months old, the SCN's activity becomes synchronized with the day/night cycle. Parents can expect that by this age, most of the baby's sleep should occur at night, although it is still fragmented into several short sleep periods, punctuated by awakenings for feeding. It is not until a few months later that babies outgrow these nighttime awakenings and finally sleep through the night."

**– Nadav Traeger, MD, FAAP, FCCP, D, ABSM, director of pediatric sleep medicine, Maria Fareri Children's Hospital**

"While research defines sleeping through the night for a 4-month-old baby as five to six consecutive hours, most parents define sleeping through the night as eight hours. When parents are told their 4-month-old should be sleeping through the night, they often expect their child to sleep eight hours a night instead of the five to six hours the experts are referring to. This misconception can cause parents to expect more than is reasonable for their child's developmental stage." With his practice, Dr. Kuhn listens to the parents' goal for their child and aims for that, as long as it is developmentally appropriate.

**– Dr. Brett Kuhn, CBSM, associate professor of pediatrics at the University of Nebraska Medical Center and Children's Sleep Center at Children's Hospital**

"When a baby sleeps for a six-hour stretch" is sleeping through the night.

**– Dr. Laura Davies, diplomate, American Board of Psychiatry and Neurology**

"Our society has changed; babies have not. In the thousands of years before clocks existed, it is likely babies and mothers napped during the day when tired, and babies woke during the night until they naturally grew beyond that stage. Unfortunately, much pressure exists to get babies to sleep through the night because mothers have to get up and go to work the next day — to places where babies are banned, and where even exhausted mothers are not allowed to nap. Parents should remember this is not the baby's fault. Today's parents are trapped between the ancient life-preserving needs of young children and modern society that is often both rigid and unresponsive to the needs of young families. When it comes down to it, what parents want to know is when they are going to get to sleep thought the night the way they used to in the 'old days.' Sleeping through the night depends on the parent's individual need for sleep."

**– Helen Neville, BS, RN, author, pediatric advice nurse, health educator, specialist in inborn temperament, and researcher**

# • Tip #4 •

## Sleep Patterns Will Change as Your Baby Grows

As shown in Tip #2, as your baby ages, her sleep needs and patterns will change. As your baby grows and develops, her natural sleep timing system, or circadian rhythm, will also mature and change. As naps are reduced or eliminated, her bedtime and wake time will also change to adapt to her new schedule. Her sleep patterns might change when her nighttime feedings stop. Though routines and consistency are preached by experts and recounted in this book, flexibility is still vital. Your baby will change and grow, as will her sleep patterns. As her parent, you must be able to adapt your sleep plan and strategy to her needs and developmental stage.

Other factors will cause changes in your baby's sleep patterns and needs. Many babies begin to experience separation anxiety between 6 and 8 months old. Although this stage is temporary, a baby who may have slept through the night without much trouble at all may seem to suddenly have difficultly sleeping. Teething, illness, potty training, changing beds, and other environmental factors may cause disruptions to your baby's sleep patterns. When evaluating your baby's sleep patterns or habits, recognize what factors could be causing a sudden change in behavior. When Mom returns to work or if Dad goes out of town on business, you may notice a change in your baby's sleep. Pay attention to other causes of stress (such as tension in the marriage, arrival of a new baby, or moving to a new house) or milestones in your baby's life that could trigger a change in sleep patterns.

# • Tip #5 •

## Do Not Expect Too Much Too Soon

Though experts do not agree on the exact age your baby should be when you begin employing sleep tactics, you should only expect as much as is feasible for your baby's age. Some experts feel you should not try to get your baby to sleep through the night until he has done so on his own. Once your baby has slept through the night even once, you will know he is capable of doing so and should feel comfortable encouraging the behavior to continue. Others say you should be flexible with your baby's sleep schedule until he is 3 to 4 months old, and you should follow your baby's schedule until then. Some recommend parents wait until their baby is 4 months old, or 14 pounds. Still, others recommend you wait until your baby is 12 weeks old and weighs at least 12 pounds. And some say you can start employing sleep strategies from Day 1. Talk to your partner and pediatrician to decide the best time for you and your family to begin using the strategies presented in this book.

While your baby is still a newborn, he will require nighttime feedings. Though these feedings will disrupt your and your baby's sleep, these feedings do not have to cause a long period of wakefulness. Nighttime feedings are vital to your baby's health and growth. Most experts feel that by 4 months old, your baby will no longer require nighttime feedings. If he is still waking and "demanding" a feeding once it is no longer necessary, begin weaning him off nighttime feedings *See Chapter 7, Tip #59 for more information on weaning your child from nighttime feedings.*

The National Sleep Foundation reports that by 9 months old, 70 to 80 percent of babies are sleeping nine to 12 hours at night. The foundation also reports that most babies do not get enough sleep. Remember: Not all babies are the same, and just because your baby does not follow the "norm" for his age does not mean he is not a good baby or a good sleeper — or that you are not a good parent. If your baby is not within or near the range expected for his age, you might need to examine whether or not he is getting enough sleep within the day. Be sure you are calculating his total sleep within a 24-hour period. Some babies will sleep more than the usual amount during the night and take shorter naps during the day. Others might take longer naps but sleep less at night. Do not worry too much over the length of each sleep session.

Instead, c[illegible]ate on the total amount of sleep your baby is getting wi[illegible]e day. If his sleep schedule is not within the appropriate [illegible] examine ways to change it. As the saying goes, "sleep beg[illegible] sleep." If he is waking up on his own, it might be because he is overly tired or not getting to bed early enough. Setting an earlier bedtime might encourage your baby to sleep in longer in the morning *See Chapter 6, Tip #49 for more information on setting a bedtime for your child.*

Some babies take longer to learn different things than others. Though one child will catch on to her ABCs in no time, another may struggle longer to grasp the concept. This same philosophy applies to sleeping. Be patient with your child and provide a loving environment where she feels safe learning at her own pace.

## CASE STUDY: WORD FROM THE EXPERTS: AGE TO START EMPLOYING SLEEP TACTICS

Canadian Pediatric Society's recommendation that a baby should be 6 months old before parents start employing sleep tactics is sound.

**– Judy Arnall, co-founder of Parenting Canada; owner of Professional Parenting Canada**

"Parents, especially those who are returning to work, can start employing sleep tactics when a baby is 12 weeks old or weighs 12 pounds."

**– Barb Dehn, RN, MS, NP**

"Parents can start employing tactics for newborns."

**– Laura Heinsohn, director of Family Bureau of Investigation Parenting Workshops**

"Although many doctors recommend waiting until 6 mo[illegible]efore beginning sleep training, many parents will start employin[illegible]s when their baby is younger. Parents should not start too early [illegible]night affect the health of a child (because a younger baby requir[illegible]nighttime feeding because of her rapid growth rate), but once a child [illegible]as slept through the night, tactics can be safely employed. Babies usually will be able to sleep through the night between 4 and 6 months old."

**– Bette Levy Alkazian, MA, licensed marriage and family therapist**

"Parents can begin sleep training when their baby is 3 months old." Fox said that she "Ferberized" her oldest child when he was 2 months old, after being advised to do so by her pediatrician. Looking back, she said she feels it was too early and she would not employ that tactic at that age again. She does, however, believe certain sleep tactics can be used at a young age, such as a warm bath before bed, a substantial nighttime feeding, a bedtime routine, white noise, and darkening shades.

**– Baby bunching experts Linda Kerr and Cara Fox.**
*See Chapter 4 for more on the Ferber method.*

"Many experts will tell parents that when their baby is 4 months old, they can start employing tactics. It will depend on your baby, but usually between 4 and 6 months is an appropriate age to begin sleep training."

**– Claudia Heilbrunn, parenting expert, author, and certified life coach**

"Parents should wait until a baby is at least 12 weeks old and weighs 12 to 15 pounds before they employ sleep tactics."

**– Karen Pollak, founder, Babies2Sleep**

Smith advised parents to start employing tactics from Day 1. "The more time you allow for bad habits to be created, the harder it will be to break them."

**– Stephanie Smith, mother of twins**

"Parents can start a regular bedtime routine when the baby is just a couple months old. At this early age, it should be a simple routine (such as a bath, pajamas, bottle, and dark room), but if done consistently at the same time, it will help cue the baby's developing internal clock to the desired sleep time."

**– Nadav Traeger, MD, FAAP, FCCP, D, ABSM, director of pediatric sleep medicine, Maria Fareri Children's Hospital**

"Parents can start employing some tactics immediately, but [I recommend] parents wait until their baby is 4 to 6 weeks old." Until that age, Kuhn suggested parents sleep when the baby sleeps and "hold on for dear life" to get through this time period. "Once a baby has reached 4 to 6 weeks old, the baby will begin to recognize environmental cues. Parents can then start making nighttime feedings dark, quiet, and boring, and can start trying to structure naptime for their baby."

**– Dr. Brett Kuhn, CBSM, associate professor of pediatrics at the University of Nebraska Medical Center and Children's Sleep Center at Children's Hospital**

Dr. Davies does not recommend sleep training until your baby is between 5 and 6 months old.

**– Dr. Laura Davies, diplomate, American Board of Psychiatry and Neurology**

Neville reminds parents that it is normal for young babies to fall asleep while nursing. "Those experts who teach 'sleep training' suggest waiting till a baby is at least 3 months of age. Before that time, a baby cannot even reliably find a thumb to suck on."

**– Helen Neville, BS, RN, author, pediatric advice nurse, health educator, specialist in inborn temperament, and researcher**

# • Tip #6 •

## Healthy Sleep Habits are Taught, Not Naturally Acquired

Although sleeping is an instinctive trait, sleeping well is a learned behavior. Some researchers have traced the need to sleep at night as an instinct for protection against nighttime predators. In modern times, most of us sleep at night because we work during the day. Shift workers adjust their schedule to sleeping during the day and working at night. Newborns do not have obligations that require them to be awake during daytime hours, nor do they even know the difference between night and day. If we want our babies to sleep at night, we must teach them to do so. Though a relationship exists between daylight and being awake, this tie can be molded by artificial light or artificial dark. A shift worker who has darkening blinds allowing him to sleep during the day and who works in a brightly lit factory at night is creating the same relationship to lightness/darkness that others get naturally from sunlight. This same philosophy can be applied to your baby's sleep; just as you would not expect your child to learn his ABCs after one lesson, do not expect him to learn to sleep in one night. Developing good sleep habits takes consistent coaching and practice. The more your child practices sleeping through the night, the easier it should become. If you are patient and remember that you are teaching your child a new skill, you will experience less frustration and more success with your sleep training.

Another important component to learning to sleep involves teaching a baby to put himself to sleep. Unless you plan to be present every night for the rest of your child's life, he will eventually need to learn to fall asleep and stay asleep without your intervention. Of course, a newborn will and certainly does need your help to fall asleep and will need feedings in the night that will prevent him from staying asleep continually. Once your baby no longer needs nighttime feedings, it will be important to his sleep (and yours) that he is able to put himself to sleep. Teaching this skill sooner rather than later will mean fewer sleepless nights for you both. *See Chapter 4 for more regarding self-soothing techniques to encourage your baby to fall asleep on his own.*

# • Tip #7 •

## Healthy Sleep Habits are Vital to Good Daytime Functioning

Healthy sleep habits should not be viewed as a luxury. As new parents, you may have been told by family, friends, and even your pediatrician to kiss a good night's sleep goodbye. That does not need to be – and should not be – the case. A good night's rest is vital to your and your baby's health. As a parent, being overly tired during the day can lead to irritability and added stress, which can cause a weaker immune system and higher likelihood for developing illness – not to mention make it harder for you to provide a loving and safe environment for your youngster. Your baby will also be stressed, irritable, and cranky if she is not getting enough quality sleep. Do not be misled to think that part of being a parent means giving up sleep. Though you and your baby may (and probably will) experience some sleepless nights as she learns to sleep, or because of illness, colic, or other issues, these situations should be temporary.

Sleep deprivation can affect you and your baby. A sleep-deprived baby can exhibit overly active or wired behaviors, fussiness or irritability, and inability to focus on play or one task. Similar signs of sleep deprivation can be seen in adults. The Nebraska Rural Health and Safety Coalition states that adults need seven to eight hours of sleep a night. Adults who do not get enough sleep at night will be irritable and less productive than their well-rested counterparts. Sleepy adults also face an increased risk of motor vehicle accidents. At the least, sleep deprivation causes less than optimal wakefulness, and the same holds true for babies and adults.

Make sleep a priority in your and your baby's life. Take the time and effort to teach your baby good sleep habits. Although it will require some effort and work and may lead to more sleepless nights at the beginning, it will be worth the effort. For new parents, sleep deprivation can cause serious side effects and may add additional problems to an already stressful time.

## • Tip #8 •

## Babies Need Practice to Develop Healthy Sleep Habits

Be patient as you teach your baby to sleep through the night. Keep in mind that you are in fact teaching your child a new skill. She will need practice to perfect this skill, just as she will need practice learning her ABCs once she is older. Put yourself in your baby's shoes and try to understand her situation. Remember that you might be contributing to her troubled sleep schedule. Be firm in your willpower to teach your baby, but keep a loving and caring attitude during the process. Different techniques will take different amounts of time to learn. And because all babies are different, learning how to sleep will require different lengths of time for each individual baby. Even as adults, we sometimes suffer from bad sleep and go through periods when we have trouble sleeping. Your baby may be going through a similar situation. She may be experiencing separation anxiety, teething, or anxiety about sleeping in a new environment or bed. Try to view the situation from your baby's point of view, and stay calm. If you are stressed or anxious about your baby's sleep (or for any other reason), your baby will sense it and might have more trouble sleeping because of it.

Using sleep logs will help you create a patient environment and encourage you to allow your baby time to learn the skill of sleeping. Sleep logs will also show you progress your baby is making, which might not be evident if you are not logging your baby's sleep schedule regularly. *See Chapter 2 for more information on sleep logs*. Most sleep strategies, if employed consistently, will produce results in a few days to a week. Producing results does not mean your baby will go from sleeping two to three hours a night to nine hours a night in just a few days; the results you see could be slight improvements. Remember to be patient and celebrate the small successes when you are sleep training your baby.

# • Tip #9 •

## Crashing is Not a Healthy Sleep Habit

As a desperate parent, you may feel that keeping your baby up more during the day will ensure a good night's sleep. But that is not at all the case. Experts, moms, and pediatricians all agree: "Sleep begets sleep." The better your baby sleeps during the day, the better he will sleep at night. Also, consider that an overly tired baby often turns into a wired baby. If you were considering this tactic, think again. This book is designed not just to get your baby to sleep, but to teach you how to develop healthy sleep habits for your baby and the rest of your family. Crashing from exhaustion is not healthy for your baby or you and should not be used as a sleep tactic.

If your baby does not seem to be sleeping well or is not sleeping long enough, chances are that you should set his bedtime earlier and encourage longer naps. Although you might be tempted to think that your baby just does not need as much sleep as other babies, this is not likely the case. In most situations, your baby is not getting enough sleep and, therefore, not sleeping as well as possible. Encouraging more sleep should help your baby to sleep longer and for more time throughout the day. If this does not work, ask your pediatrician or a sleep expert to evaluate your situation. Some other condition might be affecting your baby's sleeping (such as medical conditions or external stimuli).

# • Tip #10 •

## Remember Safety When Sleep Training Your Baby

Safety should come first in your baby's life in general, and should also come first when it comes to sleep training. One of the most important safety considerations to remember when it comes to sleep training is sudden infant death syndrome (SIDS). SIDS is the sudden death of an infant 1-year-old or younger that is unexplained after an investigation and autopsy. Most parents report that they put their baby to sleep, checked on the baby later, and found him or her dead. This situation strikes fear into the hearts of all parents. SIDS is the most common cause of death in babies under 1 year old. Babies are at highest risk of SIDS within their first 6 months of life, with approximately 90 percent of SIDS cases occurring during this time. The American Academy of Pediatrics (AAP) states the highest incidence of SIDS occurs between the ages of 2 and 3 months old.

Though SIDS cannot be explained, and no one direct cause of SIDS has been identified, certain steps can be taken to reduce your baby's risk of SIDS. The AAP has suggested many tips for parents to reduce the chance of SIDS in their homes. The following advice comes from the AAP and other baby sleep experts.

Experts recommend that babies should be put to sleep on their backs to help reduce the risk of SIDS. Babies too young to lift their heads should never be placed on their bellies to sleep, whether at night or for a short nap. Suffocation risks are much higher when babies are placed on their bellies. Since 1992, when the AAP first started recommending that babies sleep on their backs, the incidence of SIDS has dropped 50 percent.

Smoking near babies, and especially in the baby's bedroom, also increases a risk of SIDS. Parents should never smoke around their baby and should not smoke in the room the baby sleeps in, even when the baby is not present. Mothers should also avoid smoking during pregnancy. Studies have shown a correlation between mothers who smoked while they were pregnant and SIDS. Action on Smoking and Health's (ASH) Web site contains links to many articles regarding the effects of smoking on women, babies, and overall health. Visit **www.ash.org/women.html** for more information. For help quitting smoking, ask your physician and visit **www.smokefree.gov** or the American Lung Association's Web site **www.lungusa.org**. If you are pregnant, consult your physician or another organization for help in quitting smoking.

A firm mattress with no loose bedding should be used in the baby's crib. The crib should meet safety standards and should not have areas where the baby can get stuck. Keep any items that might cause suffocation out of the crib, including thick blankets, pillows, and stuffed animals. *See Chapter 5 for more information on your baby's crib, mattress, and bedding.*

The AAP recommends babies sleep in the parent's room, but not in the same bed as the parents, to better protect against SIDS. They recommend a safety-approved crib or bassinet be used for the baby to sleep in. The AAP states that studies have shown a link between co-sleeping and SIDS, although the actual increase in risk has not been determined. If parents do decide to co-sleep, safety precautions can be taken to reduce the SIDS risk. These include moving the mattress away from the wall and furniture; not allowing more than two people (Mom and Dad) in the bed with the baby while sleeping; not taking drugs, alcohol, or medications that induce heavy sleep while co-sleeping; not having fluffy pillows, loose bedding, or soft mattress or bedding; and avoiding co-sleeping if one or both parents are obese. *See Chapter 4, Tip #26 for more information on co-sleeping.*

Overheating has also been linked to SIDS. Make sure the room temperature is comfortable, and that your baby is not overly dressed for the temperature. *See Chapter 5 for more on temperature and baby sleepwear.*

The AAP recommends pacifier use for babies at highest risk of SIDS. AAP states studies have shown a correlation between pacifiers and a decrease in SIDS. Breastfeeding mothers are advised to wait until the baby is 1 month old before introducing pacifiers so that good breastfeeding skills can be established. While the exact reason for this reduction in SIDS from pacifier use is not known, some suggest that babies sleep lighter and are more easily aroused when they fall asleep with pacifiers. Deep sleeping is thought to be another contributing factor for SIDS. Though pacifier use in general can be controversial, using pacifiers only in bed and only during the baby's first year of life have not been linked to serious medical conditions, such as dental issues.

The AAP also recommends babies get plenty of daytime (awake) tummy time. They do not recommend the use of SIDS-preventer products, as none of them have been safety tested as of the date of this publication.

Caregivers and babysitters, including family members, should be reminded of these precautions before being left to care for your baby. According to the AAP, 20 percent of SIDS cases occur while the infant is being cared for by someone other than a parent. Be sure to educate all caretakers, even grandparents or relatives, about the risk of SIDS, and remind them that your baby should only be placed on his back to sleep. Relatives might say they always placed babies to sleep on their tummy and that you are being overprotective, but stay firm in your position. Only leave your baby in the care of those who will adhere to your rules for your child's safety.

For more information on SIDS and SIDS prevention, ask your pediatrician, or check **www.sids.org**, **www.aap.org**, or **www.healthychildcare.org**. Also visit the AAP's Healthy Children Web site, **www.healthychildren.org**, for more information.

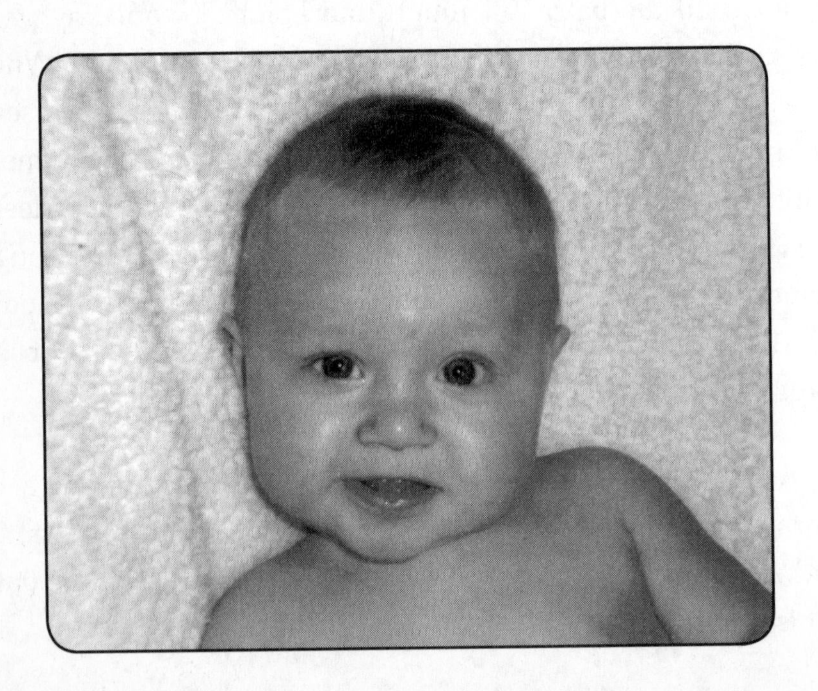

# chapter 2

## Current Sleep Habits

Before trying to change or mold your baby's sleep habits or patterns, you need to analyze her current behaviors. Many experts advocate the use of sleep logs to track or identify issues regarding a baby's sleep patterns and to evaluate the success or failure of strategies. If you are reading this book as an expectant parent, you should use this information to start formulating ideas of what sleep patterns are natural and which ones are the beginnings of bad habits.

## • Tip #11 •

### Create a Sleep Log

During your baby's first year of life, it can be helpful to log many different aspects of your baby's life, including eating, diaper changes, temperament during the day, and sleep. Of course, you will also want to record things like your baby's first smile, first laugh, first eating of solid foods, and first steps. When it comes to sleep training, creating a log will help you recognize your baby's own sleep "clock." All babies, just as all people, have an internal clock or rhythm that helps regulate what time they get hungry, tired, and wakeful. Using a log will help you easily identify your baby's natural schedule. While this schedule might not meet your lifestyle, knowing your baby's rhythm can help you match his natural schedule with yours to best suit you both.

Sleep logs will help you monitor and recognize progress once you begin sleep training. These logs also help you identify irregularities in your schedule that might be affecting your baby's sleep. This step is important to the long-term success of your baby's sleep training. Use the log in Appendix A, find a log online, ask your pediatrician for a log, or create one that works best for you. Whatever you do, do no skip this step.

When starting a sleep log, remember to log more than just sleep times. Write down the events that happened during the day that might impact your baby's schedule (such as a birthday party, doctor's appointment, or visitors). Other helpful information to write down on your log includes what, when, and how much your baby eats; what and when you change diapers; what happened one hour before your baby went to bed (such as bath, feeding, stories, or crying); timing and length of naptimes; time of bedtime; how long it took your baby to fall asleep; where your baby fell asleep (such as in your arms while being rocked, in own crib, or in family bed); number and length of nighttime wakings; number and amount of nighttime feedings; energy levels during the day; baby milestones; and other disruptions to routine.

At this point, do not analyze or make changes to your routine or sleep schedules. Simply write down what is occurring. Once you have logged your baby's daily activities for approximately a week (try to complete seven to ten days), you can begin to look at patterns in your baby's sleep schedule or habits that might be developing in your baby's life.

If creating or using a sleep log seems too tedious or time-consuming, or maybe just too rigid for your personality, consider an alternative type of log. Create a scrapbook-like sleep log if you want something more creative. This type of log could also be used for pictures and to record milestones in your baby's life. If that option does not sound appealing, consider a less formal sleep log. You might use a day planner or calendar to jot down your baby's sleep habits. Using one of these alternative methods could make tallying sleep hours more difficult and could make seeing trends in sleep habits slightly harder. However, these methods are better than not tracking your baby's sleep at all. Find the method that best suits your personality and that you will be committed to sticking to.

## • Tip #12 •

## Analyze Your Completed Sleep Log

Once you have recorded your baby's sleep habits for a week, you should be able to see patterns beginning to develop. You may notice that if your baby sleeps until after 4 p.m. during his last nap, he takes longer to fall asleep at night. Maybe you have found he starts getting drowsy at 7 p.m. but you normally do not put him to sleep until 9 p.m., and by that time, he is fussy and takes longer to fall asleep. The patterns that emerge will be unique to your baby and your family.

When you begin to analyze your log, first read through all your notes to see if any patterns or areas jump out at you as a problem. If so, write that down. Next, add up the total number of hours your baby sleeps during the day and during the night, and the total number of hours he sleeps in a 24-hour period. Record this information for each day, then get an average for the week. (To get the average for seven days, add up the total sleep for each day and divide the total by seven.) Compare your baby's average sleep to the average amount of sleep needed for a baby of his age. *See the chart in Appendix A for this average.* Remember that your baby's sleep habits may vary from the "norm," but you should make sure your baby is getting enough total sleep. As many experts and parents will tell you, sleep begets sleep. If your baby is getting too little sleep, it may be creating a cycle of less and less sleep.

Also analyze your sleep logs for any "bad" behaviors or habits that might be developing. If your baby only falls asleep while nursing, you may need to think about changing this habit. While it might work best for you now, unless you plan on nursing him to sleep every night from now on, it is best to teach him to fall asleep on his own, without relying on a bottle or breast to put him to sleep each night. Also pay close attention to the time it takes your baby to fall asleep, and the number and length of nighttime wakings. If your baby has trouble putting himself to sleep or putting himself back to sleep if he wakes at night, you will need to concentrate your training on teaching him this skill.

If, after looking at your sleep logs, you can see no pattern or find no issues, you may want to ask someone else to look at them. Sleep experts can help analyze the logs and offer advice on what may or may not need to be changed. If you cannot visit a sleep expert, try showing your logs to your child's pediatrician. If you cannot find help elsewhere, consult with a close friend or family member for help analyzing your sleep logs. Sometimes, someone who does not live in your household will be able to see the pattern you are having trouble recognizing. If your baby is still a newborn, you might not yet notice a pattern at all. If your baby is still too young to begin a regimented sleep training program, continue to log his sleep habits until he is. The more information you can gather, the better informed you will be on how to create the best sleep program for your baby when the time comes.

## • Tip #13 •

## Use Your Sleep Log to Determine the Best Plan for Your Child and Family

Once you identify your baby's pattern, you can better decide a schedule for your baby and your family. If you recognize that your baby starts getting drowsy at 8 p.m. every evening, you may decide to make this his permanent bedtime. If for some reason 8 p.m. does not work well for your family — maybe you have a book club every Monday and will not be home until 8:30 p.m. — you should not feel like you are forced to adhere to your baby's natural timing. If you decide to go against your baby's natural clock, just remember that your road to successful sleep training is still possible, but it may have a few more bumps and may take a bit longer.

Once you determine the best sleep time for your baby, work backward from that time to determine when to begin your baby's bedtime routine. If your bedtime routine will last 30 minutes and you have decided to make your baby's bedtime 8 p.m., you will need to start your bedtime routine by 7:30 p.m. each night.

Your sleep logs will help you determine more than just the best time for your baby to go to bed. If you are logging what you do to get your baby to sleep now, you can look for patterns emerging and for your baby's current sleep associations. A sleep association is an activity or object that must be present for your baby or child to fall asleep. If you rock your baby to bed every night and find that if you do not rock him to sleep, he cries, then rocking is a sleep association for your baby. If you sing a lullaby to your baby every night, but he will fall asleep easily without the lullaby, then the lullaby is not a sleep association. If you use your logs to identify your baby's sleep associations, you will be able to more easily make changes as necessary during sleep training.

• Tip #14 •

## Use Sleep Logs to Analyze the Success of the New Sleep Plan

Once you have determined which plan is best for your baby and family, keep your sleep logs going. Using a sleep log during sleep training will help you monitor the progress of your training. Depending on which plan you choose, progress might be slow. Without a sleep log, you may get frustrated with a plan, thinking it is not working when, in fact, progress has been made. Your sleep log might show that your baby is consistently sleeping 15 minutes longer at night than before training started. While you might not notice this slight change, your sleep logs will reflect it. Patience with sleep training is a must, as is determination for success. Using sleep logs during training will help you stick to a plan when you might otherwise be ready to give up. When going through sleep training, parents often remember only the bad things or bad times, like the 3 a.m. waking or the sleepless nights. Parents who use sleep logs can go back through and remind themselves of the good aspects, such as the fact that the baby fell asleep in crib without crying Tuesday night.

A sleep log might also help you realize when a plan is not working. Though success times will vary from child to child and from strategy to strategy, your sleep log will show an accurate account of what is happening. Before you give up on a plan entirely, be sure you have given the plan ample time to take hold and have followed the plan consistently. As many experts will say, most sleep training fails not because the baby is unteachable, but because the parents give up. You may have to switch plans eventually, but give each plan you try enough time. And remember that your baby might have a harder time learning to sleep than another baby. Be patient with your plan and your baby when it comes to sleep training.

## CASE STUDY: WORD FROM THE EXPERTS: NO. 1 TIP TO PARENTS

Arnall said parents should "put their baby to sleep drowsy but still awake, and to put their baby to sleep in the same location where the baby will wake up." For example, do not let your baby fall asleep in your arms or in a car seat, then put him in a crib before he wakes up. "Parents should develop more than one sleep association for their child."

**– Judy Arnall, co-founder of Parenting Canada; owner of Professional Parenting Canada**

"Each family is different, and there is no one-size-fits-all-type solution. Be sure both parents are fully committed to a strategy before they start trying it. It is too easy to abandon a strategy in the middle of the night when both parents are tired and want nothing more than to go back to sleep. If both parents are not fully committed, and a strategy is changed or not followed in the middle of the night, the parents and baby may suffer long-term consequences by training bad behaviors."

**– Barb Dehn, RN, MS, NP**

"Parents should cuddle their baby for several minutes before bedtime, holding him tightly to their chest or face. Parents should remain calm, remember to breathe deeply and not panic, sing quietly, and think good, loving thoughts before setting their baby down for bed."

**– Laura Heinsohn, director of Family Bureau of Investigation Parenting Workshops**

"Parents first should make sure their baby is able to sleep through the night. If your baby has already slept through the night but has gotten out of the habit because of teething or a cold, then you will know your baby is capable of sleeping through the night. Otherwise, make sure your baby is old enough to know how to pacify and soothe himself to sleep. Also, make sure your baby weighs enough to no longer require a nighttime feeding. Once parents are sure their baby is able to sleep through the night, parents need commitment and perseverance to train their baby to sleep through the night. Bottom line: Parents must have a stronger will than their child to be successful with sleep training. Parents must have a plan before bedtime happens and middle-of-the-night waking occurs."

**– Bette Levy Alkazian, MA, licensed marriage and family therapist**

"In the beginning, parents should do whatever it takes to get a baby to sleep through the night, such as letting him fall asleep on your chest. Once a baby gets older, parents can insist their baby sleep in his own bed. Tank a baby up before bedtime with a hearty feeding."

**– Baby Bunching experts Linda Kerr and Cara Fox**

"Parents should know their baby and take his or her temperament, age, stage of development, and sleep requirements into account when choosing a method. The sleep strategy needs to fit your particular situation (which, of course, includes parents' needs, too)."

**– Claudia Heilbrunn, parenting expert, author, and certified life coach**

"Parents should not start before your baby is ready, which means until he is at least 12 to 15 pounds, 12 weeks old, and adjusted."

**– Karen Pollak, founder, Babies2Sleep**

"Put your baby in the bed they will sleep in every night from the start. Babies need to be comfortable with their daily sleeping arrangements and the schedule they will keep."

**– Stephanie Smith, mother of twins**

"It is most important for parents to be patient, and remember that this process cannot be rushed. Trying to make this happen too soon will just lead to counterproductive frustration on both the parents and the baby. Each baby is born with a unique personality and temperament. The key for parents is to learn what works for their specific baby, and not be upset or surprised if what worked for a previous child does not work for the current one."

**– Nadav Traeger, MD, FAAP, FCCP, D, ABSM, director of pediatric sleep medicine, Maria Fareri Children's Hospital**

"Prevention is key. All sleep techniques come down to teaching a baby independent sleep initiation, which means the baby can fall asleep on her own. Parents whose children do not have this skill will experience trouble with their children sleeping through the night. Children should learn to fall asleep in their own crib, by being put in their crib drowsy but awake. Parents who employ preventive measures will be able to prevent issues from arising, and prevent tears from being shed."

**– Dr. Brett Kuhn, CBSM, associate professor of Pediatrics at the University of Nebraska Medical Center and Children's Sleep Center at Children's Hospital**

"Parents should form a united front and back each other up."

**– Dr. Laura Davies, diplomate, American Board of Psychiatry and Neurology**

"Parents should keep their expectations realistic. Most small babies need parent support during the night, and that is normal. Some babies with more challenging temperament traits (such as being sensitive, intense, easily frustrated, slow to adapt) will need more time. New parents should plan to nap or at least rest during the day to manage the effects of being awake to care for their baby at night."

**– Helen Neville, BS, RN, author, pediatric advice nurse, health educator, specialist in inborn temperament, and researcher**

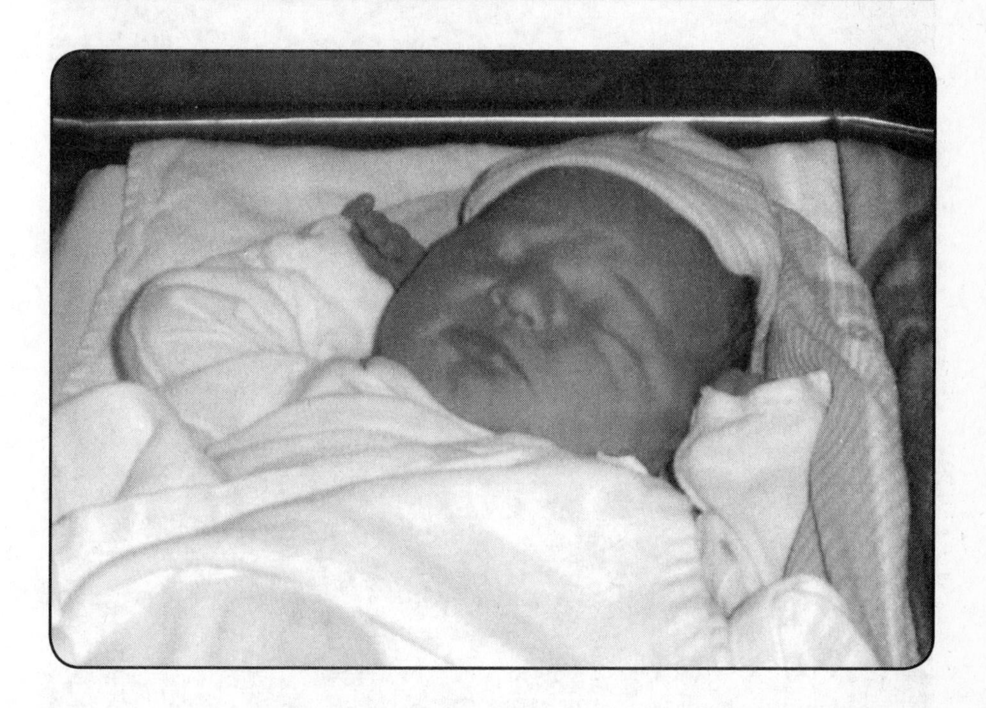

*Photo courtesy of Sivan Grosman, founder of Sivan Photography (**http://sivanphotography.com**)*

# chapter 3

## Causes of Sleep Problems

Before you begin a sleep training program, you should identify what factors, if any, are contributing to your baby's sleep problems. If your baby has not arrived yet or has not yet experienced any problems with sleeping, this chapter will help you in case problems do arise in the future, and will help you take steps to prevent problems from occurring in the first place. It is much easier to prevent bad habits from forming than it is to break them once they are set. You also want to be sure your baby is able to sleep well. Though just about every baby and child has the ability to sleep well, other factors might be getting in the way, like medical conditions or anxiety. If other issues exist, you must first solve those issues before you begin sleep training.

# • TIP #15 •

## Identify Whether Medical Issues are Affecting Your Baby's Sleep

While most sleep issues are not medically related, it is important for you to rule out medical conditions as the cause of sleep problems. Once you have ruled out medical issues, you can more confidently begin to enforce your sleep training. Some medical conditions that might cause sleep issues include colic, snoring, allergies, temporary sickness, narcolepsy, and other disorders. If you feel your baby has a medical condition outlined below, or you are concerned about other medical issues, consult your child's pediatrician. Do not attempt to diagnose your baby.

Colic occurs in about 20 percent of all babies between the ages of 2 weeks and 4 months old. This condition is commonly defined as crying more than three hours a day for more than three days a week and lasts longer than three weeks. Remember that all babies will cry, and sometimes they will cry for absolutely no reason. Just because your baby cries does not mean you are a bad parent or you have done something wrong. With colic, you might find little or nothing will soothe your baby. Most common suggestions for soothing a colicky baby include rocking, swinging, or another sort of constant motion (including walking around); sucking on a bottle, breast, pacifier or thumb; and swaddling, for younger babies. Though the cause of colic is not conclusive, one thing is for sure: It is not your fault. Well-fed and healthy babies develop colic for no known reason. If your baby develops colic, do not worry about sleep training during this time. Do what you can to get through this stage (and yes, it is just a stage), and begin sleep training as soon as possible after the colic passes, which usually occurs between 2 and 4 months of age.

Reflux, which some people mistake for colic, can also cause disruptions in sleep. Gastroesophageal reflux disorder can affect one in ten babies. This condition causes excessive spitting up or throwing up. It is usually caused by an underdeveloped gastroesophageal valve (the flap at the top of your baby's stomach). The condition is similar to colic. Your baby will outgrow this condition once the valve develops fully, which usually occurs by the time your baby is 6 months old. If you suspect reflux in your baby, consult your pediatrician for advice. Some experts recommend that parents keep their babies upright after feeding, and burp them several times during a nursing or bottle feeding. Smaller meals can also help. More severe cases may require a change in diet or the use of medication. Some pediatricians and experts also recommend elevating one side of the crib or putting a wedge under the mattress to help keep the baby slightly upright during sleep.

Snoring and allergies, which can be related, can also cause disruptions to your baby's sleep. If your baby is snoring, try to identify the cause. Your baby could be snoring because of allergies, which make it hard for her to breathe during the night. If she is prone to frequent colds, with symptoms such as a runny nose, sneezing, coughing, and ear problems, her "colds" might be allergies, not viral infections. Ask your pediatrician if allergies might be causing the snoring. Treating the allergies could eliminate snoring and, thus, lead to a restful night's sleep. In general, snoring is caused by difficulty breathing. When a baby, child, or adult "forgets" to breathe during the night, it is called apnea. Although snoring and sleep apnea are not related to SIDS, these can be serious medical issues and should not be ignored. Some occasional snoring is common among most children and can be caused by colds or mild allergies. But when snoring worsens and becomes chronic, your child will need medical attention. Chronic snoring will cause poor sleep and will affect your child's mood and performance during the day. A child who fights sleep might be doing so because he is a chronic snorer, which makes sleeping uncomfortable. Sleep training a snoring child will be difficult because falling asleep is not the issue; the issue is poor breathing while sleeping. Once medical attention is provided, sleep issues should resolve.

Your baby will undoubtedly be sick from a cold, flu, or other virus many times during her life. While sick, your baby might have a difficult time sleeping. If your baby gets sick while in sleep training or after a sleep training program has been established, put the training or program on hold until she is better. While a child is sick, she needs to know her parents are taking care of her and she is safe. Resume your training program immediately after she is better. If you do not resume training, or if you allow changes in the routine after the illness is gone, you will encourage bad habits to develop, which will make sleep training harder for you and your baby in the end. *See Chapter 10, Tip #86 for more information on resuming a sleep routine after an illness.*

Narcolepsy is a rare disease characterized by the sudden onset of sleep. Oftentimes, a narcoleptic will fall asleep while performing another action, such as reading, talking, or watching television. If your baby is nodding off in the middle of the day, chances are he is not getting enough sleep, rather than that he is narcoleptic. This disease is not usually seen in children under 10 to 14 years old. If you are concerned your child might be narcoleptic, consult your doctor and ask to see a sleep specialist.

If your baby has another diagnosed disorder that you feel is contributing to her problems sleeping, consult your pediatrician before beginning a sleep program to best decide how to cope with your individual case.

# • TIP #16 •

## Identify if Anxiety or Psychological Disorders are Affecting Your Baby's Sleep

Anxiety, nighttime fears, and other psychological disorders can make bedtime a frightening situation for your baby and a battle for you as a parent. By identifying whether these issues are affecting your baby's sleep, you will be able to treat any conditions that might exist and create a healthy sleep plan for you and your baby.

Nightmares and nighttime fears will affect almost every child at one time in his life or another. Usually peaking when your child is between 2 and 3 years old, nightmares occur as your child's imagination is developing. If your child wakes from a nightmare, comfort him, allow him to talk about his nightmare (but do not coach him while he talks), then help him fall back asleep. You should already have a nighttime routine and good sleep habits established by this age. Try not to encourage bad habits to develop because of nightmares. Comfort your child without allowing him to sleep in your bed and without your sleeping in his bed.

Once he has calmed down, encourage him to fall back asleep and have happy dreams. You can encourage these happy dreams by offering suggestions such as, "Dream about how much fun you will have playing with your friends at the playground tomorrow." If nightmares occur frequently, you might try a dream catcher, which you and your child can either make or pick out together. This can help comfort a young child while he is falling asleep. If it fits your belief system, saying prayers before bedtime can help a child not be scared at night; you can pray for happy dreams before bed. Otherwise, a book about happy dreams or another "sweet dreams" saying might help.

If your child is scared before bedtime, increase the cuddle time during your bedtime routine, and make his room feel as safe as possible. Play in the room during the day so his room is a fun place, and not just a place where he is left alone to sleep. If your child does not already have one, encourage the use of a comfort blanket, stuffed animal, or other type of "lovey" for added security, if safe for his age. During this time, do not introduce scary ideas or thoughts to your child, whether through books, movies, television, or even the news. Listen to your child's fears and help him through them without dismissing them as silly. If your child is scared of the dark, use a nightlight, keep his door cracked open at night, or try to make darkness less scary by playing with a flashlight in the dark during the day, but not right before bedtime. Identify what your child is fearful of and work to eliminate that fear. Some parents and experts advocate the use of "monster spray" by their child's bed. Others say this method only encourages the idea that monsters are real, and parents should maintain the position that monsters do not exist. An alternative is using another name for the spray with similar intent. For example, use a "nightmare spray" to ward off bad dreams or a "safety spray" to keep the child's room safe. Find a solution that comforts your child and addresses his particular fears.

Sleep terrors and sleepwalking are less common than nightmares. During a sleep terror, a child can cry, scream, and flail about with his eyes open, even though he is technically still asleep. These disorders are considered partial arousals. These episodes usually last five to 15 minutes, after which your child will return fully to sleep and have no recollection of the event when he wakes. These events are not serious medical conditions, and children usually grow out of them altogether. If you experienced sleep terrors as a child, your child might have a greater risk of having them as well. These situations are scary and hard to watch for parents. The best method for dealing with sleep terrors is to stay close to your child during the episode, but do not attempt to comfort or wake your child. He will not respond to you if you try to comfort him verbally, and he may fight you off if you try physically comforting him. Stay close to ensure his safety. If he is sleepwalking, block off stairs or gate his bedroom door so that he cannot wander about the house.

If your child has separation anxiety, practice leaving and returning during the daytime hours, so by bedtime, she is used to your leaving but always coming back. If your child is old enough to understand, tell her when you are leaving and when you will be back. Encourage her to use a lovey or comfort blanket when you are away. You can also use pictures in her room or make a picture book that she can take with her when you are not there. Encourage her to look at the pictures whenever she misses you, or look at the book together before bedtime. You can also increase cuddle time before bedtime to satisfy her need to be near you before you leave her in her room to sleep at night. When separation anxiety is high, do not try to begin sleep training. If you are in the middle of training, continue to train, but be patient with your child if she regresses in her training during this time period.

# • TIP #17 •

## Identify Trained Behaviors that are Affecting Your Baby's Sleep

More often than not, your baby's sleep issues will be caused by trained behaviors that she has come to associate with falling asleep. When she wakes in the middle of the night (as all babies and adults do), she is unable to recreate the situation that put her to sleep in the first place and wakes up crying. For example, if your baby always falls asleep in your arms nursing or feeding from a bottle, then waking up in a crib alone without you around could be scary, and she may begin crying. Think about how disoriented and confused you would be if you fell asleep in your own bed and woke in the middle of the night in a different part of the house. When you move your baby to a crib, bassinet, or bed after she has fallen asleep, you are creating a scary and confusing situation for her. By teaching your baby to put herself to sleep, and doing so in the same place where she will sleep all night, you are avoiding this scary scenario.

Other trained behaviors might be contributing to your baby's poor sleep. Use your sleep logs to identify what your baby's sleep associations are, and find out if any of these associations need to be changed to healthier habits. Do not use a sleep association your baby cannot recreate on her own in the middle of the night. Sucking on a thumb or pacifier is an example of a self-soothing sleep association. Mommy rocking baby to sleep every night is an example of a sleep association that she cannot recreate.

# • TIP #18 •

## Identify Other Factors that Affect Your Baby's Sleep

Although it is true there are no "bad sleepers," some babies will inevitably have more trouble learning to fall asleep than others. If conditions are impacting your child's sleep, try to solve those issues before you begin your sleep training. If your child is on any medication, ask your pediatrician if it will affect his sleep. You might have to change the time of day you administer the medication to lessen its impact on your baby's sleep schedule. Use your sleep log to identify other factors.

Make sure your baby's needs are met before bedtime. For example, feed her, change her, and make sure she is warm, feels safe, and knows you love her. Once you rule out other factors and you have met her needs, you can feel confident that she is well-equipped to learn how to sleep. If you are unsure about whether your baby is experiencing factors affecting her sleep, show your sleep logs to your child's pediatrician or a sleep expert to get his advice.

Be sure you are comfortable beginning sleep training. If you are anxious or unsure about whether or not your baby is ready to learn, your baby will sense your tension and might have greater difficulty learning to sleep. If you are exhausted and at your wits' end, do not start sleep training. Find a way to get some rest and wait until you feel mentally and physically capable to train your baby. Take a break by having a sitter or relative watch your baby while you catch up on sleep, or just take some time off to regroup.

Pay attention to stress or other tension within your household. If you are experiencing marital problems, are stressed about family relationships, or are worried about finances or returning to work, your baby will feel your stress. Any tension you have will rub off on your baby, who might find it hard to sleep because of your stress. Find ways to alleviate your own stress before you start sleep training. While you are training, keep a positive and loving attitude.

• TIP #19 •

## Some Babies will Take Longer to Learn to Sleep Well Than Others

Parents can often be misled to think their baby is just not a good sleeper. They might start blaming themselves and think they are bad parents. But neither of these situations are true. Your child's ability to sleep well is not a direct reflection of your parenting skills. Your child's difficulty sleeping might mean he is taking longer to learn this skill than other babies of his age. Do not doom your baby to a lifetime of bad sleep habits by succumbing to the belief that he cannot be taught to sleep or that he is just naturally a "bad" sleeper. You would not give up teaching your child to read just because he is taking longer to grasp the subject than other children his age. Remember that good sleep habits are learned, not instinctual.

Remind yourself that you are teaching your child a new skill. Some children learn by different methods than others. While some children are more hands-on learners, others will only need to be shown a task once before they grasp it. As a parent, and thus your child's first teacher, you need to learn which style of teaching and which sleep strategy will work best for your baby's learning style.

# • TIP #20 •

## Starting Sleep Training Early Can Prevent Problems From Arising

Although experts disagree on the exact age when you should begin sleep training your baby, there are things you can do from Day 1 to help prevent problems or bad habits from developing. You can start a very short and simple bedtime routine with your newborn. A simple routine might include a warm bath, diaper change, and a feeding. Many babies will fall asleep at the bottle or breast. While at a young age falling asleep while feeding might not be an issue, remember that you do not want your baby to become reliant on nursing to go to sleep. You will have to feed your baby at night for the first few months of her life, which might enforce her sleep association with the bottle or breast, so be careful not to have her overly rely on that to get to sleep. Burping your baby after her nighttime feeding may rouse her slightly. If you then put her in her bassinet or crib slightly awake and pat her belly so she falls back asleep, she will associate the crib and belly-patting, rather than the feeding, with falling asleep.

Some experts recommend varying the methods you use to soothe your newborn baby. If every time she cries, you pick her up, she will expect the same reaction from you if she cries at 3 a.m. If you vary the methods you use to soothe her, she will not become dependent on just one soothing method. You can also encourage your baby to self-soothe. At this age, it might be as simple as not rushing to your baby at each whimper or cry. With an older baby, you can encourage thumbsucking or pacifiers. If you are breastfeeding your baby, the AAP recommends waiting at least one month to introduce pacifiers.

A newborn will not yet know the difference between day and night, but you can help create this association even at a young age. Make the nights dark, quiet, and boring. Use darkening shades if you think it will help create a "night" environment. During the day, have the lights on and make it fun; perhaps not noisy, but filled with sound. Make sure your baby has a little outside time, if the weather allows. The room your baby naps in should be dark, but do not create a perfectly quiet environment outside of the room. If you tiptoe around during your baby's naptimes, you will create a light sleeper. You want your baby to get used to sleeping with some noise so she will not stir too easily during the night. And if you have older children, let them play as usual. The baby will learn to sleep through it.

# • TIP #21 •

## Parents Can Contribute to a Child's Sleep Problems

The bad news is that sometimes you can contribute to your child's bad sleep habits. The good news is that you can fix it. If you have created a situation where your child has been trained into "bad" sleep habits — for example, he knows that if he cries long enough, you will take him to your bed to sleep — know that you can fix the problem. Be patient, though; it takes longer to break a habit than it does to form one. Be honest with yourself and your partner in identifying things you might be doing to contribute to your child's poor sleep habits. Create a plan to change those habits while ensuring your child still feels safe and loved.

Be consistent when employing those changes. Inconsistency leads to longer training times and a confused baby or child. If you are continually changing the rules your child lives by, he will not know what is expected of him. Children long for routine and order; they want to know what you expect from them. Do not keep moving the target by changing the rules when it comes to sleep or any other aspect of your child's life. As the parent, it is your job to create a safe, orderly world for your baby. Make sure you are being your baby's parents, not their friend. Some experts believe the first time you truly exert parental behavior over your children is through sleep training. This is an important time to establish your role in your relationship with your baby.

# • TIP #22 •

## Understand Nighttime Behavior, and Deal with it Appropriately

Headbanging, thrashing, body rocking, and head rolling are all considered rhythmic behaviors. These behaviors are soothing to babies, much like being rocked by someone else soothes them. Most babies will rock — whether sitting up or on all fours — during the day. Some babies will carry these behaviors to bedtime and will rock, bang, or thrash before falling asleep at night, during naps, and maybe even in the middle of the night to get themselves back to sleep. Experts say that between 5 to 10 percent of babies will engage in some sort of rhythmic behavior during bedtime. Boys are more prone to headbanging than girls are. Most children begin these behaviors before their first year of life, and while most stop on their own in weeks or months, most children stop completely by the time they are 4 years old.

If you have an older child who still exhibits these behaviors, have your pediatrician evaluate him for other neurological disorders. Most children who exhibit these behaviors will go through this phase as a normal developmental behavior. Children who are more violent than others or whose behavior lasts longer than seems appropriate might be displaying this behavior for other reasons, including reacting to stress in the family, going through a developmental milestone, or undergoing another disorder.

If you are concerned for your child's safety due to headbanging, try to pad his crib so the surface he bangs against is not hard. Be prepared that if he is old enough, he might move the padding aside and continue to bang, or he might find another hard surface to bang against. While it might be painful for you to see as a parent, remember that babies or children are not causing themselves harm by headbanging. Some may develop minor bruises and occasionally have a small amount of external bleeding, but serious harm is rarely caused. If you are concerned about your child being hurt, and padding does not work, consult your child's pediatrician. In most cases, parents are feeling more pain by seeing their child engage in this activity than the child is actually experiencing.

Older children might hum along with their rhythmic behaviors, which is also a normal behavior. Most children will fall asleep within 15 minutes of their behavior. Some episodes might last as long as an hour. Remember that this behavior, like so many other behaviors your child will exhibit, is temporary and part of normal development. Do not try to coach this behavior out of your child. He will stop doing it just as he started — on his own.

## • TIP #23 •

## Remember: Almost Every Baby has the Ability to Sleep Well

Babies are not born "good" or "bad" sleepers. Sleeping is instinctual, but developing good sleep habits is a learned behavior. Some babies need less coaching than others, but all babies, barring extreme circumstances, have the ability to learn to sleep well. Even extreme circumstances can be solved with patience and expert help. Your maternity nurse might brag about how good your baby sleeps, or she might warn you of sleepless nights. Do not put much weight on either of these statements. Remember that newborns have not yet developed a sleep pattern, so her sleep patterns in the maternity ward are not a predictor of future sleep patterns. Believing your baby is not a good sleeper can actually cause your baby to develop bad habits she might otherwise not develop. If you feel your child will never learn to sleep well, you might give up on a program too soon and only half-heartedly try to sleep train her. Approach sleep training with a positive mindset and remember that while this time is challenging for you and your baby, you will be doing your baby a great disservice if you do not teach her to fall asleep. And chances are that with your positive attitude, determination, and patience, she will learn to sleep well, and you both will be happier for it.

Although some babies will be affected by medical conditions that make sleep training harder, most babies will not. Do not assume a medical condition exists just because your baby is having difficulty sleeping. Do rule out whether medical conditions exist before you begin training, and make sure your child's pediatrician feels your baby is old enough and healthy enough for sleep training to begin. Once medical conditions are ruled out, feel confident that your baby has the ability to learn to sleep and start your training program.

Illness will occur and will temporarily disrupt sleep, but most babies possess the ability to learn to sleep well; rarely do medical conditions pose long-term sleep issues. If you believe your baby does have a condition affecting his long-term sleeping abilities, ask to see a sleep specialist to accurately gauge your child's condition.

## CASE STUDY: WORD FROM THE EXPERTS: GETTING BABY BACK TO SLEEP

"When a baby wakes up crying during the night, parents should feed, soothe, and put their baby down while gently caressing them until their baby falls back to sleep."

**– Judy Arnall, co-founder of Parenting Canada; owner of Professional Parenting Canada**

When a baby wakes in the night, "Parents should rock the bassinet or jiggle the crib to try to help them fall back sleep quickly. If a diaper change is in order, parents should not turn on the lights during the change and should avoid stimulating the baby by talking, singing, or making direct eye contact. These ways of communicating with a baby should be used during playtime at daytime hours, but not at night. Many babies need a full hour to cycle from alert and crying to asleep. Parents need to remember this fact and set realistic expectations for their baby's sleeping habits."

**– Barb Dehn, RN, MS, NP**

"Quiet, classical music can be the right thing to get a baby to fall back asleep. A soft musical mobile can also be effective."

**– Laura Heinsohn, director of Family Bureau of Investigation Parenting Workshops**

"A baby will fall back asleep the same way he fell asleep initially. For instance, if you rock your baby to sleep every night, he will expect to be rocked back asleep if he wakes up at 3 a.m. Parents should put their baby to sleep tired but still awake, so he learns to fall asleep by himself. He will then be able to soothe himself back to sleep if he wakes in the middle of the night. Once other bedtime habits are created, parents may have to let a baby cry it out if he wakes in the middle of the night."

**– Bette Levy Alkazian, MA, licensed marriage and family therapist**

Parents should let their baby fuss a little so he can learn how to self-soothe. Fox said that she used pacifiers when her children were younger and would go in and put the pacifier back in their mouths if they woke up at night. Eventually, her children began sucking their fingers or thumbs to soothe themselves back to sleep.

**– Baby Bunching experts Linda Kerr and Cara Fox**

"Parents should get their baby back to sleep the same way she fell asleep to begin with," said Heilbrunn. "If you normally pat your baby's belly, then go in and pat her belly again. If you normally let her cry it out, let her cry it out again. Parents should not rush in as soon as their baby wakes. Sometimes waiting a few minutes will allow the baby time to fall back asleep on her own."

**– Claudia Heilbrunn, parenting expert, author, and certified life coach**

"Parents should provide their baby with environmental messages and cues, such as transitional objects and white noise, to encourage him to fall back asleep on his own."

**– Karen Pollak, founder, Babies2Sleep**

"Parents should remember that everyone wakes up several times each night. Those of us that are good sleepers and have good sleeping habits just turn right over and return to sleep, while those with bad sleep habits toss and turn. While it may initially appear to be counterintuitive, the key to managing those nighttime awakenings is what occurs during bedtime. Many children need to replicate the conditions of the bedtime routine during those nights. If a baby initially falls asleep with the parent present, he will again need the parent to be present for him to return to sleep during the nighttime awakening. Parents should structure bedtime so the child falls asleep in the same exact situation he will find himself in when he wakes up at night. For example, parents may read or sing to the child, place him in bed, give a kiss, say goodnight, turn off the light, and then step out of the room as he falls asleep on his own."

**– Nadav Traeger, MD, FAAP, FCCP, D, ABSM, director of pediatric sleep medicine, Maria Fareri Children's Hospital**

"If age-appropriate (after a baby is at least 6 months old), parents should work on getting their baby to fall asleep smoothly at bedtime. If a baby knows how to fall asleep on his own, he will know how to put himself back to sleep on his own during the middle of the night. Parents should make sure their baby is falling asleep in the same environment he will sleep in throughout the night. If your baby wakes and cries in the middle of the night, you should use the same strategy to get him back to sleep as you did to get him to sleep in the first place. The goal with your strategy should be to wean your baby from relying on you to get back to sleep. Your baby should be learning to fall asleep on his own."

**– Dr. Brett Kuhn, CBSM, associate professor of pediatrics at the University of Nebraska Medical Center and Children's Sleep Center at Children's Hospital**

"Parents should remember that all babies wake often during the night. Some things that help them fall back asleep include having a thumb or hand to suck, several available pacifiers, a soothing blanket, or an animal or something else that reminds baby of mother by texture and/or smell. For some sensitive babies, parents should consider using a white noise machine that masks disturbing sounds. For some children, dark blinds are helpful for the summer time."

**– Helen Neville, BS, RN, author, pediatric advice nurse, health educator, specialist in inborn temperament, and researcher**

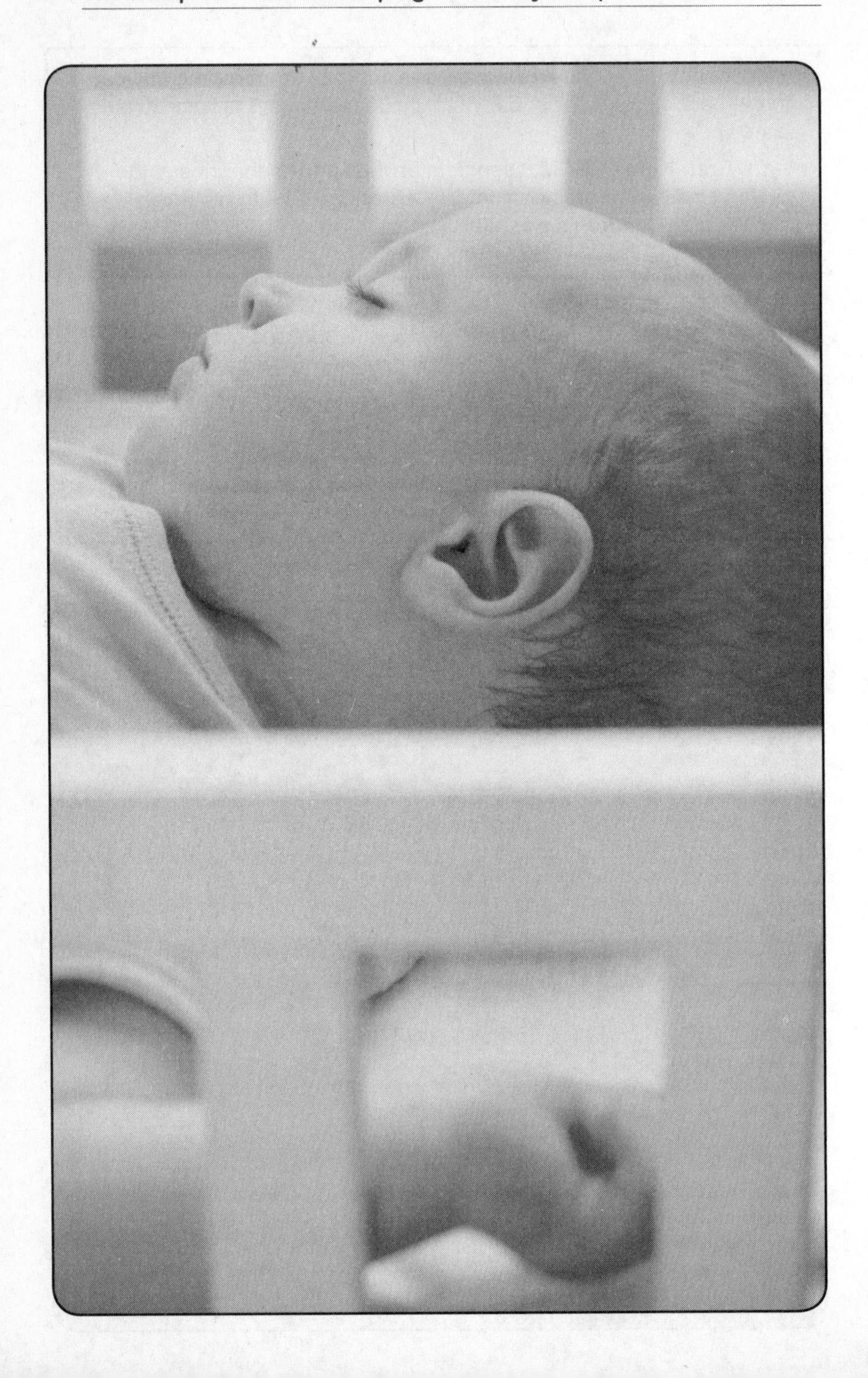

# chapter 4

## Strategies for Getting Your Baby to Sleep

This chapter will outline some of the most popular sleep strategies. Read through each strategy with an open mind, and sit down with your partner to decide which strategy might work best for your family and your lifestyle. Of course, this book does not contain all the strategies out there to help get your baby to sleep at night. The more common, popular, and proven methods have been outlined. If you have been advised about other strategies, be sure to research the strategy fully before deciding to commit to it. Remember that many strategies can work to get your baby to sleep through the night, as long as the strategy is employed regularly and is consistent with your baby's personality.

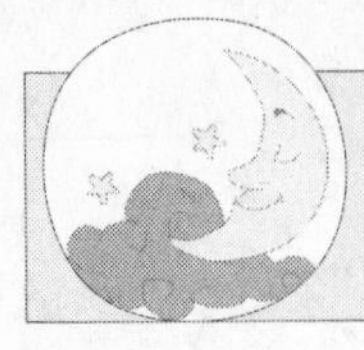

## *Sleep Strategy #1:*
### Crying it out, or the "extinction method"

Although some parents confuse the straight crying-it-out method with the Ferber method, these methods are not the same. The crying-it-out method, otherwise known as the extinction method, requires parents to let their baby cry it out at bedtime without any checks. This method is named the extinction method because it does not allow the behavior you are trying to dissuade to continue. Though other methods might take a more gradual approach and eliminate a behavior over time, this method aims to discontinue the undesirable behavior immediately. The Ferber method has a regimented schedule of progressive waiting to check on the crying baby. Both methods are similar in that the goal is to teach the baby to fall asleep on his own, without depending on his parents to put him to sleep. The Ferber method allows parental checks more for the parent's peace of mind in knowing their baby is safe and just upset.

During the extinction method, you should put your baby to bed drowsy but still awake, then leave the room. You should not return to check on your baby until he is asleep. This method, as well as the Ferber method, has been proved successful by many studies, and parents usually report success (if followed consistently) within three days. The advantage to this method is its quick success. The disadvantage is that this method is extremely hard for many parents to handle emotionally. Listening to your baby cry and not responding to his cries can wreak havoc on a parent's well-being. Many parents feel they are causing their baby emotional harm and will give in before three nights pass.

Be honest with yourself and your partner if you choose to try this method. If you are worried you will cave in, consider a less severe method, or leave the house while your partner sleep trains your baby. It is better to choose another method up front than it is to switch methods too soon or too often. *See Chapter 4, Tip#28 for more information about switching strategies.*

## CASE STUDY: WORD FROM THE EXPERTS: CRYING IT OUT

"This method increases a baby's stress levels, and it damages a baby's ability to trust and develop attachment if a baby is allowed to cry it out in his first year. If parents let a baby cry it out during the night, the parents will become conditioned to ignoring their baby's cries, even during the day." Bottom line: Arnall does not recommend this method to new parents.

**– Judy Arnall, co-founder of Parenting Canada; owner of Professional Parenting Canada**

"Parents should first ensure their baby's needs are met (for example, a clean diaper, and not sick or throwing up) before allowing their baby to cry it out. Once parents determine that a baby is safe, they can start employing this tactic. Parents should go into the baby's room keeping the lights off and pat her a few times, tell her you love her, and then leave the room without ever picking her up. Parents should stay away for ten minutes before returning if the baby continues to cry. This process is repeated with the interval between comforting the child getting progressively longer. If parents can continue this process, a child will usually fall back sleep once the interval reaches 30 to 45 minutes, if not sooner."

**– Barb Dehn, RN, MS, NP**

"Parents should never let a baby cry it out. When a baby cries, something is wrong, and parents should be sensitive and try to figure out why their baby is upset."

**– Laura Heinsohn, director of Family Bureau of Investigation Parenting Workshops**

Alkazian supports letting babies crying it out. "If a baby's needs are met and he is in a loving environment, this method will not make a baby feel abandoned or leave emotional scars. A baby will not remember in the morning that Mom or Dad let him cry it out the night before, and this method is the quickest way to teach healthy sleep habits and self-soothing techniques to a baby. Giving your baby the time and space to self-soothe allows your baby to learn to put himself back to sleep, which would not be the case if Mom was always with the baby. Teaching a baby to sleep is the first opportunity parents have to assert their role as a parent in their relationship with their baby. Defining roles is an essential part of good parenting. Parents who set healthy limits and have consistent parenting practices make their children feel safe and secure. Parents who allow children to possess too much power are more likely to be anxious."

**– Bette Levy Alkazian, MA, licensed marriage and family therapist**

"Parents have to do what works for them and their baby. The cry-it-out method works for some children, but not all children." Kerr's son did well with this method, while her daughter would "cry until the cows came home." She said that she had to find another solution to get her daughter to sleep at night. Fox had a similar situation with her children. Though the cry-it-out method worked for her oldest child, it did not work for her second-born. She said, "If my second child cried more than five minutes, he would cry all night long, although most nights, he would soothe himself to sleep before he cried for five minutes. Again, this method works well for some children and not for others."

**– Baby Bunching experts Linda Kerr and Cara Fox**

Heilbrunn has found that crying it out works well for some families, though she does not choose this method in her own home. "Contrary to what some people believe, studies do not show that this method harms a baby." But personally, Heilbrunn said there are more loving and supportive ways for parents to help their baby sleep at night. She said, "Every family and every situation is different, and parents need to find the solution that works best for them and their baby."

**– Claudia Heilbrunn, parenting expert, author, and certified life coach**

"Progressive waiting and crying it out methods can be effective for some parents based on their baby's temperament (based on the book *Healthy Sleep Habits, Happy Child)*. Babies adapt very quickly and are much happier once they sleep more productively."

**– Karen Pollak, founder, Babies2Sleep**

Smith believes in letting a baby crying it out to a point. She said that she and her husband gave their girls about 20 minutes when they first laid them down to cry it out, then they would try to soothe them. If the girls woke in the middle of the night, she says they gave them about 10 minutes or so before jumping in and soothing them.

– **Stephanie Smith, mother of twins**

"This method has been proven to work most successfully in clinical trials as opposed to more gradual approaches. This method will be tough on both the parents and the baby in the short term but easier on both in the long run. Parents are aware they need to teach their children many things (manners, reading, and writing, for example), but many overlook their responsibility to teach their children how to be good sleepers. The earlier good sleep habits are introduced, the more they will be an integral part of the child's personality."

– **Nadav Traeger, MD, FAAP, FCCP, D, ABSM, director of pediatric sleep medicine, Maria Fareri Children's Hospital**

"This method is controversial, yet effective. Studies have shown no negative effects on children, and in fact, some studies have revealed positive effects on children whose parents employed this method. This method aims to accomplish independent sleep skills." In his practice, he allows parents to choose the method that best fits them. He knows how important it is to have parents comfortable with the method they employ for successful sleep training of their children.

– **Dr. Brett Kuhn, CBSM, associate professor of pediatrics at the University of Nebraska Medical Center and Children's Sleep Center at Children's Hospital**

"Although this method is painful for parents, it is a good technique for the baby. This method should be employed in a graduated manner, with parents first waiting five minutes, then eight minutes, then ten minutes, and so on. This method gives the baby self-soothing skills, which are key in teaching a baby to sleep through the night."

– **Dr. Laura Davies, diplomate, American Board of Psychiatry and Neurology**

"Research shows babies who wake their parents at 12 months old are often doing so at 24 months. Many of these same babies are likely to have challenging temperament traits. When your baby is 3 to 11 months old, it is a good time to encourage him or her to get through the night alone. Parents should keep in mind that around the time your baby is 8 months old, the age of separation anxiety (when babies cry because you walk into the next room during the day) is an unlikely time to succeed at sleeping through the night. In fact, many babies who slept through before 8 months old start waking again for a few weeks. Due to this fact, some parents may prefer to wait and work on sleep training when their baby is between 9 and 12 months old."

**– Helen Neville, BS, RN, author, pediatric advice nurse, health educator, specialist in inborn temperament, and researcher**

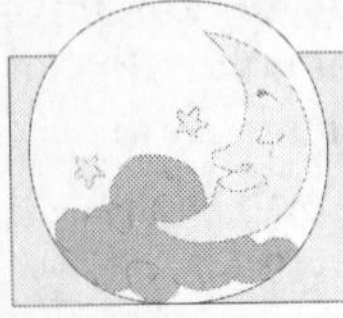

## Sleep Strategy #2: The Ferber method

This method has been around for quite a while, and as long as it has been around, it has been controversial. Dr. Richard Ferber, director of the Center for Pediatric Sleep Disorders, published his first book, *Solve Your Child's Sleep Problems*, outlining this method in 1986, which leads some of his critics to call his method outdated. He released a revised, expanded version in 2006 to clarify his method and further explain why his method works. Whether you are comfortable with his method or not is something you have to decide for yourself. Many experts, even those who do not advocate his method, believe that it works quite well for those who wish to use it – when parents stick to it consistently.

This method allows children to cry it out, so to speak, and requires that parents wait longer and longer in between checking on the baby. Like many methods, the Ferber method says the baby should wake up in the middle of the night – as we all do in a normal night – in the same situation she was in when she initially fell asleep. This means your baby should not fall asleep in your arms and then wake up in her crib. The first step in his method is to identify your child's current sleep associations. If you have already completed a sleep log, this step may be as simple as reviewing your log. Once you identify her current associations, you might need to change some of them. If your child has any sleep association that she cannot recreate on her own, you will need to help her change that association. The idea is to teach your baby to self-soothe so she can put herself back to sleep when she wakes in the middle of the night. If your baby is dependent on you to put her to sleep at bedtime, she will also be dependent on you to put her back to sleep in the middle of the night. Changing these associations will create some strain for your child, as she will no longer be getting what she wants or is used to getting. Be patient with her, and be prepared for some crying during this learning curve.

Once the new sleep association is decided upon and employed, the Ferber method says parents should use the "progressive-waiting" approach to teach their baby the new sleep association, which should be for your baby to fall asleep on her own. Basically, you will wait for longer periods of time between checking on your baby while she is learning to fall asleep. For the first night, when you put your baby in her crib while she is drowsy but still awake, you will say goodnight and leave the room. Because she is not used to falling asleep on her own, chances are she will begin crying. The first day, wait three minutes before checking in. During your check-in, spend a couple of minutes soothing your baby, then leave again. You should not stay until the baby has fallen asleep (or even stopped crying). The purpose of the check-in is to reassure your baby that you are still there to help her, and reassure yourself that she is safe. When you leave the second time, you will wait five minutes before checking in. The time between each check-in will progressively get longer. The longest the Ferber method recommends waiting for a check-in is 30 minutes, but you should not reach this time until the seventh day, according to the Ferber method chart.

Most parents and experts have found this plan to be successful in three nights, if parents stick to the plan consistently. Five minutes may not seem like a long time, but it might feel like an eternity to parents listening to the cries of their baby. Be honest with yourself about employing this technique. You cannot pick your baby up during check-ins, and you must be committed to seeing this plan through. Starting this plan and not being consistent, or deciding to switch to another plan after just a night or two, will only cause more confusion for yours baby. You might also end up encouraging your baby to cry for longer periods of time because she will learn that if she cries five minutes, you will not pick her up; however, if she cries for 30 minutes, you will pick her up and rock her to sleep, or give in to a nighttime feeding when she no longer needs to be fed at night.

The method can be used for naptimes as well. Encourage her to fall asleep during naps the same way she will fall asleep for bedtime. The Ferber method advocates set schedules for bedtimes and naps. While the method says parents might sometimes have to adjust this schedule or be somewhat flexible, parents should have set times for bedtime and naptime and adhere to them as much as possible. Though the Ferber method seems tailored more toward a baby having her own bed, the method also offers tips for families who choose to co-sleep with their baby.

## CASE STUDY: WORD FROM THE EXPERTS: THE FERBER METHOD

Arnall is not a believer of the Ferber method. She feels his method was developed on old research and reminds parents that his first book was published in 1985. She does not recommend this tactic to parents.

**– Judy Arnall, co-founder of Parenting Canada; owner of Professional Parenting Canada**

Dehn has used the Ferber method for her own son and said she found it to be successful within three days.

**– Barb Dehn, RN, MS, NP**

"While this method absolutely works to get a baby to sleep through the night, it does not always work for the parents. Oftentimes, parents experience more stress trying this strategy than they feel it is worth, and end up giving up before the process has time to stick. When consistently employed, this technique usually works in three days. Parents who commit to this method and stick to it consistently swear by its effectiveness. On the other hand, some parents have reported their baby crying for up to two hours in a row. This situation can be hard for tired parents to tolerate and can cause stress within the marital relationship. In some cases, having one parent sleep out of the house for a few nights while the other parent stays committed to this method can be an effective way to get a baby to sleep through the night without overly stressing both parents. Most importantly, parents should make a decision about what strategy they will use to get their baby to sleep ahead of time. Decisions should not be made, or strategies changed in the middle of the night, when parents are tired and not thinking clearly." Alkazian also suggests that parents use humor to get through those tough nights and reminds parents that giving up partway through a strategy will only create habits that will be harder to break later on.

**– Bette Levy Alkazian, MA, licensed marriage and family therapist**

"The advantage to this technique is that if parents can get through it, this technique will work within a couple of nights, and if parents employ this tactic sooner rather than later in the baby's life, they may have less, if any, sleep issues later on. The disadvantages are that it is heartbreaking to listen to your baby cry, and it takes willpower. The best method to implement when using the Ferber method depends on the child," Kerr said. Fox recalls that with her oldest child, going in his room to soothe him just made him more upset, so she had to just let him scream until he fell asleep. On the other hand, her youngest child responded well to going in to soothe him, with the increments between soothing increasing over time.

– **Baby Bunching experts Linda Kerr and Cara Fox**

"While this method has been very effective for some families, it has not worked for all families. The advantage to this method is that the process is usually short term and results in a child that will sleep through the night. The disadvantage is that some parents simply cannot follow through with the process. These parents often feel it is painful and nerve-wracking to let their baby cry it out. Some parents may feel they are causing harm to their baby by not responding to his cries. In such cases, parents who are not consistent with their sleep strategy confuse their baby and make sleep training harder for the baby. Parents who choose this method need to be consistent."

– **Claudia Heilbrunn, parenting expert, author, and certified life coach**

"The Ferber method has absolutely been proven effective. The advantage is quick success, while the disadvantage is listening to your child cry, which may cause you to question whether you are hurting your child. Parents who choose to implement this plan should fully understand this method and use it precisely as it was designed." She cautions against parents who want to pick and choose elements of the plan and said that parents should not abandon efforts too quickly."

– **Karen Pollak, founder, Babies2Sleep**

"Yes, this method has been proven to work in clinical trials. Several variations of the original method exist. These variations are more gradual and perceived to be more 'gentle' on both the child and the parents. But the bottom line is that these 'gentle' approaches tend to fail much more often than the more 'harsh' method, and even when they do work, it takes much longer to do so. Thus, the advantages of the Ferber method are that it is more likely to work and that it will work faster. The disadvantage is that during those few days while it is being applied, parents may feel that they are doing the wrong thing — perhaps even that they are somehow causing the baby 'harm' by letting them cry. The fact is they are doing just what their baby needs them to do — teaching them how to sleep — in the shortest possible time."

– **Nadav Traeger, MD, FAAP, FCCP, D, ABSM, director of pediatric sleep medicine, Maria Fareri Children's Hospital**

"Fourteen research studies, comprising nearly 750 children, found this method effective. This method teaches children to sleep independently. Unlike the straight crying-it-out method, this technique allows parents the peace of mind to check on their baby. The disadvantage is that this method is more difficult for some parents to adhere to, and being inconsistent with this method can teach children to cry for longer periods. Parents that choose this method need to follow the protocol exactly. If parents offer more attention during their middle of the night check-ins than is allowed, or if they do not manage their child's sleep schedule appropriately during training, they might not only sabotage the effectiveness of this program, but cultivate bad sleep habits in their child as well."

– **Dr. Brett Kuhn, CBSM, associate professor of pediatrics at the University of Nebraska Medical Center and Children's Sleep Center at Children's Hospital**

"This method has been proven effective. While the advantage is that it works, the disadvantage is that it is hard on the parents emotionally. Parents who choose this method should be consistent and have any other caretakers implement it as well."

– **Dr. Laura Davies, diplomate, American Board of Psychiatry and Neurology**

"Parents who are interested in this method should look for Ferber's newest edition of his book." Given her own experience with inborn temperament, whether or not the system works easily depends on the child's temperament.

– **Helen Neville, BS, RN, author, pediatric advice nurse health educator, specialist in inborn temperament, and researcher**

## Sleep Strategy #3:
12 hours a night by 12 weeks

This method, based on the book *The Baby Sleep Solution* by Suzy Giordano, claims to have babies sleeping 12 hours a night by 12 weeks old. This technique touts less crying than the Ferber method, but there will still be some crying involved. It also will be a slower method than the Ferber method should be. Parents, again, must fully dedicate themselves to this plan for the duration if success is sought. If parents start this method from Day 1 and continue through their baby's 12th week, they should be feeding their baby four times a day, with no night feedings, and should have a baby who stays in bed either asleep or quiet for 12 hours a night.

According to this method, when the baby is 1 to 6 weeks old, you will not be sleep training your baby, but you should be concentrating on not creating bad sleep habits that will require more time and effort to break later on. This method encourages parents not to co-sleep, at least until your baby is completely sleep trained. Switching beds during sleep training will make learning to sleep more difficult for the baby and training harder for the parents. Parents should vary the methods they use to soothe their baby at this age so he does not get accustomed to being soothed by just one method. This method also encourages regular feeding times and states that these regular feedings are important in establishing routine and healthy sleep habits. At this age, parents should be feeding their baby every two-and-a-half to three hours. If you feed more often, your baby will get used to snacking throughout the day, instead of eating a full meal during feedings. You might have to wake up your baby for feeding to keep this schedule. If feeding at night, keep the lights low, do not interact with your baby, and put him back to sleep immediately after the feeding is done. For this method to be employed properly, parents should keep sleep logs and record food intake amounts and times for the duration of the training.

From 6 to 8 weeks old, you should encourage feedings every three hours, but not more frequently. You should not have to wake your baby for night feedings. If he wakes up on his own for a feeding, you should feed him. If your child's pediatrician feels he still needs night feedings and tells you to wake him for the feedings, you should do so. Because of the high prevalence of colic during these ages, this method does not suggest any intense training take place yet.

The period between when your baby is 8 to 12 weeks old is what this method calls "baby boot camp." During this time, parents will go through a four-step process. Parents must go through these steps in the order outlined for this plan to be successful. The first step is to feed your baby every four hours, four times per day during 12 daytime hours. The process to get your baby to feed every four hours instead of every three hours might be a slow one. The method suggests distracting your baby if he gets fussy and is ready for a feeding before the four-hour mark. When you first start moving his feeding times, do so slowly. Try waiting 15 minutes past his old feeding time, and when he gets used to that time, move it back 15 minutes more until you are feeding every four hours, four times per day. Your baby's total intake of formula or breast milk should be 24 ounces. Pick your target feeding times, and do not move to Step 2 until you have reached those times (for example, 8 a.m., 12 p.m., 4 p.m., and 8 p.m.).

Step 2 is to gradually eliminate nighttime feedings. She outlines a method to taper these feedings off by slowing reducing the amount and number of feedings that take place. If your baby eats less than usual on his own, do not offer him any more than that amount at future nighttime feedings. Breastfeeding moms might find it easier to taper off feeding if they use measured pre-pumped breast milk instead of continuing to allow nursing at night. Once nighttime feedings have been eliminated, parents can move to Step 3.

The third step is getting your baby to sleep or rest quietly for 12 hours each night. You should have already picked the times you want your baby to sleep during the night because you will base your daytime feeding schedule on those times. With this plan, you will never wait longer than five minutes to go in and soothe your baby. The goal during these check-ins is to get your baby to settle down, but not to fall asleep while you are in the room, and not for you to pick him up. Soothe your baby by talking quietly to him or rubbing his belly. When his cries quiet a bit, leave again, then wait for another five minutes before returning and repeating this process. This same method should be used if he wakes in the middle of the night or too early in the morning. You will probably need to slowly adjust the morning wake up time to reach the 12-hour mark. Just as with the feedings, increase the time by 15 minutes a day until your baby can wait the 12 hours. Your baby does not need to sleep the entire time. He can play quietly in his crib the last hour, as long as he is not crying. The idea is that you are setting the time that he goes to bed and wakes up. Just because he wakes up does not mean he gets to leave his crib, according to this plan.

The fourth and final step is getting your baby to nap one hour in the morning and two hours in the afternoon. This method strongly advises parents to not let their baby nap between the third and fourth daytime feedings, as that will make bedtime more difficult. Use the same process for getting your baby to nap, although an abbreviated version, as you do for bedtimes. Remember that the goal is quiet crib time and not necessarily sleep; your baby can be awake as long as he is quiet and not crying.

Though this method is designed for younger babies, the same techniques can be used in older children. Babies 3 to 9 months old should be able to adapt to the same process, but it might take longer to see success. For children 9 to 18 months old, parents should log their baby's sleep schedule for one week before beginning training. This method still advocates feeding four times during the day, although this process might be harder for babies who have started eating solids. Consider having another family member help out in training instead of Mom. At this age, be sure not to bargain with your child, and make sure not to pick him up during nighttime soothing. For the first night, you should soothe your baby every 30 seconds to one minute, then increase the intervals to three to five minutes. This process should still work if used consistently, but it will require added patience on the part of the parents — and added commitment and dedication to the plan.

## *Sleep Strategy #4:* No-cry sleep solution

Elizabeth Pantley, author of the *No-Cry Sleep Solution* book, recommends parents teach their baby to sleep without allowing their baby to cry. In this method, much like other methods, parents will need to teach their baby or child to fall asleep without parental help. Her method may take more time to have full success and may require more repetition to get a concept to stick with your baby. She suggests parents should not always allow their newborn to fall asleep nursing or bottle-feeding. Instead, she suggests you stop nursing your baby and put her to bed when she is sleepy but still awake. This concept is not different from many other sleep methods. With this method, however, if your baby cries when you try to put her down, she suggests you pick her up, rock her, and give her the bottle/breast again. Once again, when she is sleepy, try to put her in the crib. These steps will need to be repeated as often as necessary to allow your baby to learn to fall asleep alone. She suggests parents who co-sleep also teach their baby to fall asleep without the aid or presence of her parents.

Though this method does not promote parents letting their baby cry, it does suggest parents learn how to *read* their baby's cries. Many babies make crying-like sounds when they are sleeping. Parents should learn to recognize the difference between these "sleep sounds" and true cries. According to this method, if your baby is truly crying, you should offer support. If your baby is only making sleep sounds, let the baby sleep. Responding to these sounds can actually cause your baby to wake more during the night. Some other tips include not letting your baby nap too long and helping your baby distinguish day from night. She advises parents to differentiate nighttime sleeping from daytime naps by making bedtime dark and quiet, and making naps take place in a lighter room with some noise. This method also suggests parents learn their baby's drowsy signs and use these to signal bedtime instead of the clock. *See Tip #24 in this chapter for more on recognizing when your baby is drowsy.*

## CASE STUDY: WORD FROM THE EXPERTS: BEST OR WORST STRATEGIES FOR YOUR BABY TO SLEEP THROUGH THE NIGHT

With five children of her own, Arnall has plenty of experience in how to get a baby to sleep through the night. The method she believes is best is a form of co-sleeping, where one parent sleeps in the room with the baby (making a small sleep area on the floor next to the bed for the baby) while the other parent sleeps in a quiet room. Parents take turns getting undisturbed sleep. The parent in the same room with the baby should comfort the child every third night.

**– Judy Arnall, co-founder of Parenting Canada; owner of Professional Parenting Canada**

Dehn said she waited until her son slept through the night on his own before trying any strategies to have him continue to sleep through the night. Once he started waking up in the night (at about 9 months old), she used the Ferber method to get him to fall back asleep and start sleeping through the night on his own again. The Ferber method worked for her within three days. The method that worked the worst for her was picking him up and comforting him. This method prolonged the time she spent trying to get him settled and back to sleep.

**– Barb Dehn, RN, MS, NP**

Heinsohn said she has found rocking a baby and singing to her before bedtime the most effective method for getting a baby to sleep through the night. She cautions against creating an environment that is too quiet. Parents who create such an environment for their babies can end up with children who are very light sleepers and need complete silence to get sleep. On the other hand, parents who allow music, television, or other noise to continue while their baby is sleeping are more likely to raise children who are heavy sleepers.

**– Laura Heinsohn, director of Family Bureau of Investigation Parenting Workshops**

Alkazian said her three children are all great sleepers. In the "Mommy & Me" classes she teaches, sleep questions are the most frequently asked questions she receives. She has found a combination of letting a baby cry it out, establishing and maintaining a consistent bedtime routine, and giving a baby transitional objects for comfort work best in getting a baby to sleep through the night. Waiting a problem out seemed to work the worst. Babies and children need to be taught how to soothe themselves back to sleep. Parents who maintain the philosophy that they know what is best for their baby and who do not give up trying to teach their baby to sleep through the night seem to have the most success. She also believes these parents create a long-term relationship of safety and comfort with their baby.

**– Bette Levy Alkazian, MA, licensed marriage and family therapist**

Kerr said with her first child, she used the cry-it-out method — and it worked. She read the book *Healthy Sleep Habits, Happy Child* by Marc Weissbluth, M.D., and employing the techniques in that book worked well for both of her children. If they were well rested during the day, they slept better at night, even from a young age. Fox said she Ferberized her oldest child, but her second child did not need that method. Her third child required environmental changes, including a white noise machine and darkening shades.

**– Baby Bunching experts Linda Kerr and Cara Fox**

"Since no two babies are alike, no one solution exists that will work best for all babies." For her own daughter, Heilbrunn nursed her to sleep while she was young. Once her daughter got older, she substituted a soft doll (that her daughter picked out) for the nursing and gradually taught her to fall asleep on her own. Heilbrunn's technique started with her staying next to her while she fell asleep. She then moved to patting her on the back, and finally stayed in the room with her for a certain amount of time (lengths that gradually got shorter and shorter). If her daughter was still awake after the designated time passed, Heilbrunn would kiss her, say goodnight, and leave the room (promising to check on her in ten minutes).

**– Claudia Heilbrunn, parenting expert, author, and certified life coach**

As an infant and toddler sleep coach, as well as the mother of three, Pollak found the progressive waiting or Ferber method worked best.

**– Karen Pollak, founder, Babies2Sleep**

"Many new mothers are told by their own mothers and friends that giving the baby solid foods (such as cereal) before bedtime will help the baby sleep better because their baby will not be as hungry. Several studies have actually refuted this philosophy. The nighttime awakenings for feedings will continue until the expected maturational process reaches a point when they no longer occur (which will not be sped up or delayed by varying the baby's diet). Another common misconception is the use of 'noise machines' or playing music. Besides the dangers of causing permanent hearing damage, these tactics are simply not useful. Instead, he advises parents wait until the baby starts displaying a change in behavior (crying, whimpering, or wanting to be held, for example) that occurs at around the same time every evening.

That should cue the parents the baby is starting to get synchronized to the day/night cycle. Once this occurs, parents will know it is time to begin a regular bedtime routine. An appropriate bedtime routine for this age might be a bath, dressing the baby in sleep clothing, reading him a book — yes, even to a baby just a few months old — in a quiet, soothing voice, and/or singing some lullaby songs, feeding if the baby seems hungry, and putting him to bed. At first, it is important to time the bedtime routine according to the baby's inner clock/schedule, but as the baby matures, lessen the variability at which this occurs. There will be plenty of occurrences, especially initially, when the baby may cry for a few minutes when placed in the crib, but with time and consistency, this becomes less common." Dr. Traeger said he and his wife used these techniques with both of their boys, and bedtime has become soothing, effective, regular, and enjoyable to all.

– **Nadav Traeger, MD, FAAP, FCCP, D, ABSM, director of pediatric sleep medicine, Maria Fareri Children's Hospital**

Dr. Kuhn raised three children of his own and has first-hand experience both in his own home and with his practice in helping children sleep. He admits that although he is an expert in childhood sleep patterns in his practice, he could not be an expert in his own home. After months of sleepless nights, his wife agreed to let him use the cry-it-out method. Within three nights, all were sleeping better. When his second child was 2 ½ months old, his wife suggested the cry-it-out method again. It was too soon and so they waited another month before employing the cry-it-out method. Again, they found success in three nights. With their third child, his wife started preventive measures — which she had heard him lecture about — from Day 1, and they never had to employ the cry-it-out method. Instead, they placed their daughter in her bassinet drowsy but awake and allowed her to fall asleep on her own. She never became dependent on her parents to put her to sleep and thus never developed sleep issues. In his practice, Dr. Kuhn listens to the parents' concerns and issues, discovers the cause of the sleep problems, and develops a plan tailored specifically for that family and their specific issues and goals.

**– Dr. Brett Kuhn, CBSM, associate professor of pediatrics at the University of Nebraska Medical Center and Children's Sleep Center at Children's Hospital**

Dr. Davies said she has personal experience with the incremental cry-it-out method, or the Ferber method, which gradually increases the time a baby is alone. "Not sticking to a plan, whether you do not stick to it, or the babysitter or the father undermines it, is the worst 'strategy' to employ."

**– Dr. Laura Davies, diplomate, American Board of Psychiatry and Neurology**

Neville said that although she cannot explain it, somewhere between when her babies were 7 to 9 months old "felt" like the right time for her to begin training. Her babies were sleeping in their own room by that time, and waking her to eat once a night. With her son, she prepared to grit her teeth and listen to him cry for at least 15 minutes. What really happened is that he cried for two minutes, for one night only, and to her complete amazement, that was the end of night waking. Two years later with her daughter, Neville said she could not stand the thought of her crying it out. According to Neville, her daughter had a blood-curdling scream and had screamed for the first six months of life any time she was awake and not being carried on a walk — including when she paused to load the washing machine or sit on the toilet.

By the time her daughter was 6 months old, she could crawl on her own and stopped screaming. Neville's solution was to leave home and spend the night with friends, knowing that her husband would wake up if things got really bad. Neville reports her husband slept through the night — although she is not positive her daughter did. The next night, Neville returned home and slept through the night as well, and night waking was a thing of the past. She believes her method worked because she did not try it too soon, and her children were both of pretty flexible temperament.

**– Helen Neville, BS, RN, author, pediatric advice nurse, health educator, specialist in inborn temperament, and researcher**

# • TIP #24 •

## Recognize Your Baby's Drowsy Signs

Though most parents would recognize certain signs their baby is drowsy, like fussiness or rubbing her eyes, other signs can be easily overlooked. Some babies will not signal their sleepiness overtly. Losing interest in activity is an example of a drowsy sign that is easily overlooked. Some babies will look away or lose interest in playing or interacting with others when they are tired. If nursing, pay attention to when your baby stops sucking with as much enthusiasm as she first started. Her eyes may start to close, and her sucking slows. Other signs of sleepiness include becoming more quiet, slowing down or lessening of play or movement, getting a glazed look in their eyes or staring into space, heavy or droopy eyes, and fussing.

Overlooking these drowsy signs or keeping a baby awake longer than his biological clock wants can create a fussy, overtired baby who will be harder to put to sleep and who will not sleep as well. Recognize the difference between your baby's drowsy signs and his overly tired signs. Learn to put your baby to bed when drowsy, and before he is overly tired and crashing from exhaustion.

Although maintaining consistency with your routine and bedtimes is important, you should allow some flexibility based on your baby's drowsy signs. If your baby's normal bedtime is 8 p.m., but he is displaying drowsy signs at 7 p.m., you might need to run through a quick bedtime routine to get him to sleep. If you miss this drowsy window, you could end up with a wired baby who will not go to bed at his appropriate time and then wakes earlier than usual the next morning. If you make an adjustment such as this one, try to resume your normal schedule the next night. If your baby seems to be getting tired at the same earlier time each night, you should consider switching his bedtime to this earlier schedule. If not, examine what other factors are present that could be contributing to his early drowsiness. If you recently changed naptimes or eliminated the evening nap, you might be seeing such changes in his bedtime routine. Remember that although your goal is to maintain consistency in your routines, you do not want to be so rigid in your schedule that you are ignoring your baby's signs. Keep an eye on the clock when it comes to bedtime, but remember that your baby's drowsy signals are more important.

## • TIP #25 •

## Do Not Give Up on Sleep Training if the First Strategy Does Not Work

Some parents will say, "We tried to sleep train our baby, but it did not work." These parents might have tried a sleep training program, but they almost certainly did not try the right sleep strategy, or they gave up on a sleep training program too soon. If your first attempt at sleep training does not work, you should not give up on sleep training altogether. Though experts do not recommend strategy jumping, you should not be discouraged if your first sleep strategy attempt does not work. All babies and children are different, and different techniques work for some and not others. Some babies respond great to the cry-it-out method, while others just seem to cry longer and longer. Use your sleep log to decide whether your strategy is working.

Do not decide to switch or quit strategies in the middle of the night, and do not make changes when you are tired and frustrated. Using your sleep logs will help you make a decision on the success or failure of your strategy accurately. During these trying times, you might only remember the sleepless nights. Without the logs, you might not realize your baby is waking up less frequently and falling asleep more quickly than before you started training. Depending on your strategy, success might be slower than you expect (or hope). Remember to give your strategy adequate time to work. Some will take weeks, while others will usually see success in days. Usually some improvement should be seen within the first seven to ten days. If you are not seeing success or even improvements, take an honest look at your implementation of the plan. Consistency is key for the success of any sleep strategy.

## • TIP #26 •

## Decide if Co-sleeping or the Family Bed is Right for You

Co-sleeping is another area that is highly controversial and debated among experts and parents. When considering whether co-sleeping is right for your family, you should weigh the advantages and disadvantages to make your decision.

**Advantages of co-sleeping:**

- Cuddling with baby/partner and more time with baby
- Convenience for breastfeeding mothers
- Quick response for any baby nighttime waking

- Better sleep for baby and parents (if baby was keeping parents up when sleeping in a crib)
- Could create an easier sleeping arrangement for a colicky baby

**Disadvantages of co-sleeping:**

- Increased risk of injury and SIDS to baby (such as from parents rolling over on baby, baby getting stuck between mattress and headboard, or suffocating on pillows or covers)
- Baby might become dependent on parents' presence to fall asleep
- Bad sleep habits might be harder to break if co-sleeping (for example, nighttime feedings will be harder to stop if Mommy and breast are "available" all night long)
- Your baby or child might sleep well but keep you and your partner up all night (children are often restless and noisy sleepers)
- If both parents do not want to co-sleep, one parent may resent the other or the child for having to share a bed
- Loss of intimacy for the parents; parents unable to have sex in family bed
- Earlier bedtime for parents
- Parents might not be able to go out at night if child cannot fall asleep without them present

Co-sleeping is a decision that each family needs to make for themselves. Parents need to agree that co-sleeping is right for them. If one parent forces another into co-sleeping, tensions could arise within the marriage, or one parent might resent the child. This decision is best made before your baby arrives, but should at least be made before sleep training decisions are finalized. Co-sleeping sometimes results in one parent sleeping in another room. Parents should address this potential issue before they begin co-sleeping. If one parent is unable to sleep in the same bed as their partner and child, parents should have a pre-determined plan to deal with this situation.

But reactive co-sleeping is not a healthy habit and should not be a part of any sleep-training plan. Reactive co-sleeping is when exhausted parents give up on their sleep strategy in the middle of the night and bring the baby into their bed as a last effort to get some sleep. Reactive co-sleeping will encourage your baby or child to push you past your limits so you will give in to their demands. This method teaches that your rules as a parent can be broken or bent if the child tries hard enough. When it comes time for your child to switch from the family bed to a crib or bed of their own, the transition will be much easier if co-sleeping was a preemptive decision rather than practiced reactively.

If you decide to co-sleep, you should still set appropriate parental boundaries. You might decide to allow your child to sleep in your bed, but not with the same bedtime as you. This means the child should be able to fall asleep without you or your partner present. This method is not safe for young babies, so be sure to ask your child's pediatrician or sleep expert if your baby is old enough to sleep in your bed without you present. Other parental boundaries might be limiting the number and times of nighttime breastfeeding. Though co-sleeping can make breastfeeding easier for both mother and baby, if not monitored, your baby can turn into a nighttime grazer. While this might not seem like an issue at first, it will be harder for you to discontinue nighttime feedings if your baby is accustomed to grazing all night long.

Before you start co-sleeping, set a time limit for when you will stop co-sleeping. Experts' recommendations vary when it comes to the time to end co-sleeping. Some suggest parents stop co-sleeping when their baby is 6 months old. Others say parents should stop co-sleeping when their child is 1 year old. Most will suggest by age 3, a child should no longer sleep in the family bed. As parents, you should determine your goal for co-sleeping and decide when you feel it is appropriate to end co-sleeping. If you are co-sleeping to make breastfeeding easier, you might decide to move your baby to a crib as soon as nighttime feedings are no longer necessary. When deciding when to move your child out of the family bed, consider this: The earlier you make the transition, the easier the transition will be on you and your baby.

Parents who decide to co-sleep also need to make safety their first priority. A parent can suffocate or smoother a baby by overlying, especially if a parent uses any type of drugs (including medications or sleep aids) or alcohol that cause a deep sleep. Some experts recommend parents move their bed away from the wall and any furniture or headboard in the room so the baby cannot get stuck in crevices created where the bed meets the wall. Parents who co-sleep should have a firm mattress and avoid using pillows or heavy covers around the baby. The baby should still be placed on his back to sleep, just as a baby should be placed if a crib is used. Loose sheets and comforters should also be avoided. Parental obesity can also create a hazard when co-sleeping. Some experts recommend parents convert a whole room into a co-sleeping bed by covering the entire floor of the room with mattresses to make co-sleeping roomier for everyone and safer for the child.

Prevention of SIDS should be a consideration whether co-sleeping or using a separate bed. The AAP does not recommend co-sleep. Instead, the AAP suggests that parents who want to sleep close to their baby should keep their baby in their room, but in a bassinet or crib instead of in the same bed. Some studies have shown a connection between co-sleeping and an increase in SIDS. To lessen the risk of SIDS while co-sleeping, use the precautions listed to avoid suffocation or overlying by a parent. Parents should also prevent anyone from smoking in the house with the baby, especially in the bedroom the baby sleeps in.

## CASE STUDY: WORD FROM THE EXPERTS: CO-SLEEPING/FAMILY BED VERSUS CRIB

Arnall feels this decision should be made by each individual family. "Families considering using a family bed need to remember that safety of the baby should be the first and foremost consideration. A great way to ensure the safety of the baby is for parents to use a co-sleeping safety checklist." See the one available on her Web site at **www.professionalparenting.ca**.

**– Judy Arnall, co-founder of Parenting Canada; owner of Professional Parenting Canada**

As a former pediatric ICU nurse, Dehn cautions against this popular method for getting a child to sleep through the night. She said she has treated too many babies whose parents accidentally rolled over him or her at night, and the consequences are too frightening to make this tactic worthwhile. She said it occurs frequently enough that most SIDS experts discourage co-sleeping. Another disadvantage of co-sleeping, according to Dehn, is the parents' quality of sleep may suffer.

– **Barb Dehn, RN, MS, NP**

"The decision to allow co-sleeping really depends on the child." From the time Heinsohn's son was 2 to 5 years old, he would crawl into bed with her and her husband. Heinsohn recalls letting him fall asleep in their bed, then carrying him to his own bed. Eventually, Heinsohn placed blankets next to the bed where her son could sleep instead of in the bed with her and her husband. Her son soon outgrew this behavior altogether. Her daughter was a heavier sleeper, and although she too went through a similar phase, it did not happen as often.

– **Laura Heinsohn, director of Family Bureau of Investigation Parenting Workshops**

"This is a very personal choice for a family. Teaching a baby to fall asleep by himself is an important lesson," said Alkazian. She also said that she does not sleep as well with a baby in her bed because she feels she has to say a little bit awake all night and, of course, her space is more limited. "Studies have also shown that a baby's life could be at risk while sleeping in a family bed. Teaching a child to sleep on his own helps teach self-reliance and independence. Teaching a baby healthy sleep habits leads to a happier family environment and better-behaved children."

– **Bette Levy Alkazian, MA, licensed marriage and family therapist**

Kerr said that while she never used this method, "some families will find this technique works best to ensure the whole family is well-rested. This is especially important for "baby buncher" parents — parents who have children less than two years apart — who have to be focused the next day to take care of a baby and a toddler." Fox said that the family bed method did not work for her family. Her baby was too noisy, and she stayed awake all night worrying that someone would roll over her baby. She also said some experts do not recommend this method, based on an increased risk of SIDs. "As much as I adore snuggling," Fox said, "I try to stay away from it [the family bed]."

– **Baby Bunching experts Linda Kerr and Cara Fox**

Heilbrunn only recommends that parents determine what method is right for them. "Because all families are different and have different needs, no one method is best. If both parents love the idea of having a baby in their bed, then they should try it. If parents want the bed to themselves, then the baby should sleep in a crib."

**– Claudia Heilbrunn, parenting expert, author, and certified life coach**

Pollak advocates letting the baby have his own bed when parents are ready to have their child sleep independently. "Once the baby is sleeping in his own bed, everyone sleeps better. Sleep training is much easier if your baby is sleeping in his own bed."

**– Karen Pollak, founder, Babies2Sleep**

Smith and her husband decided not to use a family bed or co-sleeping. She said they felt that having their own bed was the best situation for her family. "Everyone needs his or her own space and room to sleep at night." Another advantage she sees to giving a baby her own bed is that it also allows parents time to themselves.

**– Stephanie Smith, mother of twins**

"While most families in this country choose to have each child sleep in his or her own bed, this decision is a very personal choice based on cultural, ethnic, and personal experience," said Dr. Traeger. "Some families opt to have a communal bed shared by the whole family or just the children. Neither method is wrong or right, as long as at the end, everyone gets a good night's sleep within the setting of the parents' choosing."

**– Nadav Traeger, MD, FAAP, FCCP, D, ABSM, director of pediatric sleep medicine, Maria Fareri Children's Hospital**

Dr. Kuhn does not recommend any certain technique, but instead thinks the family needs to decide what method best fits their philosophy and beliefs. "Couples should decide for themselves if they want to co-sleep with their baby." Depending on the situation, Dr. Kuhn sometimes will recommend parents consider co-sleeping. He does advise that children have a higher tendency to become dependent on their parents' presence to fall asleep when the co-sleeping method is used, and some children do not get as much sleep when they sleep with their parents rather than sleeping alone. However, no studies have shown that children who co-sleep have more sleep issues than those who do not. "The problem arises when parents practice reactive co-sleeping.

This practice is when parents bring their child into their bed in the middle of the night as a 'last resort' measure to get a good night's sleep."

– **Dr. Brett Kuhn, CBSM, associate professor of pediatrics at the University of Nebraska Medical Center and Children's Sleep Center at Children's Hospital**

"This decision should be based on family preference. Some risks are present with the family bed, including a slight increase in mortality." Davies advocates having a parent be a co-sleeper with the baby if a family chooses to have their baby in the family bed.

– **Dr. Laura Davies, diplomate, American Board of Psychiatry and Neurology**

When it comes to co-sleeping, Neville reminds parents that the overall goal is to maximize sleep for the whole family. "Some sensitive moms cannot sleep well in bed with an active, noisy baby. Conversely, some babies sleep longer when in bed with parents. It comes down to your particular family and what method works best to achieve the overall goal of better sleep for the whole family."

– **Helen Neville, BS, RN, author, pediatric advice nurse, health educator, specialist in inborn temperament, and researcher**

# • TIP #27 •

## Know When Your Baby Needs You

As a parent, you need to learn to cultivate your inner parental instincts. If this is your first baby and he is still a newborn, you might still be learning to read your baby's signs. It will take time to develop this skill, but it is a skill worth developing. You should try to start distinguishing between your baby's cries for help and cries for attention. You soon should know when your baby is crying for hunger, for a diaper change, or for some good-old-fashioned Mommy time. To understand why your baby is crying, you must first understand the different reasons babies cry. Babies cry to communicate a want or need. They cry because they are hungry, tired, need to burp, need a diaper change, want to be held, want to be rocked/walked/moved, are too hot/cold, want attention/to be able to see you, want to suck, are feeling sick, and many more reasons. Basically, they cry because they have no other way to communicate feelings. Pay attention to when your baby cries and which cries signal certain wants or needs. By paying attention to your baby's cries during the day, you will be better equipped to decipher his cries at night.

When your baby cries at night, use the skills you have learned to know why your baby is crying. Remember that not all cries mean something is wrong. If he is crying because he wants you to rock him to sleep, you might need to let him cry (if you are employing the cry-it-out method). If he is crying because his diaper is dirty, you should change him and then put him back to sleep. Knowing the difference in these cries will also help you know when your baby is sick and should not be left to cry and when he is crying for attention.

Oftentimes, you baby will first exhibit signs of illness by being fussy for what seems like no reason. If your baby is crying and you cannot figure out why, see if onset of an illness might be the reason. Take your baby's temperature even if he does not feel particularly warm to see if he is starting to develop a low-grade fever. Pay attention to any body parts your baby is grabbing while crying. If he is pulling on his right ear, he might be trying to tell you he has an earache, which could indicate an ear infection.

## • TIP #28 •

## Avoid Strategy Jumping

Strategy jumping is best avoided by carefully considering all sleep strategies and picking the one you and your partner are most comfortable with. If you or your partner are not fully committed to a plan, or not comfortable with the plan you have chosen, you will be more likely to abandon your plan at the first sign things are not going well. For instance, if you are not comfortable with hearing your baby cry at night but decide to try to the cry-it-out method anyway, chances are good you will give up on the strategy after just a night or two.

A great way to prevent switching strategies or abandoning one too quickly is by using sleep logs to evaluate the strategy you have chosen. While sleep training, it is easy to get caught up in the negative aspects of training, like the sleepless nights or listening to your baby cry at 3 a.m. With your sleep log, you can accurately evaluate the progress or lack of progress of your sleep strategy. If you feel your sleep strategy is not working and feel like switching strategies, first wait until morning to evaluate the situation with a clear head. Second, ask the opinion of your child's pediatrician or a sleep expert before deciding for sure if you should switch plans. Bring your sleep log with you so they can accurately evaluate your situation. Remember that different strategies take different lengths of time for your child to learn; children learn to sleep well at different rates.

Strategy jumping is not a good idea because it can cause your baby or child to develop bad sleep habits you later will have to break (which ultimately causes sleep training to be harder on you and your baby). Switching strategies also creates a confusing situation for your baby or child. If you change strategies often, you are changing the rules for your child, and he will not know what is expected of him from day to day. This lack of structure can create a stressful environment for your child, which also makes sleep training more difficult. Sticking with one strategy might work within seven to ten days, but switching strategies continually will make success take longer.

## • TIP #29 •

## Gradual Approaches are More Prone to Cause Relapses

This tip is true only if you are consistently sticking to your sleep strategy. If you are being inconsistent in your implementation of a strategy, chances are neither cold-turkey nor gradual approaches will have much success. Experts have said this tip is true for consistent implementation because by their very nature, gradual approaches take longer for your child to learn. It might be more accurately said that gradual approaches take longer to teach. For example, if you decide to teach your child to swim by throwing him in a swimming pool, he will have a shorter learning period than if you teach your child to swim in slow steps, starting with teaching him to blow bubbles in the bath water. Because gradual approaches take longer to teach, they are more prone to have small relapses as the child is learning.

Also, parents might be more likely to give up on a gradual sleep-training approach because successes are not seen as quickly as with a cold-turkey approach. This does not mean cold-turkey approaches are better than gradual approaches. The best approach for you and your baby is the one that you will be able to stick to consistently until you reach success. When you decide on a sleep strategy, take into consideration the amount of time it will take to see success with that plan. Weigh the pros and cons honestly and decide what is most important to you. If you cannot stand the idea of hearing your baby cry, you might choose a no-cry method that is more gradual and will take longer to be fully successful. If you would rather find a plan that works quickly, and you can manage a few nights of hearing your baby cry, you might choose the extinction or Ferber method.

## • TIP #30 •

## Parental Inconsistency Often Leads to Bad Sleep Habits

Inconsistency in parenting can lead to bad habits. Much the same, inconsistency in sleep training can lead to poor sleep habits for your child. Once you have selected a sleep strategy, follow the plan exactly as prescribed. Do not pick and choose certain elements of a sleep plan unless you are working with an experienced sleep coach or sleep trainer who is tailoring a plan to your baby. Otherwise, stick to your plan. If your sleep strategy does not allow you to pick up your baby during middle-of-the-night check-ins, and you do pick your baby up one night, your baby might expect to be picked up subsequent nights. She might also cry longer and harder to get you to pick her up as you did previously. Other inconsistencies can include rocking your baby to sleep or letting your baby fall asleep nursing instead of in her crib.

Once you begin your sleep training, be disciplined enough to stick to the plan. If you do have a moment of weakness and pick up your baby or rock your baby to sleep, do not worry. Remind yourself the next morning that you need to get back on track with your plan. Be sure not to repeat this same inconsistency more than one night in a row and get back on the original plan for your sleep training as soon as possible.

Keeping your sleep logs up will also help you determine whether parental inconsistencies are affecting your baby's sleep training. You might not be aware of how you are being inconsistent or subconsciously sabotaging your sleep strategy if you are not keeping accurate sleep logs. Be honest when filling out sleep logs. The purpose of the log is to provide an accurate account of your sleep training program. Your effectiveness as a parent is not being judged through these logs. Without this accurate account, you could be setting your baby up for sleep training failure without realizing it. Remember that your goal is having a family who sleeps well the whole night.

*Photo courtesy of Sivan Grosman, founder of Sivan Photography (**http://sivanphotography.com**)*

# • TIP #31 •

## Combat Stalling Tactics Before Your Child Tries Them

For babies, this tip is easy to follow. Before bedtime, make sure your baby's basic needs are met. He should be fed, have a clean diaper, be in a comfortable environment, and know he is loved. For older children, and especially for talking children, this can pose more of a challenge. Try to anticipate your child's bedtime wishes or requests before bedtime. It is best to incorporate these requests into the bedtime routine — brushing teeth, taking a potty break, drinking a glass of water, and reading bedtime stories, for example. If your child asks for additional acts beyond his usual requests, he is most likely stalling bedtime.

Do not give in to your child's tactics. For example, if he is asking for one last bedtime story, explain to him that you will always read one story before bedtime. Remind him that at bedtime tomorrow, you can read another story. If you give in to these requests — even one night — he will learn that he can push your limits and that your bedtime rules are bendable. This situation could encourage your child to view bedtime as a challenge to push your limits and could result in a challenge for you to continually find ways to meet the new requests each night. If you never give in, your child will learn that bedtime is bedtime, and he will eventually stop pushing the limitations.

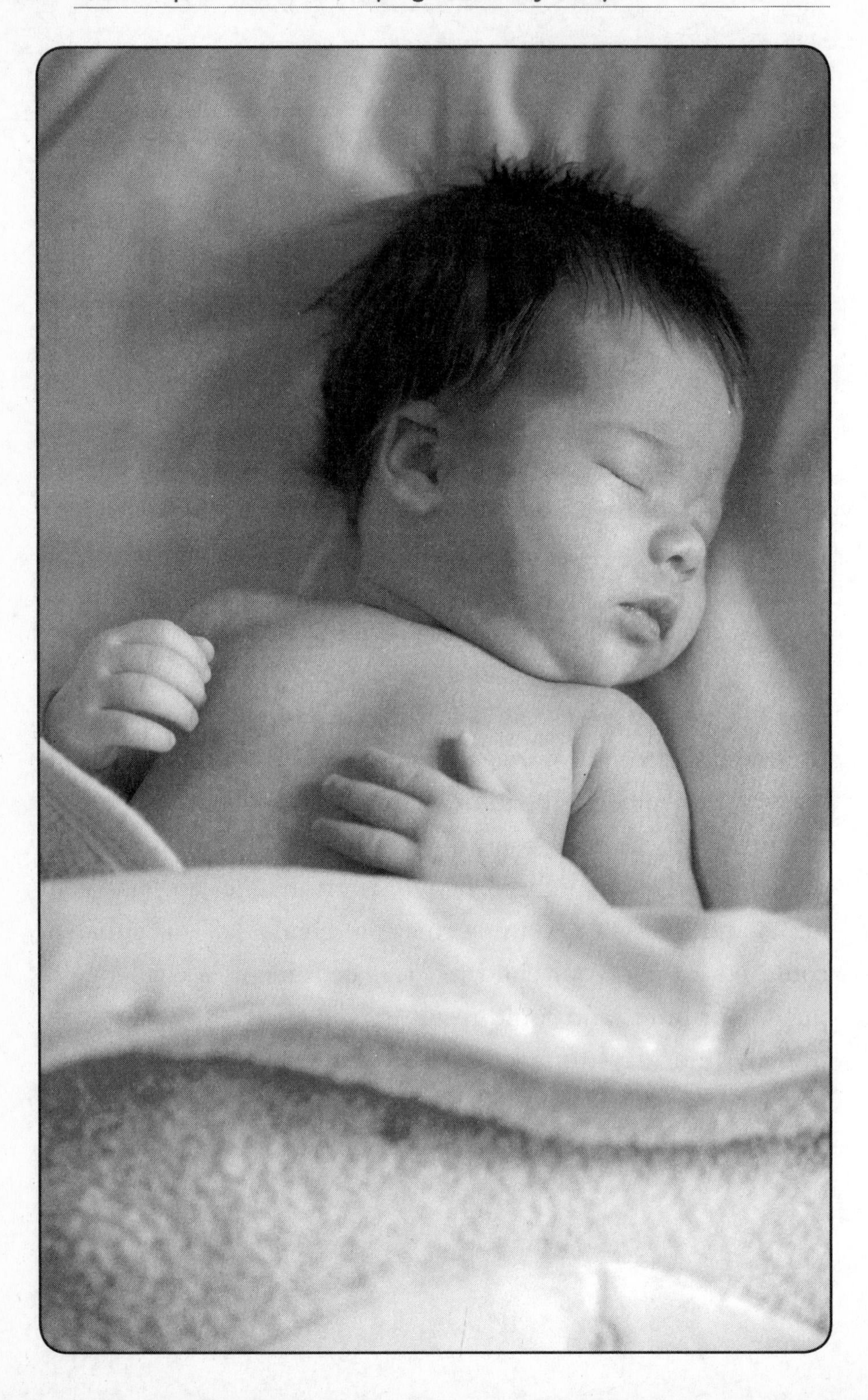

# • TIP #32 •

## Pick a Sleep Strategy that Both Parents are Comfortable With

Many emotions can be involved with picking the right sleep strategy. One parent may not believe in using the cry-it-out method, while the other is convinced it is the best and quickest method. Remember that as parents, you must create a united front. Pick a solution you both are comfortable with and committed to. If one of you agrees to a solution you are not truly comfortable with, chances are you will not be as committed to it as you should be. This parent could subconsciously sabotage the sleep plan or see every minor setback as complete failure of the plan. Sleep training can be hard enough without adding in the complication of marital stress. Never agree to a sleep plan you and your partner are not 100 percent in agreement on.

If you are hesitant about a strategy, but believe that it is the best for your child, you might need to remove yourself from the sleep training program. For instance, if you believe your child will respond best to the cry-it-out method, but you cannot stand the thought of hearing him cry at night, have your partner lead the training, and consider wearing earplugs while your partner carries out the plan. If you are unsure whether this solution will work, consider sleeping elsewhere for a night or two while your partner is sleep training the baby. Do not try to force yourself through the sleep training process if you are not comfortable with it. You will only add stress to your life, which your baby will sense. Even if you do commit to the plan and carry it out consistently, your high stress levels can cause your baby sleepless nights.

You also might start resenting your partner for "making" you go through with a plan that you did not want to do. Creating stress in your relationship will create stress in your family unit. Your baby will pick up on the stress, which will also sabotage whatever sleep method you choose. Be honest with yourself and your partner. Do not force your partner into any method he or she is not comfortable with. Remember that sleep training is important for the whole family.

# • TIP #33 •

## Do Not Make Decisions About Sleep Strategies or Change Sleep Strategies in the Middle of the Night

During those trying nighttime hours when both you and your partner are exhausted and at your wits' end, do not make decisions about your sleep strategy. Keep with your plan for at least one more night. Be committed to your plan, and make all your decisions about sleep strategies and techniques during the day – and when you both are as well rested as possible. No good decisions can be made during those high-stress times when all you can think about is getting to sleep as quickly as possible.

Be determined to at least get through one night, and discuss changes in the morning. The following morning, take an honest look at the situation the previous night and at your sleep training plan's big picture. Remember to give a strategy enough time to take hold. Look through your sleep logs to see if any progress has been made, or if inconsistencies might be contributing to your baby's lack of sleep. Determine if other factors contributed to the previous night's situation or caused your baby to have more trouble sleeping than usual.

Try to keep at least one parent well rested at all times so that the well-rested parent can step in when the other is beyond his or her limit. If Mom usually handles all sleep training so Dad can get sleep, consider having Dad step in for a night or two while Mom catches up on sleep. If you are too tired, frustrated, or stressed to deal with sleep training, ask your partner for help. Even one night off can make a difference and relieve some built-up stress so you will be able to handle sleep training the next night.

If no one can help, and you cannot handle another night of training, take a break. Let your baby cry while in a safe place such as his crib, take some deep breaths, or scream into a pillow. It is better to let your baby cry longer (and maybe put himself to sleep in the end) than to risk your baby's safety by pushing yourself past your limits. Do not take your frustration out on your baby. If you need a break, take it. Shaking your baby will not make him stop crying and poses a severe risk for long-term damage or death.

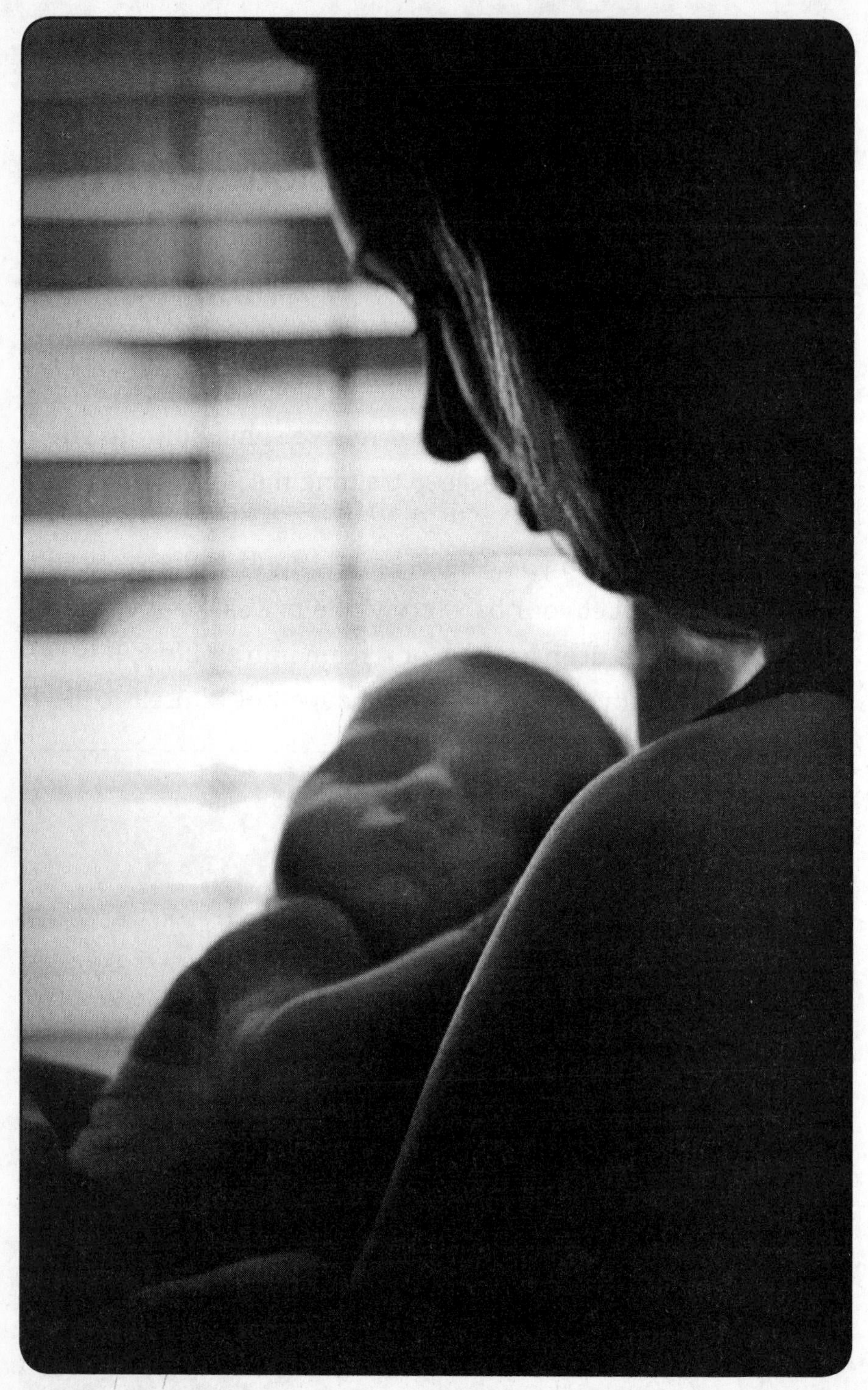

*Photo courtesy of Sivan Grosman, founder of Sivan Photography (**http://sivanphotography.com**)*

# chapter 5

## Setting the Mood for Sleep

An important component to getting your baby to fall and stay asleep throughout the night is making sure the mood is right. If you pick the right strategy and employ it consistently, but put your baby down for bed in a distracting environment, you could be setting yourself up for failure. Before you begin sleep training your baby, make sure you have created the best sleep environment you can. Help make sleep training easier for you and your baby by creating a place where your baby will feel safe, secure, and bored enough to fall asleep. Designing the cutest nursery on the block might make you the envy of your friends, but it may end up sabotaging your baby's sleep. And when it comes down to it, sleep – for you and your baby – is more important than a cute nursery. Plus, you can save the money you would have spent designing a nursery for more important details, like diapers or a college fund for your child. Setting the mood for sleep involves having all the right ingredients. *See the "Setting the*

*Mood Checklist" in Appendix A for a quick guide to ensuring your baby is prepared for sleep.*

# • TIP #34 •

## Understand that a Baby's Environment Can Enhance or Detract From Her Sleep

Your baby's nursery (or the room he sleeps in) should be designed to encourage sleep. Loud noises, brightly lit mobiles, and toys can create a stimulating environment where your baby will want to play, not sleep. But the room chosen for sleeping should also be a place where your baby feels safe and where she associates good times or memories. Many experts recommend that most of the bedtime routine take place in the nursery and should consist of positive, fun, and quiet activities. Fancy wallpaper or murals on the wall are not necessary. Turn out the lights and look at the room from your baby's point of view. A big, cuddly stuffed animal in the corner of the room might look cute during the day but could look very scary to a young child when the lights are off.

Most parents and experts agree that less is more when it comes to nursery design. Keep in mind the objective is to get your baby to sleep, not to have the cutest nursery on the block. Avoid aquariums in the baby's room or any stuffed animal in the crib for newborns. Once a child is no longer at risk for SIDS, a safety-approved stuffed animal or blanket might be useful to help your child fall asleep. Some experts suggest Mommy or Daddy sleep with the stuffed animal or blanket before giving it to the child so that it has a comforting scent. Older children should be allowed to pick out their own stuffed animal or blanket – keeping safety in mind – so they are playing an active role in their bedtime routine and sleep training.

Stay away from loud colors and designs in the baby's room. Though a poster of cartoons or animals might be cute, these items could create a stimulating environment for your baby, and any item or design that could keep your baby's interest or occupy his time should not be in the room. Remember that you are designing an environment for sleep. Everything in the room, even the color of paint on the walls, should signal sleep to your baby. If you put your baby to bed in a room full of interesting pictures and stimulating colors, you are setting him up for a night of wakefulness, not sleep.

# • TIP #35 •

## Pick the Right Room and Furniture

Safety should be your No. 1 consideration when it comes to picking out furniture for the nursery or choosing which room to make the nursery. Although it might be tempting to use an antique crib that has been passed down in your family, it might not be the safest option, and it may in fact pose a serious risk to your baby. Also be wary of hand-me-down cribs from friends and family or bargain cribs from a neighborhood garage sale. Check to be sure the crib meets U.S. Consumer Product Safety Commission (CPSC) standards (**www.cpsc.gov**). This Web site also lists up-to-date recalls and other product safety news. The crib should be put together correctly without missing pieces or broken parts. It should have no sharp edges or corners. Crib slates should not be wider than a soda can (2 3/8 inches), and no corner posts higher than 1/16 inch, according to CPSC.

The mattress should fit tightly in the crib (you should not be able to fit more than two fingers between the mattress and the crib frame) and should be firm. *See Tip #36 in this chapter for more information on the mattress and bedding*.

The room should be a place where your baby feels safe and associates it with good memories. Your baby should not associate the nursery with a place where she is left alone each night. Make sure you create good times and memories in your child's bedroom. During the day, spend some time playing in the room. Make sure lots of cuddling, hugs, and kisses take place in this room. If your baby or child associates good times with her bedroom, you will not have to fight each night to get her to go there. When deciding on your bedtime routine, make sure more of the routine takes place in the bedroom. Be sure the routine is pleasant and comforting for your child. You want your baby to feel safe and comfortable in her room.

Carefully decide which room of the house to make your baby's nursery. Consider how much noise will carry into the room while the baby is sleeping. If you have a noisy dog for a neighbor, you might not want to put the baby's room closest to the barking. While you do not want to create a completely noise-free environment, you do not want to set your baby up for failure by placing her in the noisiest spot in the house. This could include keeping her room away from the laundry room or garage.

Set up the room to make for quick nighttime feedings and diaper changes. Have a dim lamp or light in the room you can use during these nighttime interactions. You want to have enough light to see what you are doing without stimulating your baby to a fully awake state. Your nighttime interactions should be as dimly lit as possible.

You might also consider having a baby-wipe warmer device in the room for nighttime diaper changes. You could easily fully wake a baby by wiping him with a cold baby wipe during a nighttime changing. Design the room to make easy nighttime interactions so you can get in and out quickly without fully waking your baby. Bottle warmers can also be helpful for times when nighttime feedings are still necessary.

# • TIP #36 •

## Pick the Right Bed

When considering the right bed, including the right mattress, sheets, and crib, two main factors should be considered: safety and sleep. Your first priority should be creating a safe environment for your baby. Your next most important consideration should be finding bedding that provides a good sleep environment for your baby. Many experts suggest the use of flannel sheets rather than cotton sheets so you will not be placing your sleepy baby on cold, cotton sheets, which may wake them up.

You can also pre-warm cotton sheets by placing a heating pad or hot water bottle in the crib before the baby's bedtime. Any heating devices should be removed from the crib before the baby is placed in it. Check the temperature of the sheets before putting baby to bed to ensure sheets are a little warm rather than hot. The point of the heating device should be to get rid of the coldness of the sheets rather than to heat the sheets.

Crib bumpers should be avoided for newborns unless they are firm (not soft or cushy) and should be safety-approved, as some can increase the risk of SIDS. Babies who can stand on their own or pull themselves up in the crib should not have crib bumpers in case they pull themselves up on top of the bumper and risk falling out of the crib at night. Babies 1 year old or younger should not have any blankets or pillows in the crib with them.

A firm mattress without loose blankets or bedding is an important safety tip for young babies when the risk of SIDS is still high. The mattress should have a tight-fitting bottom sheet only. The fitted sheet should be designed to fit the mattress you are using and should not come loose during the night if your baby moves around. Blankets are not recommended for babies at risk for SIDS. If you choose to use a blanket, be sure to tuck the blanket in tightly at the foot-end of the crib. Place your baby's feet against the end of the crib, and do not allow the blanket to reach higher than his chest. Consider sleepwear for warmth instead of using a blanket. No other comforters or fluffy blankets should be allowed in the crib, especially for babies 6 months old or younger, when the risk of SIDS is highest.

Consider safety and sleep when deciding if a crib, bassinet, or family bed is the best match for your baby.

# • TIP #37 •

## Pick the Sound

Experts do not agree on whether white noise or music helps babies sleep. Most experts do agree babies should not have complete quiet during nighttime or naptime sleeping because the child may not learn to sleep through noise that might occur from someone outside the room. With some noise occurring during sleeping, your baby will be more likely to develop into a deep sleeper. This trait is a very important one to cultivate if you plan to have more children and need the older child to be able to sleep through the new baby's crying.

Although experts might not agree, as a parent, you should decide what seems to be the best answer for your baby. Many experts and parents have reported success with using white-noise machines or soft music. Avoid any music or crib mobile that stimulates the baby, as this is counterproductive to creating a good sleep environment. Some experts also suggest using machines that mimic the heartbeat, much like what a baby hears in the womb.

Find what works best for your baby. If you live in a particularly noisy neighborhood, white noise might help block out much of the background and help your baby sleep. You might not even need to buy a machine to create white noise; a fan or air purifier in the room can create the same effect. Some clock radios also have functions that play wave-like sounds, which create a similar effect to a white- noise machine.

Remember that if you decide to use music or white noise to get your baby to fall asleep, it should play throughout the night.

When your baby wakes in the middle of the night, everything that got her to fall asleep in the first place should be the same. If white noise or music was playing when she first fell asleep but is no longer playing when she wakes up, she might be scared or confused and not be able to put herself back to sleep. Using white noise or music is creating a sleep association. While not all sleep associations are bad, all sleep associations must be present during the night if you want your baby to be able to fall asleep on her own after a middle-of-the-night waking.

## • TIP #38 •

## Pick the Right Sleepwear

For babies still at risk for SIDS (under 1 year old), you should put the baby to sleep in as little or as much clothing to keep him a comfortable temperature throughout the night without needing any blankets. You want the room temperature to be comfortable but not too hot. Overheating could be linked to SIDS, so avoid creating a hot baby. Space heaters should never be used in the baby's room. The age and mobility of the baby will determine the type of pajamas a baby should wear to bed.

Any pajamas you use for your baby should be flame-resistant, safe, and comfortable for your baby. Babies who are mobile might not enjoy sleeping in a sleep sack because they could become tangled in the pajamas in the middle of the night. For these babies, consider using a footed-blanket sleeper. If it is summertime and warm in the house, you might be putting your baby to sleep in a diaper only.

Check the temperature of the room before you put your baby to bed and ensure your baby is a comfortable temperature during your nighttime checks. Some experts recommend against using sleepers as nighttime wear. These types of pajamas are considered blankets by regulating authorities and are not held to the same standards (such as being flame-resistant) as other "true" pajamas because they are not classified as clothing. Loose nightgowns can also pose a hazard to young babies. Use tight-fitting pajamas so your baby will not get tangled in loose clothing and risk suffocation.

# • TIP #39 •

## Pick the Right Crib Accessories

As previously discussed, toys are a distraction and should not be present in the nursery, and especially not in the crib. Blankets should not be used for infants at risk for SIDS and should be used for older children only when safe. The use of pacifiers is another widely debated issue among child experts and parents. In 2005, the AAP began recommending parents encourage their babies to fall asleep with a pacifier because pacifier use might help protect against SIDS in young babies.

The AAP did not recommend parents reinsert pacifiers in their baby's mouth in the middle of the night, but rather allow the baby to reinsert it himself if he so chooses. Studies do not show any decrease in SIDS if pacifiers are reinserted by parents throughout the night. If your baby does not reinsert the pacifier himself at night, you might find it easier to wean him off pacifiers when the time comes to do so. If he is able to put himself back to sleep in the middle of the night without the pacifier, he should also be able to put himself to sleep initially without a pacifier.

If you decide to use pacifiers, experts recommend placing several around the crib but not attaching them to your baby or the crib. Limiting pacifier use to bedtime only might create less dependence on the pacifier than allowing use throughout the day. AAP suggests breastfeeding mothers wait until their baby is 1 month old before using pacifiers, even for sleep. This recommendation allows time for the baby to establish good breastfeeding skills.

Older children who use pacifiers (especially if they use them throughout the day) might have difficulty developing speech properly and can experience trouble with their teeth. Expert recommendations on the age to discontinue use of pacifiers vary. Some say by age 2, your child should no longer use a pacifier. Others recommend weaning your child off pacifiers between 12 and 17 months or waiting until age 3. This is based on the fact that your baby will go through many stressful changes between 18 months and 3 years old, and trying to also wean from a pacifier will add to the stress.

Other crib accessories, such as mobiles or toys, are unnecessary and often can create a stimulating environment for your baby. When shopping for the nursery or looking at crib accessories, ask yourself whether the item is needed and whether it will enhance sleep or contribute to a stimulating environment for your baby. The goal is to make nighttime boring and quiet. Do not buy any product that does not meet that goal. Do not use any item in the crib that is best reserved for daytime play.

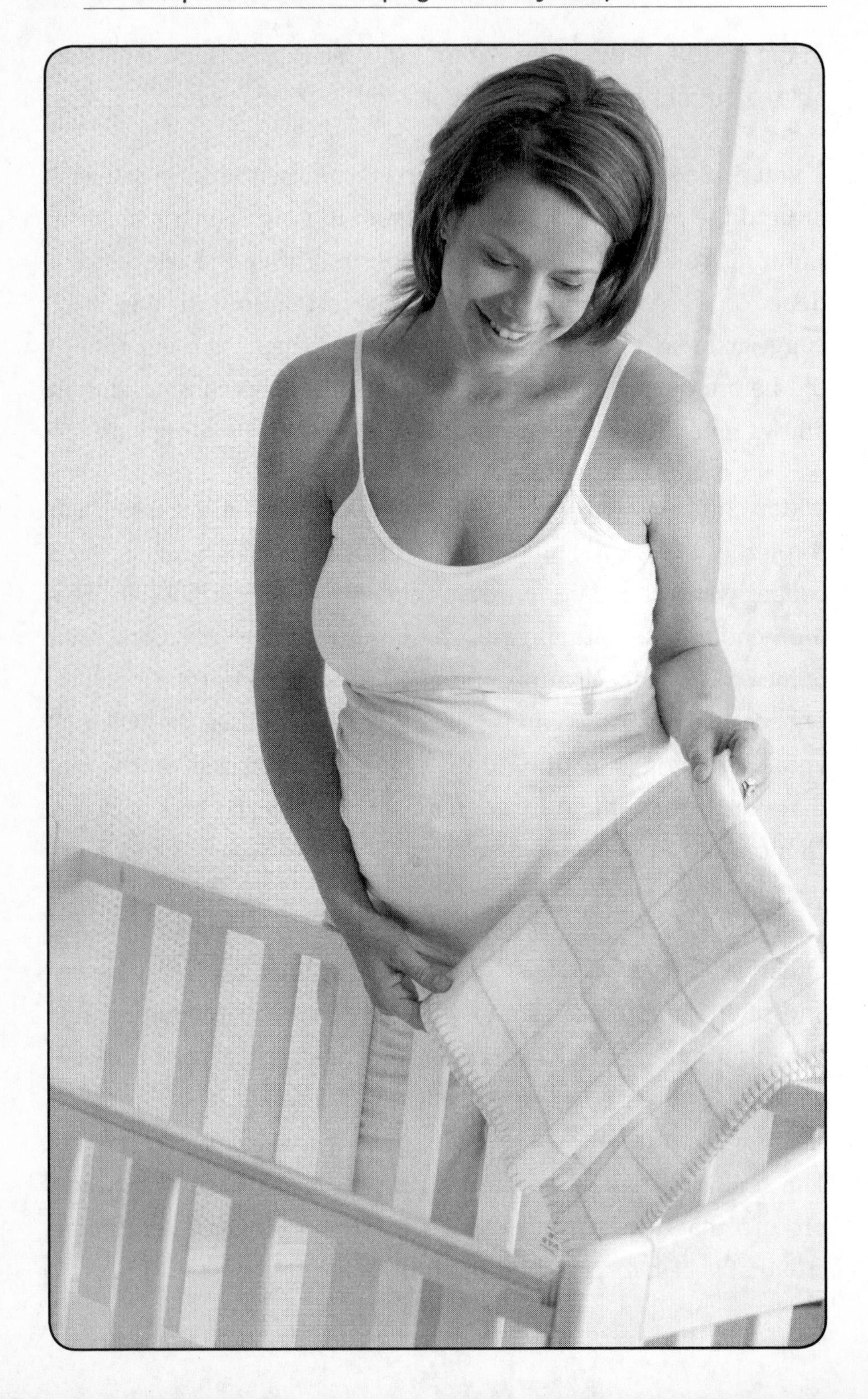

# • TIP #40 •

## Pick the Right Bedtime Story

When picking a bedtime story for your baby, choose one that is quiet and soothing and will help set the mood for bedtime. Stay away from books that create excitement or stimulation for your baby or child. An example of a good bedtime story is *Goodnight Moon,* by Margaret Wise Brown.

Not all books that involve sleep are good bedtime stories. A story that involves bedtime but also involves yelling and jumping on the bed would not be an ideal candidate for a bedtime story. Books that excite children do not lead to soothing bedtime sleep. While these stories might be a great daytime story, they should not be used as part of a soothing bedtime routine.

If your child is old enough to pick out her own bedtime stories, make sure you have predetermined which stories are suitable for bedtime stories, and have her pick only from the predetermined bedtime stories.

For older children, it is also important to have a set number of books that you will read at bedtime and not read any more than that amount. If you allow the one extra book tonight, chances are that when tomorrow night arrives, one extra will turn to two extra, and stalling techniques will get worse with time.

# • TIP #41 •

## Pick the Right Lighting

When you put your baby down for bed, the room should be nearly pitch-dark. Most experts recommend that on a scale of one to ten (ten being complete darkness), your baby's room should be an eight or nine. If streetlights, sunlight, or moonlight shine into the windows, consider installing darkening shades. (You can substitute a heavy blanket over the window for darkening shades, as long as it will not pose a safety hazard to your baby.)

Babies do not need nightlights. As your child ages, he might become scared of the dark, in which case nightlights might be helpful. For young babies, you might help them learn the difference between night and day by adjusting the amount of darkness in the room during naptimes. While bedtime darkness ranks an eight or nine, you might make naptimes a six or seven. You still want to create a dark environment for naps, but creating a slight difference in the amount of darkness might help your baby learn when he is being laid down for a short sleep time (naptime) or a long sleep time (bedtime). Because newborns do not know the difference between day and night, you might find this a helpful tool to teach them the difference, thus teaching them to sleep longer at night than during the day.

## • TIP #42 •

## Pick the Right Temperature

The temperature of the room should be comfortable enough so your baby is warm without being hot and will not need blankets to stay warm throughout the night. Most experts recommend the baby's room temperature stay around 68 to 72 degrees Fahrenheit. Check your baby's temperature throughout the night by placing your hand on her tummy or the back of her neck. If she is hot or sweaty, adjust the temperature lower or remove some of the baby's clothing.

Air circulation can also help keep the room from having a stale smell. If a ceiling fan is in the baby's room, it can work to circulate the air and provide white noise for the baby. You might not need to install a ceiling fan or have another fan placed in the room if the air is circulated by the vents. Be sure the vents are clean so dusty air is not being blown about the baby's room. Do not place furniture in front of vents. Consider where the vents are located when placing the crib in the room. Do not place the crib in the direct line of the vent. While your room temperature might be appropriate, you could overheat or overcool your baby if the vent is blowing directly on her.

In colder months, adjust the thermostat to keep the room warm without needing additional heaters in the baby's room. Do not place space heaters in the baby's room. Overheating a baby increases the risk of SIDS.

# • TIP #43 •

## Pick the Right Smell

Research shows babies are more sensitive to smell than adults, and babies can recognize their mother's smell. Be aware of the smell of the nursery or room where your baby sleeps. Do not make any scent overpowering, and remember that your baby will be more sensitive to the room's smell than you are. Older babies can benefit from a blanket or stuffed animal that smells like Mom. Be careful about using this technique with younger babies when the risk of SIDS is still high. Ask your pediatrician if you are unsure if your baby is still at risk for SIDS. Moms can sleep a night or two with the blanket or stuffed animals to get their scent on it, then place it in the crib so the baby will smell them throughout the night.

Another option might be the use of aromatherapy to help your child associate a certain soothing smell with nighttime. Proponents of this idea suggest once your baby has associated the smell with a comforting environment and sleep, it will be easier for another family member or sitter to put your baby to bed in your absence. A couple of drops of lavender oil placed on a tissue or cloth near your baby while you feed him his last meal of the night might help this association. Remember to keep the scent faint, and recall that your baby's senses will be more sensitive than your own. *For more information on aromatherapy for babies, see Appendix C for a list of helpful Web sites.*

Although you might not decide to use any sort of aromatherapy in your baby's nursery, you do want to make sure there are no offensive smells in your baby's room. Make sure the air has a fresh smell, and do not use overpoweringly scented plug-ins or aerosol sprays in the nursery.

# • TIP #44 •

## Pick the Right Position

A newborn baby should always be put to sleep on his back, whether at bedtime or for a short nap. The AAP began its "Back to Sleep" campaign in 1994, after which the incidence of SIDS was reduced by more than 40 percent. Babies are at the highest risk for SIDS within the first six months of life, but are still at some risk until age 1. Once a baby is able to roll over, placing him on his back to sleep can seem less important (or less effective, because he is able to change positions at night). If your baby resists sleeping on his back, try swaddling your baby. The swaddling method should only be used if your baby is still a newborn and your pediatrician approves that this is a safe method for your baby.

Also consider having your baby sleep in a car seat or stroller. Babies are used to sleeping curled up in the womb, and car seats can mimic this position while not posing a safety risk. If you use an alternative method to sleeping on the back, try not to allow the baby to alternate positions every night. Intermix the car seat with trying to get your baby to fall asleep on his back. While experts do not recommend having your baby sleep in a car seat every night or as a long-term solution, it can help in the short term to get your baby to sleep through the night.

If your baby simply will not sleep on his back, try having him sleep on his side. Sleeping face-down, before a baby is old enough to turn over by himself, poses the highest risk for SIDS. For SIDS prevention, the best sleep position is for your baby to sleep on his back. Sleeping on his side is the next best solution.

## • TIP #45 •

## Pick the Right Feeding Times

Depending on the sleep strategy you have chosen to implement, your plan may guide you in setting very specific times to feed your baby. If you have chosen a plan that does not lay out specific feeding guidelines, you may need to create your own. Creating a regular feeding schedule for your baby ties in with developing her circadian rhythm.

Remember that circadian rhythm also governs when we get hungry and eat. If you are feeding your baby at the same times every day — and at appropriate times — it can enhance her ability to sleep and help her establish her circadian rhythm based on the schedule you have developed for her.

When selecting feeding times, your baby's age will determine the interval between feedings and the number of feedings he has throughout the day (and possibly night). Your newborn will feed every two-and-a-half to three hours, night and day, even if you have to wake him up to feed.Once your baby is older, you can begin spacing feedings out more and more. By the time your baby is 12 to 15 months old, and thus 12 to 15 pounds, he should no longer require nighttime feedings. Wean your baby off these feedings as soon as possible so you can start encouraging him to sleep through the night without your assistance, and so you can create a regular schedule for his daytime feedings.

Many experts recommend feeding your baby four times a day. Your child's pediatrician or sleep coach might suggest a different schedule of feeding, possibly three or five times a day. Avoid letting your baby snack constantly throughout the day. While some feedings might be larger than others, if your baby is a grazer during the day, he may very likely want to be a grazer during the night as well. This situation could cause sleep training to be a bigger challenge than it already is.

Be sure your baby is taking in enough food during the day. For your baby's first four months of life, do not introduce other foods besides breast milk or formula. If you are breastfeeding your baby, time the length of nursing to determine the amount of milk your baby is getting. Consider using pumped breast milk for nighttime feedings to more accurately measure your baby's intake — especially when you are beginning to taper off the feedings. After 4 months old, your baby might be ready to try a few alternative foods. Check out Baby Center's Web site for a guide of when to introduce new foods to your baby at **www.babycenter.com/0_**

**age-by-age-guide-to-feeding-your-baby_1400680.bc**. Be sure to ask your child's pediatrician if she is ready for new foods before you introduce them.

## CASE STUDY: WORD FROM THE EXPERTS: SETTING THE MOOD FOR SLEEP

Dehn suggests parents use flannel sheets instead of cotton because they will be warmer when a baby is first put down.

**– Barb Dehn, RN, MS, NP**

"Too much stimulation will keep a baby awake, and what makes one baby sleepy could keep another baby awake. Parents should be aware of what works and what does not work for their baby. Parents should look at the room from a baby's perspective. Something that looks cute and harmless to an adult might look big and scary to a child when the lights are turned out.

"Window blinds that block out all the light will help when trying to get a baby to sleep during times when it is not dark outside. Parents should not tiptoe around during their baby's sleeping times. Parents should make noise from the beginning of baby's sleeping time so he will learn to sleep through noises."

**– Bette Levy Alkazian, MA, licensed marriage and family therapist**

"A nursery should be designed for good sleeping for a baby," Kerr said. She used shades to block out sunlight and put on white noise during naps and bedtime for her children. Because she sleeps better this way, she thought her children would, too, and it seemed to work well. "Trying to get a toddler to nap was much easier when naptime was in a darkened room." Fox said she listened to Kerr when she endorsed the dark shade and white-noise method and finally adopted it for her youngest child. She has found this method is working very well.

**– Baby Bunching experts Linda Kerr and Cara Fox**

"Often parents create a stimulating room environment without knowing it. While this situation can frequently detract from a baby's sleep, parents might never make the association between the stimulating environment and their baby's poor sleep.

"Some examples of stimulating environments include mobiles over the crib with strong, contrasting colors such as black/white/red, high-contrast art on the walls, or orange/black/white clown fish painted all around the room. On a scale of one to ten, the room should be an eight in darkness (room-darkening shades can accomplish that). If there are sudden external noises that can be heard from the room — such as a dog barking, cars or motorcycles roaring by, or doorbells ringing — having an ambient, white-noise element can mitigate wakings on the baby's part. Room temperature should hover between 65 to 68 degrees Fahrenheit. Rooms too cold or too warm can cause sleep disruptions."

– **Karen Pollak, founder, Babies2Sleep**

"The nursery should be a place that your baby feels comfortable [in]. Parents should keep the bed away from windows and be sure to allow for movement of air around vents."

– **Stephanie Smith, mother of twins**

Dr. Traeger recommends the nursery be designed so while the child is asleep, the room will be cool, comfortable, quiet, and dark.

"Any item in the room that detracts from this can lead to poor sleep, including noise or music machines, mobiles, nightlights, and excessive toys or decorations. Many new parents get the wrong message from advertisements, friends, and baby supply stores and buy a whole bunch of accessories, thinking that otherwise they will be 'bad parents' because their baby would be deprived. The bed should be a place where the child sleeps, and nothing else."

Dr. Traeger tells parents their baby will not be deprived if these items are missing, but will certainly be deprived if these items cause missed sleep, which is so important to development. Newborns need their parents' love, nutrition, and ability to be left alone to sleep in a soothing environment.

"Parents should use the money they would spend on baby 'necessities' for other uses — saving for college, for example."

– **Nadav Traeger, MD, FAAP, FCCP, D, ABSM, director of pediatric sleep medicine, Maria Fareri Children's Hospital**

"No one design is needed to help sleep; in fact, no design is even necessary. Your baby does not need 400-thread-count sheets to sleep well. Babies do not need special mobiles, pillows, or designs on the wall. A baby does need a relatively dark, mostly quiet, safe room. The room should be at a comfortable temperature in an environment where the baby feels protected and safe."

**– Dr. Brett Kuhn, CBSM, associate professor of pediatrics at the University of Nebraska Medical Center and Children's Sleep Center at Children's Hospital**

"The nursery should be just like 'Goldilocks' — not too hot, not too cold, not too bright, and not too dark. The designs do not matter. If they parents are comfortable, their baby will be comfortable. Parents should not put a lot of stuffed toys and pillows in the crib because of the risk of SIDS."

**– Dr. Laura Davies, diplomate, American Board of Psychiatry and Neurology**

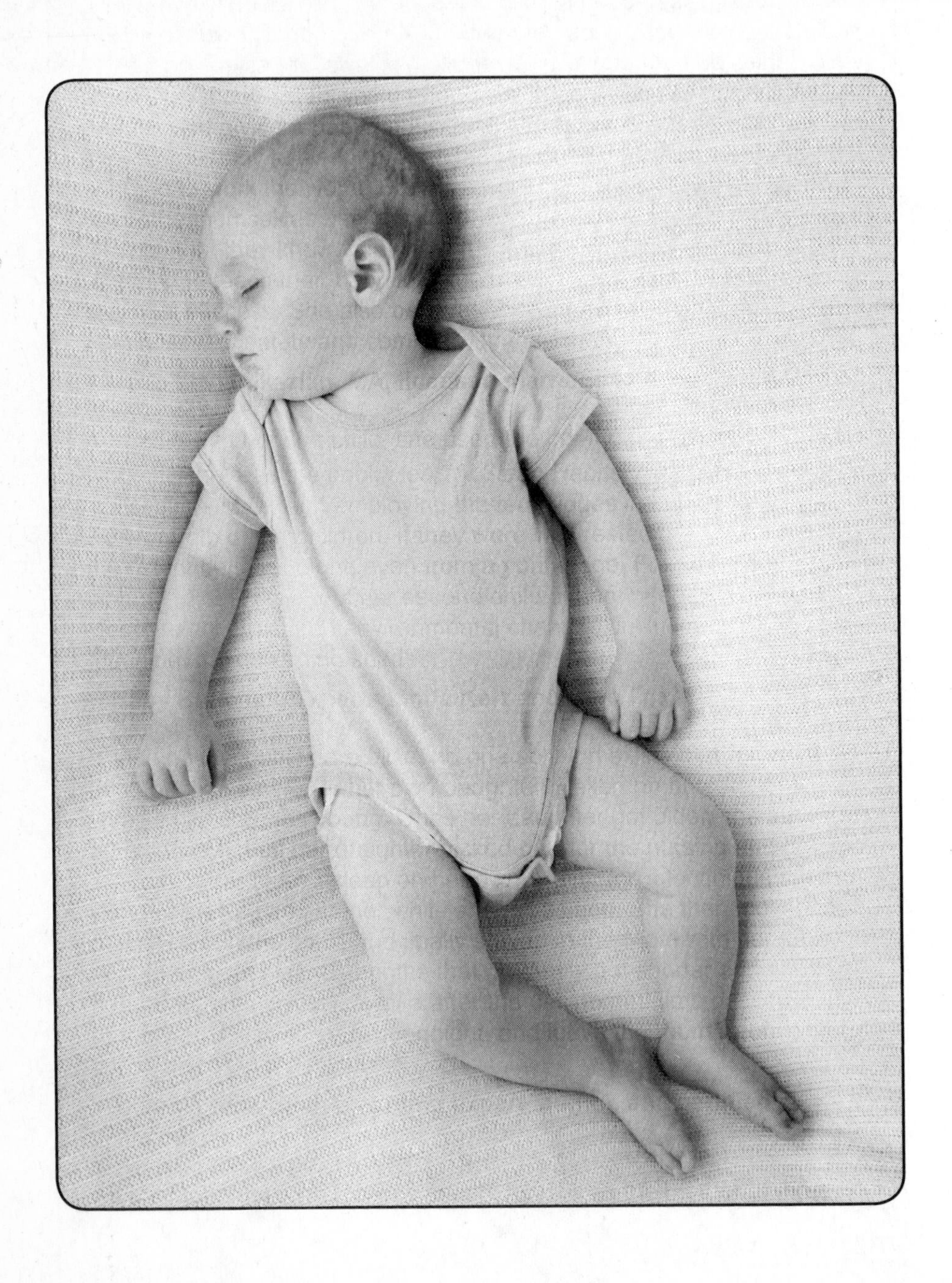

# chapter 6

## Establishing a Routine

Many experts believe in the success of a bedtime routine. Some believe the routines should be more formal than others, and some like to suggest specific activities your bedtime routine should include. Most agree that consistency in the routine itself is more important than the details of the routine. The idea of a bedtime routine is that it communicates to your baby that bedtime is coming. Your baby will learn that after this sequence of events, he will be put down for bed and will be expected to sleep through the night. Without a routine, your baby might be confused about what is expected of him and be surprised when he is suddenly left alone in his bed.

### • TIP #46 •

### Plan Your Baby's Bedtime Routine Before Bedtime

When planning a bedtime routine for your child, take his specific needs into account along with your personal needs and the needs of your family as a whole. Experts agree there is not one bedtime routine that is best. Bedtime routines can vary from family to family and child to child. What experts do agree on is that the bedtime routine should be planned ahead and should be one that works for your family's own unique needs.

This routine should be one that signals bedtime is coming; it should be predictable and consistent. To maintain consistency each night, you must plan ahead and create a routine you know you can employ each night. Avoid routines that will not work every night. If your partner's work schedule is unpredictable and might include late nights, your partner should not be the primary employer of the bedtime routine.

While the routine might involve both parents, some families might find it better to have it led by just one parent. In families with multiple children, one parent might put the youngest to bed while the other parent takes care of the older children. If one parent works during the day, that parent might want to lead the bedtime routine to spend some quality time with the baby. Decide what fits best for your family situation. Both parents should be at least minimally involved if possible, even if this means just a hug and kiss goodnight before the actual routine starts.

The bedtime routine should at least partially, and some say mostly, take place in the room the child will sleep in. While your routine might start with a bath and pajamas, it should move into the baby's room so she will have happy memories in the room where she sleeps. If your entire bedtime routine occurs in another part of the house and ends with you putting her down in her bedroom and leaving, she might start to associate her room with the place you leave her alone at night. Create happy times in the bedroom both during the day and during the bedtime routine. If you decide to read books, play quietly, or sing as part of your routine, do so in the room where your child will sleep. Have the lights dimmed during these events to signal quiet time and the upcoming bedtime.

Listen to your baby's natural rhythm for sleep times to make bedtime easier for you and your baby.

Remember that your routine will start to change as your baby grows and matures. Although maintaining a routine is important, you must also be flexible to change over time as your baby ages.

Some experts also recommend involving other family members in the bedtime routine. If you and your partner plan to go out at night and want to be able to leave your baby in the care of a trusted babysitter or family member, it is a good idea to get your baby used to having other people put her down for bed at night. If Mom usually handles bedtime, have Dad occasionally take the reins. If you have another family member who will be watching your baby from time to time, have him or her "practice" putting your baby down for bed while you are home to avoid issues once you leave the family member alone with your baby.

# • TIP #47 •

## Maintain Your Routine Even When Life Gets in the Way

While stringently maintaining your routine might not always be possible, try not to let life get in the way unless absolutely necessary. If disruptions to your routine are unavoidable, try a shortened version of your normal routine. You might skip the bath and read just one book instead of your normal three books on nights when you do not have time to complete your whole routine. Aim to still get your baby to bed at the same time. If you miss the drowsy window, you could end up with a baby who will be hard to get to fall asleep. Determine the element or elements that are most important to your child during his bedtime routine. When conducting a shortened version of the routine, be sure not to eliminate those elements. Some babies and children are more flexible than others when it comes to routines and especially to their bedtime routines. Learn to read your baby's flexibility when it comes to routine and, in particular, to his bedtime routine. If your baby does not handle changes in routine well, work even harder not to disturb it. Each baby, child, and person is different. Working within your baby's temperament and personality will make bedtime (and life in general) easier.

Other events such as birthday parties, doctor's visits, and traveling might also cause disruptions in your baby's bedtime. Try to minimize the disruptions as much as possible. If bedtime routines are disrupted due to events, resume your normal routine as quickly as possible — the next night, if you can. Remember that while you are sleep training your baby, disruptions will cause more severe setbacks. Be patient as you continue training. Minimizing disruptions will make sleep training easier for you and your child.

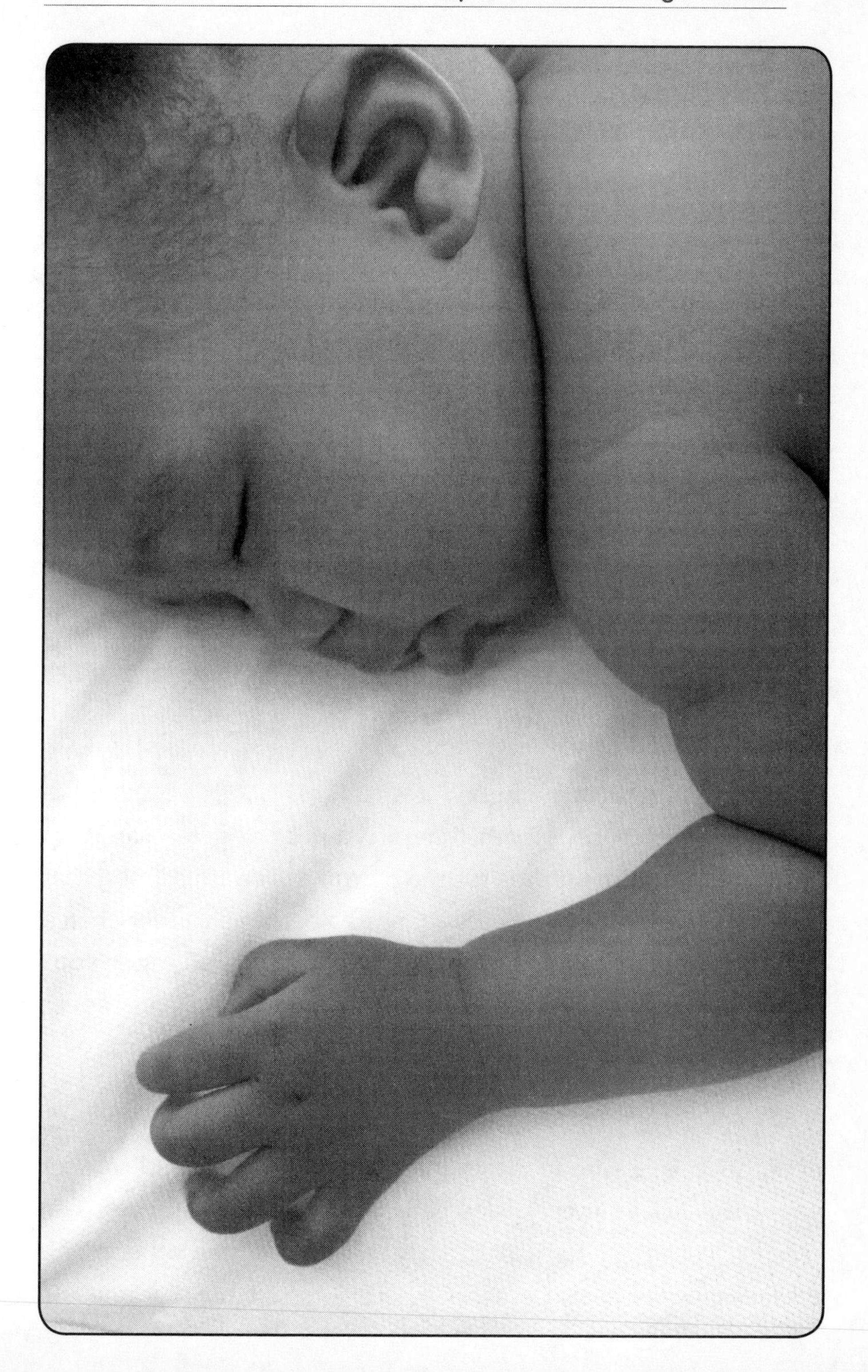

# • TIP #48 •

## Make Sure Your Baby Knows She is Safe, Cared for, and Loved Before Bed

Your bedtime routine should be one that encourages sleep and helps your baby wind down after a full day. Horseplay, loud sounds, and bright lights have no place in a good bedtime routine. Your routine should make your baby feel safe, loved, and cared for. She should know that all her needs have been met, that she is in a safe place, and that you love her. Cuddling, hugs, and kisses are a great way to remind your baby that she is loved. Changing her diaper, feeding her, and making sure she is comfortable where she sleeps will let her know that her needs have been met. Making the room she sleeps in a happy and comforting place during the day and conducting her bedtime routine in her room will ensure she knows she is safe.

Though some babies might find a warm bath soothing, other babies will be excited by bath time. If your baby gets geared up after a bath, save bath time for the morning. You might find that a massage with lotion is a better part of a bedtime routine than a bath. Be sure you are designing a routine that is soothing to your individual baby and not just doing a routine because an expert, pediatrician, or family member suggested it.

If you decide to make a massage or lotion a part of your bedtime routine, be sure to pick a lotion that is healthy and safe for your baby. Ask your child's pediatrician for recommendations on whether your baby has particularly sensitive skin or other medical conditions or allergies. Most experts recommend avoiding any nut-based oils or lotions due to possible allergies. Consider using oils or lotions made with grape seed, wheat germ, sunflower, or olive oil for your baby. Experts also recommend any lotion or oil that is edible, as babies will often end up with fingers, toes, or other body parts in their mouth.

## CASE STUDY: WORD FROM THE EXPERTS: BEDTIME ROUTINES THAT WORK

Arnall suggests parents put their baby in pajamas, read a book, give her a last bottle or nursing, wipe her gums, rock or cuddle her, then put her in the crib or co-sleeping bed with music playing. This song should be the same song each night.

**– Judy Arnall, co-founder of Parenting Canada; owner of Professional Parenting Canada**

"The keyword is 'routine,'" said Dehn. She suggests parents dim the lights and turn off the television. Even if the baby is not watching it, the light from a television can stimulate him or her. "A warm bath or a warm blanket while being held for a last feeding often helps a baby fall asleep. Parents should put their baby down for bed before he is fully asleep so he will start learning to fall asleep by himself. Babies sense fear and anxiety and will feel anxious or scared if Mom or Dad is feeling that way. Parents should be confident, hold their baby close, and whisper comfortingly to him while helping him fall asleep."

**– Barb Dehn, RN, MS, NP**

"Parents should spend several minutes calmly cuddling and talking sweetly to their baby. As you talk, start slowing your speech down and lower your tone while repeating the same 'love phrases.'" Heinsohn stresses that parents need to be in the moment and try hard to be loving and peaceful to their baby, even when stressed or sleep-deprived.

**– Laura Heinsohn, director of Family Bureau of Investigation Parenting Workshops**

Alkazian's routine with her three children started with a bath. "Even a playful bath is fine because the warm water will relax the baby," she said. The bath was followed by a feeding, books, then quietly speaking about the day or saying a prayer, and ending with kisses. "Younger babies will often fall asleep during the feeding, and parents may want to put books before a feeding in this case. Parents should turn out the lights after the books are read and only speak quietly from then until bedtime. Ultimately, the routine itself does not matter as long as it is about winding down for the night and quiet energy. The routine should end with putting the baby down right before he falls asleep. As children get older, parents need to plan ahead for a child's 'delay tactics,' such as needing water or having to go to the bathroom. Parents should deal with those issues before bedtime so it is not up for discussion later."

**– Bette Levy Alkazian, MA, licensed marriage and family therapist**

"A bath always signaled that bedtime was coming in my household," Kerr said. The bedtime routine was: bath, book, bottle/breast, song, and bed. If I strayed from this routine at all, I would have problems putting my children to sleep." Fox agrees that bath and then stories is a successful recipe for bedtime. She said her 3- and 4-year-olds run around like crazy after their baths, but by the time they are in bed for stories, they wind down. Because her children are older, she allows them to look at the books by themselves after being read a story.

**– Baby Bunching experts Linda Kerr and Cara Fox**

"Parents can find success with many different techniques," Heilbrunn said. She has seen success with co-sleeping, patting and singing, staying in the room and saying "Mommy's here," leaving the baby in his own room (knowing he will fall asleep in ten minutes), and Ferberizing. Her biggest recommendation to parents, no matter what method they choose, is that they should have a bedtime ritual planned out before bedtime starts and they should be consistent with their ritual. One example of a bedtime ritual Heilbrunn offers is bath, pajamas, book, lullaby, kiss, give baby his "comfy" — a blanket or stuffed animal, for example — and sleep. "Parents should remember that no technique will stop a baby from waking up forever. Just as sometimes adults have trouble sleeping, so will children. And, as children, they need parents to take care of their needs during the night just as parents would do during the day. Parents need to find out why a baby is crying at night to ensure the baby's needs are met."

**– Claudia Heilbrunn, parenting expert, author, and certified life coach**

"Parents should get their baby ready for sleep in a dimly lit room with white noise playing. The baby should be cleaned and changed, swaddled, and offered a pacifier (as a transitional object). Parents should then rock or cuddle their baby until she is drowsy, but still awake, and lay her in her crib so she can fall asleep independently." Pollak said she has used this routine hundreds of times.

**– Karen Pollak, founder, Babies2Sleep**

Smith said her own bedtime routine begins with a bath about 45 minutes before bedtime. After the bath, she gives the girls a snack and lets them watch television for about ten minutes. Next, they read books as a family. Afterward, Smith and her husband take their girls up to their room and let them choose a doll or stuffed animal to sleep with. Lastly, the girls are tucked in for the night.

**– Stephanie Smith, mother of twins**

"Parents may read or sing to the child, place them in bed, give a kiss, say goodnight, turn off the light, and then step out of the room as the child falls asleep on his own." He and his wife use this routine every night for both of their boys and he says it works wonders.

**– Nadav Traeger, MD, FAAP, FCCP, D, ABSM, director of pediatric sleep medicine, Maria Fareri Children's Hospital**

Dr. Kuhn said he does not place much emphasis on the specific bedtime routine. "What parents do during the routine is not as important as it is to perform a sequence of activities in the same order each night so your baby can predict bedtime. Parents should make sure the last activity in their routine is a positive one that occurs in the child's bedroom, so the child will look forward to going to their bedroom and will not fight it."

**– Dr. Brett Kuhn, CBSM, associate professor of pediatrics at the University of Nebraska Medical Center and Children's Sleep Center at Children's Hospital**

Neville said she wanted her children to sleep in their own room. She never used a crib because it looked too much like jail to her. After a few months in a bassinet in her room, she moved her children to a mat on the floor in a well-childproofed room. This arrangement allowed her to lie next to them and snuggle them to sleep when they needed it. Their pad on the floor became a place they associated with comfort, relaxation, and sleep. Part of her routine was to always sing the same repetitive lullaby at bedtime when they were young. The fact that there were no no struggles about sleep helped assure her that they slept easily and well. However, she noted, neither of her children had a "difficult" temperament.

**– Helen Neville, BS, RN, author, pediatric advice nurse, health educator, specialist in inborn temperament, and researcher**

# • TIP #49 •

## Establish a Realistic Bedtime

Remember that making your baby stay up later will not mean she will sleep longer at night or later in the morning. In fact, setting an unrealistic or late bedtime for your baby will most likely lead to less sleep for you and your baby. Use your completed sleep logs to determine the best time for bed for your child. Read your baby's drowsy signs so you are putting her to bed at the time when she is naturally drowsy but not overly tired. Most newborns and young babies will be ready for bed between 6:30 to 8 p.m. Many parents wait until closer to 9 p.m. to put their baby down to sleep. Waiting until a later bedtime may create a fussy baby who is harder to get to sleep and who will not sleep as long. Find a bedtime that is appropriate and early enough for your baby so you both will get a good night's rest.

If you set a bedtime for your child that goes against her body's natural rhythm, you might struggle more with getting her to sleep well. Make sure you leave time for the bedtime routine to occur before the actual bedtime so your child's routine ends at the appropriate bedtime each night.

If your baby's current bedtime is late, adjust the time to an earlier hour. Most experts recommend adjusting bedtimes slowly, in increments of 15 to 20 minutes. If your child is exhibiting signs of sleep deprivation, you can make the bedtime adjustment all at once — moving the bedtime from 10 p.m. to 7 p.m. in one night, for example. When trying to find the right bedtime for your child, allow four to five days before evaluating the effectiveness of the new time.

# • TIP #50 •

## Establish a Realistic Wake-up Time

Just as you need to set a bedtime, you will need to set a wake-up time. This time should be the same every day and should be determined by you, the parent, not your child. Most babies and toddlers will naturally wake up between 6 and 7:30 a.m. If your child is currently within that range, you should not try to alter it — even if you would rather sleep in until 9 a.m.

When deciding on an appropriate wake-up time, use the bedtime and sleep recommendations for your baby's age. If your baby should be sleeping 11 hours at night, set the wake-up time for 11 hours after the bedtime. If your baby is waking before this time, you need to identify the cause of the early rising and work to establish a healthier wake-up hour. Your baby could be waking early due to sleep deprivation, especially if nighttime sleeping is still an issue or if you set a bedtime too late in the evening. If your baby is 4 months old or younger, colic might be the culprit of the early waking. Wait until after colic has passed before employing sleep training methods or trying to adjust your baby's wake-up time. Other factors could be causing an early rise, such as noises, light, or other external factors. Once you identify the cause of the early rising, you can work to eliminate the cause and begin training your baby to sleep later. If your child is sleeping too late in the morning, you might need to adjust his wake-up time earlier. You can do this by creating an exciting morning ritual. A baby who sleeps too late in the morning might not nap well, which could lead to a fussy baby during the day.

As with adjusting bedtimes, you can choose to move the wake-up time slowly or all at once. Use your same sleep method to get your baby to sleep to the desired time in the morning as you would during a middle-of-the-night waking. If your child is old enough to understand, set an alarm clock and tell your child it is not time to get out of bed until the alarm goes off.

# • TIP #51 •

## Getting Your Baby to Sleep Well Starts First-thing in the Morning

If your baby's day is full of chaos and stress, chances are she will not sleep well at night. Creating a happy and loving environment during the day will help your baby feel safe and loved, which will lead to better sleep at night.

Routines and schedules during the day can also lead to better sleep at night for your baby. If you are consistent with your baby's daytime schedule, including playtime, feeding time, and naptime, she will learn the entire routine, which includes bedtime. Consistency helps children learn what is expected of them and helps them recognize environmental cues as to what will come next. When babies are surprised by schedule changes or inconsistencies, they often react by crying or getting fussy. Because babies are too young to communicate unhappiness with their words, they will react with tears.

Many experts recommend creating a morning routine, just as you create a bedtime routine. The morning routine should be the complete opposite of the bedtime routine. It should be light and loud, fun and playful, and with loads of interaction. You might use this early morning time as a special playtime for a parent who might get home too late at night to enjoy interactive play. Lifting the blinds, playing energetic music, and partaking in light horseplay are examples of good morning routine activities.

• TIP #52 •

## Establish Appropriate and Consistent Naptimes

An important component to your routine will include the number of naps and the time those naps occur. Your child's age will largely govern his naptimes and the number of naps he takes. Remember that while you will establish naptimes and schedules for your baby, the number and length of naptimes will change as your baby grows.

Like bedtime, maintain consistency with naptimes as much as possible, even when other events get in the way. Try to schedule doctor's appointments around your baby's nap schedule. During sleep training, do not alter naptimes to compensate for shorter or longer nighttime sleeping. If your child gets up earlier than usual in the morning, try to keep her awake until her normal naptime. If you adjust her schedule because she woke up early, you will throw off the whole day's schedule and possibly create an even longer-term issue. Once you have established your child's naptime schedule, stick to it as closely as possible.

Examine your child's sleep from a big picture point of view. Consider the amount of time he sleeps during the day and night to get a total amount of sleep within a 24-hour period. Make sure your baby is getting enough total sleep. If he is not, adjust bedtime or naptime lengths as appropriate. If your baby is getting enough total sleep but sleeps too much or too little during the day, you might need to adjust bedtime or naptimes to get a better split of his sleep during the day and night. Babies do need naps. Even when getting enough total sleep, a baby can be fussy during the day if he is not napping enough. Babies can only be awake for so long before they need to sleep. If they are not getting sleep often enough, they will not function as well when they are awake.

*See Chapter 8 for more information on your baby's naps.*

## CASE STUDY: WORD FROM THE EXPERTS: ESTABLISHING ROUTINE TIMES FOR NAPS, BEDTIME, AND WAKING

Arnall does not believe it is necessary for parents to establish set routines. "Most babies will settle into their own unique routine by about 6 months old."

**– Judy Arnall, co-founder of Parenting Canada; owner of Professional Parenting Canada**

"Parents should ask themselves if they are on a routine and if they have set clear boundaries. Parents should establish clear boundaries early in their baby's life so that the baby feels safe and secure."

**– Laura Heinsohn, director of Family Bureau of Investigation Parenting Workshops**

"Newborns will not have a normal schedule. As a baby grows older, a routine will begin to emerge so that parents can start to plan sleep times (with some flexibility). Depending on the age, after a certain amount of awake time, the baby will need to sleep."

**– Bette Levy Alkazian, MA, licensed marriage and family therapist**

"Parents need to recognize and adhere to their baby's sleep schedule for naps and bedtime," Kerr said. With her oldest child, if she strayed even a half-hour from his nap or bedtime schedule, she would face significant problems. "Parents need to take advantage of their window of opportunity to get their baby down for a nap. By recognizing their baby's groggy or drowsy signs, parents can put their baby down for nap before he gets a second wind," Fox said. She also said she sticks to the sleep, eat, play, sleep, eat, play cycle.

**– Baby Bunching experts Linda Kerr and Cara Fox**

When it comes to establishing routine times, Heilbrunn reminds parents that routines will change as their baby ages and his sleep needs change. "While parents should establish a routine and should be consistent with that routine, they should not be so attached to oneway of doing things that they will have trouble changing routines as the baby grows and matures. Parents should take cues from their baby as to when naptimes and bedtimes should be. For newborns, parents should not expect much of a routine at all, since young babies will need to sleep and eat around the clock.

As babies grow, they should take two to three naps during the day (one or two in the morning and one in the afternoon). For consistency, parents can establish set naptimes for each day and use the same sleep method that they use for bedtime. Most babies will have the tendency to wake up early in the morning (at 4 a.m., for example). If this is the case for your baby, try getting your baby back to sleep, just like you would if he woke up in the middle of the night. Resist the temptation of putting your baby down for bed later at night to get him to sleep longer in the morning. This strategy often backfires, as babies tend to have more fitful sleep if they are overly tired before bedtime. Sleep begets sleep. If you have a baby or child that will not nap, make naptime a rest time."

**– Claudia Heilbrunn, parenting expert, author, and certified life coach**

"Parents should understand the circadian rhythm of their child (based on age). Parents should read sleep books that support their parenting philosophy, and work with a sleep coach."

**– Karen Pollak, founder, Babies2Sleep**

Establishing naptime routines can be very tough, so Smith feels that a nighttime and wake routine for the baby is best. "While babies need naps and parents should try to keep the naps on a schedule, the naptimes can be driven by the day or how the night went. Parents should set a schedule that they know will work for them and try stick to it.

This might require giving a few things up or not going somewhere so that their child can get to bed on time, but in the end, it is worth it."

**– Stephanie Smith, mother of twins**

"Parents should enforce set naptimes and bedtimes gradually with younger babies. Parents walk a fine line between listening to the clock and following their own child's sleep patterns when it comes to establishing schedules. Parents should remember the importance of knowing the sleep requirements for their child based on her age. Inappropriate naptimes can create bad behavior. A child that is not getting enough sleep overall will likely exhibit behavioral issues that could be solved with more sleep. Parents cannot always abide by a rigid schedule, but they should ensure their child is getting enough sleep within the day."

**– Dr. Brett Kuhn, CBSM, associate professor of pediatrics at the University of Nebraska Medical Center and Children's Sleep Center at Children's Hospital**

"You are the grown-up. Parents need to be rigid and [know] that their friends with children will understand. If other friends think parents are a little kooky, they should remember the reward is a much calmer life. Parents should watch their baby and see when he or she becomes cranky. Babies often need two naps, which become consolidated into one midday/early afternoon nap as they are older. As for nighttime, parents should remember that they may end up spending a lot more nights at home than they had been accustomed to pre-baby."

**– Dr. Laura Davies, diplomate, American Board of Psychiatry and Neurology**

When it comes to scheduling naps and bedtime, Neville said individual differences again play a large part. "Some babies are so biologically regular that they put hang-loose parents on a schedule. On the other hand, some babies are biologically extremely irregular. There were no clocks for most of human society, and babies do best if put to bed when they are tired regardless of what the clock says."

**– Helen Neville, BS, RN, author, pediatric advice nurse, health educator, specialist in inborn temperament, and researcher**

# • TIP #53 •

## Do Not Stimulate Your Baby Before Bed

Although this tip might seem like common sense, you might be stimulating your baby before bedtime without realizing it. While you might be reading stories as a bedtime routine, you could be reading stories that are not conducive to sleep. Remember to keep everything quiet and low-key, and think of your bedtime routine as winding down to when your baby goes to sleep. Keep all talking and singing quiet and soothing. Avoid flashing lights from toys or a television that is on in the room. Do not engage in horseplay, tickling, or other active play close to bedtime.

Parents who work during the day might find that by the time they get home, they only have enough time to put their baby to bed. This situation might tempt parents to play and horse around with their baby when they get home from work, even if it is too close to bedtime for such play to be appropriate. Resist the temptation to play with your baby close to bedtime or to set your baby's bedtime later so you can have this time to play. A better option is to try to get in bed earlier yourself so that you can wake up earlier and enjoy some morning playtime before you go to work.

Examples of good bedtime routine activities include a warm bath, reading books, singing songs, playing soft soothing music, quiet play, massaging your baby, breastfeeding or bottlefeeding, rocking, talking quietly, and hugging, kissing, or cuddling. As your bedtime routine gets closer to sleep time, slow down your talking and speak in a lower, softer voice.

# • TIP #54 •

## Remember: Routines Will Change as Your Baby Ages

With your young baby, your bedtime routine should be simple and might include a bath, diaper change, feeding, then bed. As your baby grows older, your bedtime routine might become more involved and last longer. When your baby is 1 year old, you might have a routine that lasts 30 minutes to an hour and includes a bath, pajamas, book reading, cuddle time, and a massage.

As your baby grows older, her bedtime routine will continue to change. She might start reading books to you as she learns to read. Once your child is talking, make bedtime a time to share things about life. Bedtime can be a time of sharing and bonding between a parent and child. Talk to your child about her hopes and dreams, or her fears, future plans, or fights with friends. Even talking about your plans for the next day can be a loving and soothing way to end the day.

Eventually, her routine will involve you less and less. As a teenager, your child will not need you to help her go to sleep. Even so, you should continue some routine. As a teenager, your child's routine might involve you peeking in to wish her goodnight before heading to bed yourself. Try to continue the tradition of talking about your day or other events before bedtime.

Try to make bedtime routines a special time you and your child spend together. This time should be enjoyable for you and your child. Bedtime routines should not involve fights and arguing about bedtime. By establishing pleasant routines early on, you will create an environment where bedtimes are happy times for you and your child.

# • TIP #55 •

## Do Not Give in to Pleading

When older children are being put down for bedtime, they will often try stalling techniques to push the limits of their bedtime routine. Oftentimes, these tactics include asking for "one more" of something, whether it is a book, a song, a glass of water, a hug, or a kiss. Recognize these stalling tactics and resist the temptation to give in to your child's pleas. If you do give in, chances are you will face the same request the next night, and the requests will get more and more extensive. Anticipate your child's needs or requests before bedtime, and set clear expectations for your child. Make sure your child knows that when you set rules, you keep them. This applies to bedtime as well as all aspects of parenting. If your routine includes only one book before bed, do not read two, no matter how many times he asks. Explain your bedtime rules and your child's bedtime routine beforehand so no issues arise during bedtime. Make sure your child knows the rules ahead of time so there will not be any debate later on.

If your child is testing his limits during the day, be prepared for him to test the limits at bedtime. Be strong in your willpower both during the day and during bedtime. Remember that though giving in to your child's pleas one night might be easier at the time, you will create more issues in the long run. Set your rules and stick to them. If you do give in to your child's wishes one night, be prepared to say no the next night. Resume your normal routine the next day and recommit to your sleep strategy.

# chapter 7

## Breaking Bad Habits

While it is always easier to prevent bad habits from forming than it is to break them, chances are that some bad habits will form. If you began reading this book because your baby is not sleeping well, this chapter should be especially helpful. If you are reading this book before bad habits have formed, try to use the advice in this chapter to prevent them from developing. Some habits discussed in this chapter are not necessarily "bad" in and of themselves. Bad habits can be classified as any sleep association your baby has that he either cannot recreate on his own during the middle of the night – and thus will require parental assistance to fall back asleep – or something you cannot or do not wish to continue doing every night. For instance, if you began getting your baby to sleep during the night by rocking him until he fell asleep, and now he will not fall asleep unless you are rocking him, you might wish to change that sleep association. Though rocking is not actually a *bad* habit, it is a sleep association your child cannot do alone, and something you might not want to do each time he wakes at night.

# • TIP #56 •

## Recognize Your Child's Sleep Associations

A sleep association is any activity, routine, or item that must be present for your child to fall asleep. Breastfeeding, rocking, music, darkness, or a blanket/stuffed animal are all examples of possible sleep associations. Your sleep logs should be the best way to recognize your child's current sleep associations. If you have been writing down your bedtime routine every night, you should be able to identify your child's sleep association.

Not all routine activities are sleep associations. For instance, if you always sing to your baby to get him to fall asleep at bedtime, but he does not need you to sing him back to sleep in the middle of the night, then singing is not a sleep association for him.

Before you can make changes or adjustments to your child's sleep associations, you must be able to identify what his current associations are. If you have not been tracking your sleep routine on your sleep logs, or if you are not sure what your child's associations are, you can easily test to find out. Try removing one item of your child's bedtime routine. For instance, if you want to find out if singing to your child is one of his sleep associations, go through your bedtime routine as usual, but skip the song. If your baby goes to bed as usual without fussing, then you know that singing is not an association. Be sure you are only testing one sleep association at a time so you can identify the specific associations your child currently has. Once you have established what these associations are, you can determine whether you will need to change any associations for your sleep strategy to work.

Sleep associations will most likely change as your child ages. You might need to readjust his associations numerous times over his childhood. As long as his sleep associations allow him to fall back asleep on his own, no adjustment should be necessary.

# • TIP #57 •

## It is Not Too Late to Change Sleep Associations

No matter what age your baby or child is, it is not too late to change her sleep associations or habits. Do not feel forced into the path you began just because your baby has become accustomed to it. Do have patience, especially with older children, when trying to change sleep associations. Your child will probably resist your changes and might suffer relapses along the way. Remember that you are teaching your child a new way of doing things, and this process will take time.

Sleep associations can be changed through a gradual process or through a cold-turkey process. The gradual process to changing habits will take longer, but most likely will result in fewer tears. The cold-turkey approach will likely be successful more quickly, but you could face many more tears and more resistance from your baby.

# • TIP #58 •

## Replace Bad Sleep Associations with Good Ones

If your goal is to have your child sleep through the night, then you need to create sleep associations your child can recreate in the middle of the night to put himself back to sleep without your assistance. Although breastfeeding should not be a sleep association (if your baby is no longer in need of nighttime feedings), sucking on a pacifier would be a good sleep association because your baby, if old enough, could reinsert a pacifier at night to fall back asleep.

When your baby is younger than 4 months old, you should not worry too much about changing sleep associations. Instead, concentrate on preventing bad sleep associations from developing. You can prevent your baby from developing sleep associations by varying the method your use to get him to sleep at night. Though he might fall asleep nursing one night, you might rock him to sleep the next night. Once your baby is older than 4 months, be sure to work toward changing bad sleep associations. Ignoring bad sleep associations can create more sleepless nights and more work to correct them later on in your child's life.

In his book, Dr. Ferber compares changing your baby's sleep habits to adults trying to learn to sleep without a pillow. He says parents should keep this analogy in mind as they try to reteach their children sleep habits. Eventually you could get used to sleeping without a pillow, but it would be a difficult transition and would result in quite a few sleepless nights. The more nights you would do it, the easier it would become.

This same principle applies to your baby's sleep patterns. The more nights you consistently employ the new sleep tactics or sleep associations, the easier it will be for her to fall asleep. If you are not consistent in changing her sleep associations, it will take longer for the changes to stick.

# • TIP #59 •

## Taper Off Nighttime Feedings as Your Child Ages

During your baby's first few months of life, she will need to feed about every two to four hours and, for a time, should never go longer than five hours without eating. During this time, your baby is growing rapidly, and these feedings are vital to good development. You should consult with your child's pediatrician to discuss their recommendations on how often your newborn should eat and whether you should wake your baby at night to eat. Once your child has reached 12 to 15 weeks old, she should no longer require nighttime feedings. Ask your child's pediatrician when you think your baby might be ready to end nighttime feedings. Although she might no longer need feedings, she might continue to wake up during the night to feed.

Once your baby no longer needs nighttime feedings as determined by your child's pediatrician, start tapering them off. If your baby no longer needs feedings but is still waking up for a feeding, begin the tapering-off schedule. If your baby does not wake on his own for a nighttime feeding, do not continue to wake your baby to feed him. You can reduce the amount of formula you offer or start watering down the formula until you are only giving your baby water at nighttime feedings. Begin to reduce the number of feedings during the night at the same time you are reducing the quantity of feedings. When your baby wakes for a feeding, use your soothing bedtime techniques to get him to fall back asleep. If you are breastfeeding, consider having Dad handle nighttime wakings so your baby will not be tempted by a food supply when you go in to comfort him.

You can approach this process as gradually or dramatically as you want. A gradual approach, again, will most likely result in fewer tears. Once your baby no longer needs to eat at night, you can discontinue nighttime feedings altogether. If you choose to quit feedings without a tapering-off method, plan to face more resistance from your baby. If you are using the Ferber method, wait the appropriate amount of time in between check-ins, and do not pick your baby up to console him. Your baby will learn to sleep through the night without waking for feedings if you maintain your sleep strategy and resist giving in to feeding your baby during the night.

# • TIP #60 •

## You Baby Should Fall Asleep in the Same Place He Will Sleep Throughout the Night

A common mistake parents make that can lead to sleep issues for their child is to let their baby fall asleep in an environment different from where he will sleep throughout the night. If your baby falls asleep every night in your arms and is placed in his crib only after he is fully asleep, he will wake in the middle of the night in a completely different environment than the one he fell asleep in. This environment change can be scary and very disruptive for your baby. Your baby will cry out for you so that you will once again pick him up and let him fall asleep in your arms. This scenario might be repeated several times throughout the night.

Although you might think you are doing the best thing for your baby by letting him fall asleep in your arms, you are not allowing him to learn to fall asleep any other way. You are also creating an unpleasant night waking for him. Babies who are moved after they fall asleep might also start to resist sleep entirely. These babies might become scared to fall asleep because every time they do, they wake up in a different place from where they fell asleep.

Teach your baby to fall asleep in the same place he will wake up during the night. You can still help soothe him by rubbing or patting his belly, but remember that he needs to learn to fall asleep on his own; try to recreate the situation in the middle of the night without your assistance.

## • TIP #61 •

## Your Willpower Must be Greater Than Your Baby's

If you have been up most nights trying to get your baby to sleep well, you are probably sleep-deprived. Experiencing sleep deprivation will create a situation where it will be harder for you to stay strong in your willpower. Willpower will be needed to break bad habits. Keep your willpower strong and your attitude positive and loving.

When you start trying to make changes in your baby's sleep patterns, you will most likely face resistance from your baby. Be patient as your baby learns the new techniques, but do not give in to his demands to return to the "old" way of doing things. Be consistent yet gentle, and remember that the skill of sleeping is one that is worth the work for you and your baby.

# • TIP #62 •

## Ask for Help

If you begin to feel overwhelmed by your child's sleep habits or lack of sleep altogether, do not shy way from asking for help. You might just need a night or two away from home to catch up on your own sleep before tackling sleep training with your child. Asking for help does not make you a bad parent or any less of a parent; asking for help is often the most responsible and loving thing you can do for your child.

It would be much better to put off beginning training for a couple of nights while a friend or relative watches your baby than to begin training, only to give in due to exhaustion. Once you begin sleep training, it is important to stick with your plan and consistently employ your chosen tactic.

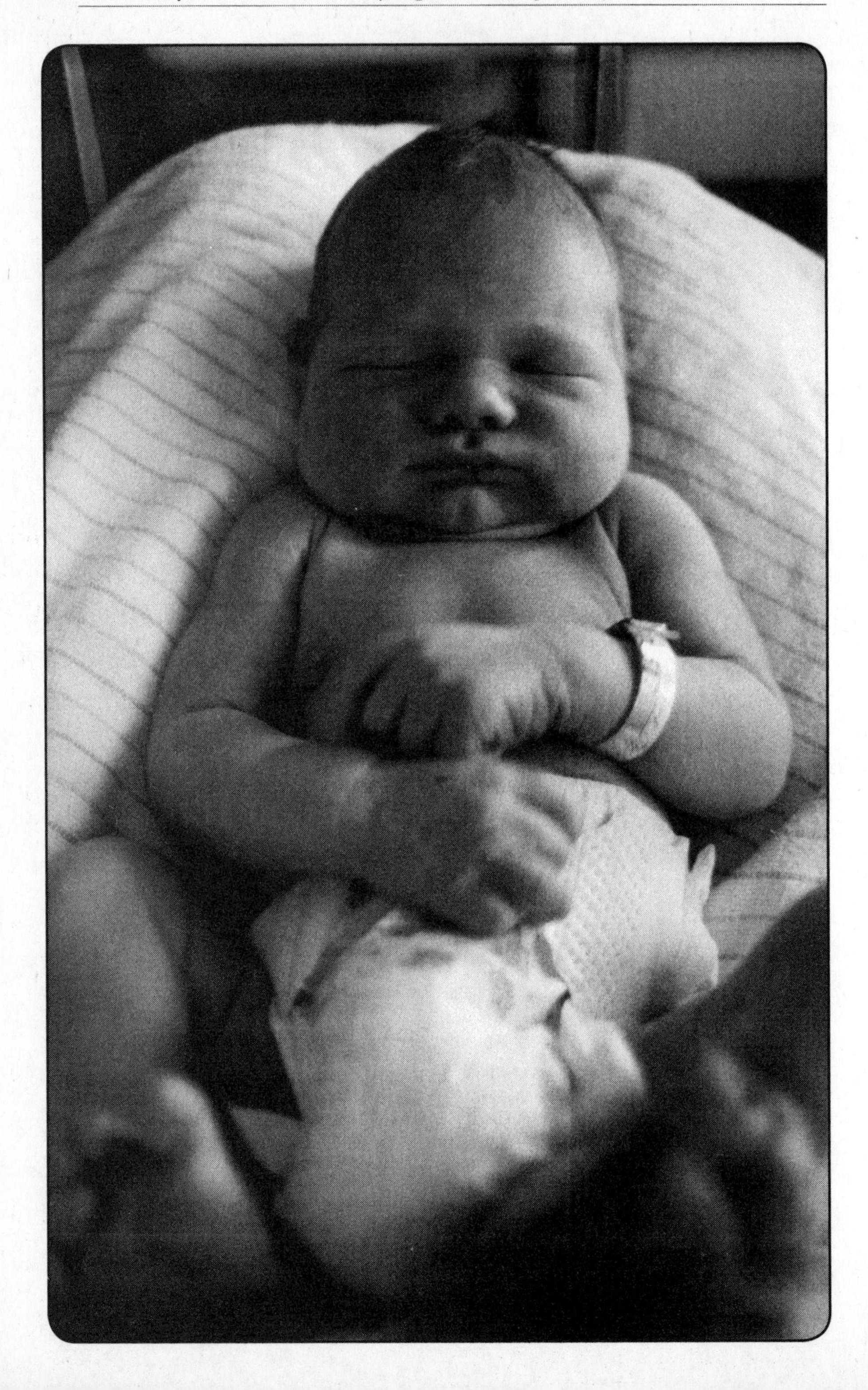

# • TIP #63 •

## Put Yourself in Your Baby's Shoes

While you are sleep training, and especially while you are working to break bad habits, be empathetic to your baby's situation. Your baby cannot communicate the way older children and adults can. She will not understand why things are changing and will fight to get things back to the way they were. While you should not give in to your baby's wishes, you should be understanding of her situation. Love and comfort your baby while you make changes to her sleep patterns.

If your child is old enough to understand, explain the changes to her before you make them. Let her know what the new rules will be and consistently employ them. Remind your baby or child you love her, and make sure plenty of hugs and kisses are part of the bedtime routine. Remember that you can be loving while being firm and consistent. Giving in to your baby's wishes is not the best thing for your baby. As the parent, you know what is best for your child, and teaching her to sleep well is definitely best.

# • TIP #64 •

## Do Not Take Frustration Out on Your Baby

Sleep training your baby can be mentally taxing. It is natural to become frustrated with the situation and even to become aggravated with your baby. Though this emotion is common, do not take your frustration out on your baby. Your baby will also pick up on any tension or aggravation you are feeling, which will make it harder for him to fall asleep. If you find yourself getting frustrated with your baby, take a break. You might decide just to let you baby cry safely in her crib until you can calmly take care of the situation. You might need to let your partner or another member of the family handle sleep training – whether permanently or temporarily – until you can catch up on rest and can handle the situation more effectively.

Do not get into a situation where your frustration is impacting the health or safety of you or your baby. No matter how frustrated you might become, you should never shake your baby or cause him harm in any other way. Be honest with yourself and take a break if your frustration level is rising to an unsafe level.

## • TIP #65 •

## Exercise Your Child or Stimulate Your Baby During the Day

Exercising your baby during the day will also lead to a better night's sleep. For a young baby, interacting and stimulating her during the day will help her to sleep better at night. Make daytime the opposite of nighttime. Daytime play should be louder, brighter, and involve all the activities you should avoid during the bedtime routine. If weather permits, let your baby get some outside time. Whereas nighttime should be dark and boring, daytime should be bright and full of activities.

Just as you feel extra tired when you have had a full day, extra stimulation can lead to a better night's rest for your baby. This could be as simple as going for a long walk in the evening, playing at the park with children her age, or providing extra tummy time in the morning.

## CASE STUDY: WORD FROM THE EXPERTS: COMBATING BAD HABITS AND NIGHTTIME FEEDINGS

Arnall recommends parents make nighttime boring and dark. To dissuade nighttime feedings (only after a baby is about 8 months old and no longer needs a nighttime feeding), "parents should start giving their baby a non-nutritious feeding, such as a bottle of water instead of breast milk or formula, to start weaning babies off feedings during the night."

– **Judy Arnall, co-founder of Parenting Canada; owner of Professional Parenting Canada**

"Parents should be sure that their baby is old enough to go through a night without a feeding before they employ these tactics. Parent should ask their child's pediatrician for advice on whether their baby still requires nighttime feedings. Parents should give a baby water in a bottle or nurse for five minutes or less and gradually decrease either the amount of water in the bottle or the time of nursing over a few nights. Sleep deprivation can cause mood swings and irritability, can contribute to postpartum depression and, overall, can create anarchy in the home. Teaching your baby to sleep through the night is teaching her the world is a safe place, so she can soothe herself back to sleep. To combat other bad habits that cause a child to wake and not fall back asleep during the night, parents should identify the cause of their baby's crying. If a baby cries when his pacifier falls out of his mouth in the night, teach him to sleep without a pacifier. Likewise, if a baby cries because she is too cold, turn up the temperature in the room at night or add extra pajama layers."

– **Barb Dehn, RN, MS, NP**

Alkazian believes the best way to combat bad habits is to recognize them and get things back on track quickly. When it comes to nighttime feedings, Alkazian suggests switching to water or letting your baby cry it out until the habit is broken. "The keys are perseverance and patience. Remember that children will often get off track. Your job as a parent is to get them back on track as quickly as possible."

– **Bette Levy Alkazian, MA, licensed marriage and family therapist**

Fox said she tries hard to avoid creating bad habits. With her children, Fox had them sleep in a bassinet next to her for the first two months or so. After that, Fox moved the baby to a crib. She would not allow her children to fall asleep on her or in a swing. She tries to schedule errands around her baby's naptimes so her baby would always nap in his bassinet or crib. With baby No. 3, she is having a harder time working around naptimes. Another tactic she has for not creating bad habits is to not wake a baby to feed. Her only exception is when she is establishing her milk supply while breastfeeding a newborn, in which case she will wake her baby every three hours. She said that her 2 ½-month-old sleeps eight to nine hours a night, but he eats all day long to make up for it.

**– Baby Bunching experts Linda Kerr and Cara Fox**

"Parents should use a gentle method to wean their baby from a bad habit, or decide to stop the habit all together. Parents should be sure their baby still feels they are available for her and will meet her needs. Your baby will learn that her needs can be met, even if it is in a way that she is not used to."

**– Claudia Heilbrunn, parenting expert, author, and certified life coach**

"Parents should understand what their baby needs during the day and then find ways to eliminate that need during the night."

**– Karen Pollak, founder, Babies2Sleep**

"Parents should not start a habit they are not willing to continue for their life." Smith said she was told this same message from the start and even hung a sign with those words to help her remember that each day.

**– Stephanie Smith, mother of twins**

"The best general approach to any behavioral change is to reward behaviors that one would like to encourage with positive reinforcement/attention, and ignore behaviors that one would like to extinguish. When an older child shows improvement during the bedtime routine or sleeping through the night, parents should tell them how happy that makes them feel and how proud they are. For the younger ones, parents should take more direct control of the behavior. Once the parents feel that the baby no longer 'needs' that nighttime feeding, they can either phase it out slowly over a week or two — by giving less volume and/or watering it down — or just go cold-turkey and let the baby cry it out for a couple of nights. For those babies that learned that they need a bottle to fall asleep, it may also be necessary to get rid of the bedtime bottle to break that learned association."

**– Nadav Traeger, MD, FAAP, FCCP, D, ABSM, director of pediatric sleep medicine, Maria Fareri Children's Hospital**

"Parents can combat bad habits gradually." Kuhn has spent 15 years trying to develop gradual and positive strategies to make changes in a child's sleep behavior, as opposed to a cold-turkey approach to making changes in your child's life and sleep schedule. "Parents should work on any bad bedtime habits during the day. If trying to reduce or eliminate nighttime feedings, parents can space feedings out more during the day and not let the baby graze. Parents should also reduce the time of a nighttime nursing or dilute the formula gradually until nighttime feedings are eliminated."

**– Dr. Brett Kuhn, CBSM, associate professor of pediatrics at the University of Nebraska Medical Center and Children's Sleep Center at Children's Hospital**

When it comes to changing bad habits, Dr. Davies said, "Parents should employ basic behavioral training. As for discontinuing nighttime feedings, parents can try mixing cereal in with the milk at bedtime to tide them over. The first few nights, the non-breastfeeding parent can go in and soothe the baby, and then after that let the baby soothe herself."

**– Dr. Laura Davies, diplomate, American Board of Psychiatry and Neurology**

"If a baby is used to a 3 a.m.-feeding, parents should gradually shift when the baby gets those needed calories. Mothers who nurse do so for gradually shorter times, or gradually give less in each 3 a.m.-bottle, for those who use formula. The baby will adjust by taking in more calories during the day. Once babies no longer need those calories during the night, they are more likely to be able to get themselves back to sleep."

**– Helen Neville, BS, RN, author, pediatric advice nurse, health educator, specialist in inborn temperament, and researcher**

*Photo courtesy of Sivan Grosman, founder of Sivan Photography (**http://sivanphotography.com**)*

# chapter 8

## Napping

When working on getting your baby to sleep through the night, you will have to consider how naps will affect his nighttime sleep. Many experts believe naptime and bedtime sleeping should be viewed not as entirely separate sleeping periods, but as different blocks of sleep that make up the collective sleep your child gets within a 24-hour period. Consult the sleep charts in Appendix A to see the average sleep requirements for your child's age, and be sure your baby is meeting her overall sleep requirements for a 24-hour period. You might need to adjust your baby's sleep schedule so bedtimes and naptimes are appropriate.

## • TIP #66 •

### Know How Long Your Baby Should Nap for His Age

When your baby is 4 months old, you can start implementing a schedule for naptimes and bedtimes, according to most experts. By this age, your baby should sleep the longest period at night –

aim for nine to nine-and-a-half hours — and have three naptimes during the day — a long midmorning nap, a long midafternoon nap, and a short evening nap.

By the time your baby is 6 months old, you should be able to drop the evening nap. You might need to adjust his bedtime slightly earlier or allow the second nap to last slightly longer to make this transition easier and ensure your baby is still getting enough sleep within a 24-hour period.

By 1 year old, your baby might be napping only once a day. If so, the two naps will merge into one nap and usually will occur between the times of the previous two naps and last the length of the two naps combined. If your baby previously napped at 10 a.m. for one-and-a-half hours and at 2 p.m. for one-and-a-half to two hours, he may now nap at noon for three to four hours. When you eliminate naps, be sure that your child is still receiving enough total sleep during the day.

The last nap is dropped at different ages for different children. Most children will no longer need any naps once they are between 3 to 4 years old. Some children will drop their last nap at age 2, or not until after 4 years old.

Not all children and babies will be ready to give up naps at the same age. Learn to read your child's signals to appropriately consolidate or eliminate naptimes.

If you notice resistance to a certain naptime, or your child no longer seems sleepy at his appropriate bedtime, it might be a signal that he no longer needs one of his naps. The evening nap is the first nap to be eliminated. If your baby start resisting this nap or seems to not be ready for bedtime at the same time he used to be, consider eliminating this nap altogether.

You might also notice he has started consolidating or eliminating naps on his own. He might start going down for his midmorning nap later than usual and sleep longer, but then resist his midafternoon nap. If you notice this trend, determine whether it is time for certain naps to be consolidated. Be aware of your child's cues to know when naps can be reduced or eliminated.

## • TIP #67 •

### Identify Your Baby's Naptime Associations

Identifying your child's nighttime sleep associations was an important step in teaching your baby to sleep through the night. The same concept applies to teaching your baby to nap well during the day. Again, while sleeping is instinctual, taking healthy naps during the day is not. Your child can develop different sleep associations for naps than for bedtime. Evaluate your child's naptime sleep associations separately from his bedtime sleep associations. Though the associations might differ, the principle for changing these associations is the same.

## • TIP #68 •

### Remember: Almost all Babies and Children Need Naps

Some parents believe their child does not need naps or does not need as much sleep as other children her age. While this situation might occasionally be the case, more often than not, these parents have an overly tired, sleep-deprived child. An overly tired child will appear to have excessive energy and will have a hard time settling down for a nap or bedtime.

If you believe your child does not need naps, look for any signs of over tiredness. These signs include excessive energy (getting a second wind), being fussy or displaying other behavioral issues after long periods of wakefulness, and falling asleep during car or stroller rides. If your baby is napping at all during the day, including short naps in the car or stroller, chances are he needs naps during the day. Remember that most children suffer from not getting enough sleep, not the opposite – sleeping too much. *Consult the sleep charts in Appendix A.*

If your child is sleeping enough within a 24-hour period but is not napping an appropriate amount of time for his age, you might need to adjust his nighttime sleep schedule. Babies and children need naptimes after being awake for certain lengths of time. These naptimes or rest times help rejuvenate them, which leads to better functioning while awake. If your child exhibits crankiness or signs of being overly tired during the day and is not napping, change his sleep schedule to incorporate the appropriate naptimes.

## • TIP #69 •

## Keep Naptimes and Lengths Consistent — Even When Nighttime Sleep is Not

When you are sleep training your baby or child, there will be nights of inconsistent sleep, whether less or more than usual. Even when the nighttime schedule is off due to training, keep naptimes consistent. By maintaining naptime consistency, you will encourage nighttime sleep to the schedule you are aiming for. You will also begin to set your baby's internal clock. If your baby is sleeping and waking at different times every day, her internal clock will not know when it is supposes to sleep and for how long at each period.

If your baby is not sleeping well at night, she might compensate by trying to sleep longer during her first nap. You might have to wake her during her first naptime to maintain her normal schedule. Letting her compensate for missing nighttime sleep during the day can set her timing system to adjust to sleeping longer periods during the day than at night. You also might set yourself (and your baby) up for another challenging night and face the same issue the next day. Instead of letting your baby sleep longer during naptime, put her down to bed earlier for bedtime than usual. This method should encourage her to sleep more through the night and not develop bad habits of sleeping too long during the day. Chances are better that using an earlier bedtime will result in your baby's sleeping until later in the morning.

## • TIP #70 •

## Put Your Baby to Sleep for Naptime Using the Same Method You Use for Bedtime

Use the same sleep technique and consider an abbreviated bedtime routine. If you are using the Ferber method to sleep train your baby at night, follow the same rules for getting your baby down for naptime. Put your baby in his crib (on his back – even for short naps), kiss him, and leave the room. If your baby cries, wait the appropriate interval of time before checking on him. Follow this method throughout the entire naptime. If your baby never goes to sleep, wait until the naptime has passed before allowing him out of his crib. For instance, if he was supposed to nap for two hours, keep using your sleep techniques to encourage him to sleep throughout the two-hour period. If he is still awake after two hours, take him out of his crib and try again at his next scheduled naptime or bedtime.

Although you will not have quite the same ritual for naps as you do for bedtime, you should employ the same basic concepts to get your baby to sleep during naps as you do at night. Consider using a slightly different version during naptime to help your baby know when she is expected to nap or sleep for a short period rather than when she is going to bed to sleep for a longer period. Instead of saying "night-night," you might tell your baby "nap-nap." You can use other environmental cues to signal that naptime is different from bedtime. Try using slightly more light in your baby's room during a naptime. Play soft music during naptime if you do not play music during the night. Using these types of cues will help teach your baby whether he is expected to sleep for shorter or longer periods of time.

Your child might not need such a routine during naps and might go down very easily during the day. Be flexible enough to do what works best for your baby.

• TIP #71 •

## Do Not Let Your Baby Nap Too Late in the Day

If your baby is napping late into the evening, he might have difficultly going to bed at the appropriate time at night or might resist bedtime until late at night. If your baby has this issue, adjust his evening naptime earlier in the day. Do not let your baby sleep too long, and adjust his bedtime earlier if needed, such as if your baby is showing drowsy signs before his scheduled bedtime. Most experts recommend the evening nap end before 4 or 4:30 p.m. You might need to wake your baby up if he starts sleeping too late in the day. Remember that keeping your naptimes on schedule is vital to your baby's nighttime sleep.

It will be easier to transition the late nap and bedtime if you make the changes by 15 to 30-minute increments and do so slowly, over time. Adjust his naptime to end 15 minutes earlier on day one. Do not move his naptime again until he is comfortable with the earlier time. Once he has adjusted to the 15 minutes, move the time up another 15 minutes and continue this process until you have reached your target time.

The alternative plan is to make the schedule change all at once. You can move the naptime to begin and end earlier without the gradual change in time. You might encounter more issues at first, but your baby should catch on to the new schedule and adjust within a few days. During this change, you might notice your baby is ready for bed sooner than usual, especially if he is still resisting the earlier naptime. If this is the case, let your baby go to bed at an earlier time. He should sleep more at night and later into the morning than if you force him to wait until his scheduled bedtime. Making him wait for bedtime can also lead to an overly tired baby who will have trouble falling asleep and will wake up earlier than usual in the morning.

# • TIP #72 •

## Do Not Rush to Comfort Your Baby if He Stirs During Naptime

If your baby wakes or begins to stir before his naptime should be over, be careful not to rush into the room before necessary. Implementing this tip depends on which sleep method you have chosen. If you are using a cry-it-out method, wait your appropriate time, based on your nighttime sleep method. Use the same tactic to get your baby to nap the appropriate amount of time as you would to get him to sleep through the night if he woke up at 3 a.m. Once the set naptime has passed, even if your baby never fell back asleep, allow him to get up.

If you are using a no-cry method, be sure your baby is making a crying sound and not just stirring in his sleep. If you rush in to help your baby because you heard him stir, and he is making noises in his sleep but not actually crying, you could be causing him to wake up early.

Remember that many babies and children are noisy sleepers. Your baby might make crying-like sounds in his sleep. If you think he is crying, try waiting another minute or so to see if he stops on his own. Learn to read your baby's noises and cries, and use the same sleep method you use at night to get your baby to sleep through naptime.

# • TIP #73 •

## Not All Children are Impacted the Same by Naptime Discrepancies

Some children will not cope well with change to their naptimes, whereas others will not be affected at all by slight naptime inconsistencies. As a parent, you will need to learn how your child is affected by naptime inconsistencies and adjust your schedule to meet your child's needs. Keeping a sleep log can assist you with this. Countless events and circumstances can interfere with your baby's naptimes. Errands, doctor appointments, visiting friends or relatives, or birthday parties can get in the way of your normal naptime routines. Though you should try to avoid such disruptions when possible, chances are naps will ultimately face disruptions. Find out how your child is affected by these disruptions.

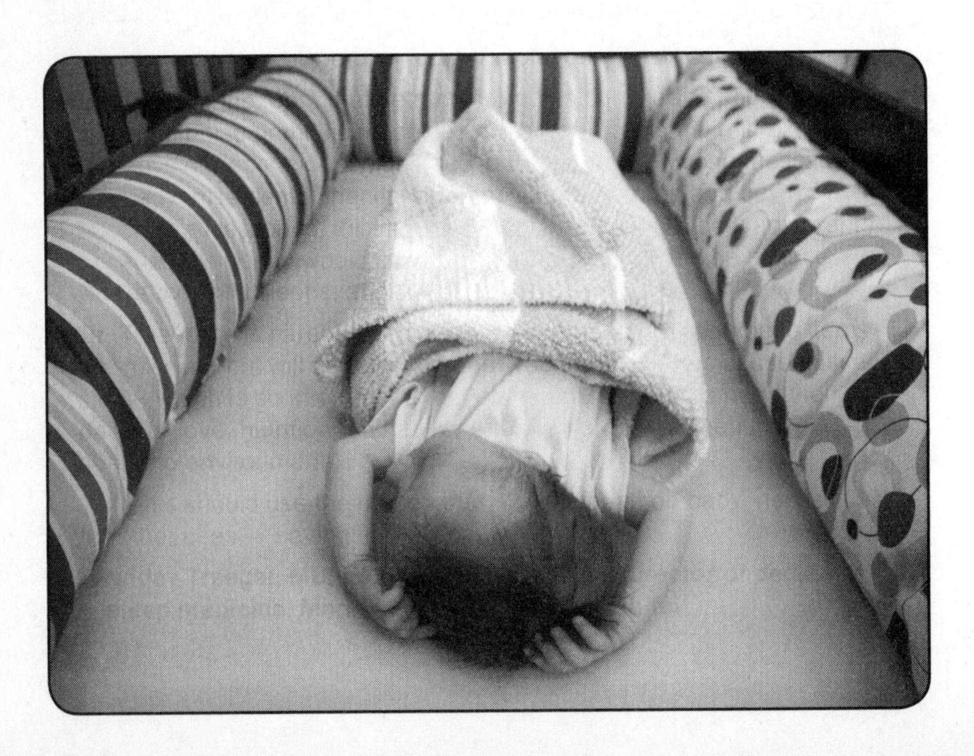

If your child is not affected much by naptime adjustments, you might be able to push his naptime back one day to accommodate a visiting relative or a friend's birthday party. You might also be able to let him nap in a different place than usual. He could start his nap in the car and finish his nap in his crib once you get home. If you are visiting friends or relatives, you might be able to let him nap at their house. If your baby is more flexible with naptimes, you will have more options available to you when disruptions do occur.

If your child does not cope well with changes in his nap schedule, you might have to schedule events and visits around his normal schedule. If you find you must alter his nap schedule to make a doctor's appointment or other such occurrence, resume his normal schedule as quickly as possible. Remember not to let him compensate for one shorter or missing nap by napping longer later in the day. Resume his normal nap schedule and consider putting him to bed earlier that night. The next day, aim to return fully to his usual routine.

# • TIP #74 •

## Do Not Skip Naps in Order For Your Baby to Sleep Better at Night

Skipping naps should be avoided whenever possible. While some circumstances might arise where naptimes are disturbed, this practice should never be done intentionally to make your baby sleep better at night. This method will only serve to sleep-deprive your baby and will lead to an overly tired and wired baby.

Experts agree that babies who nap better also sleep better at night. Conversely, babies who do not nap well do not sleep as well at night. Be sure your baby is receiving the right amount of sleep both during the day and during the night. Missing sleep can create a vicious cycle of missing even more sleep. Much the same, sleeping well creates a cycle of sleeping well.

If your baby misses a nap due to some disruption in his schedule, resume a normal nap schedule and let him go to bed earlier that night if he is showing drowsy signs before his appropriate bedtime. Resist the urge to let him take a five-hour afternoon nap because he missed his morning nap due to a doctor's appointment.

# • TIP #75 •

## If Your Baby Refuses to Nap, Insist on a Rest Time Instead

If your baby simply will not nap, then instead, your baby should rest quietly for the appropriate nap length. If he should nap for one-and-a-half hours, make sure he stays in his room or crib and rests or plays quietly (without you) for that amount of time. Your baby might eventually sleep during that period or might nod off if left alone in a dark and quiet room. Unlike some sleep strategies for nighttime, you should not leave your baby alone and crying until he falls asleep if that means keeping him in his room all day or for more than the length of his nap.

If your baby or child is resisting naptime, consider other factors that might be causing this resistance. Your baby might be old enough to drop one nap, especially if he is still napping three times a day and is having trouble falling asleep for the last nap.

Also consider the total hours your baby is sleeping within a 24-hours period. If your baby is sleeping an excessively long period of time at night, he might be meeting his 24-hour sleep requirement during nighttime sleep and resisting naps because of it. If this is the case, and your baby is fussing during the day or gets fussy later in the day, you might need to adjust his nighttime sleep schedule so he will start napping during the day. Babies and young children need naps to make daytime hours more productive and happy. Even if your baby is sleeping his full 24-hour requirement at night, you might have a bad sleep habit that should be corrected. By adjusting your child's bedtime later and waking him up earlier, you should see a happier, less fussy child.

## CASE STUDY: WORD FROM THE EXPERTS: HOW NAPS AFFECT BEDTIME

"The more sleep babies get, the more they sleep." In other words, sleep begets sleep. So, if your baby sleeps well during the day for naps, he will also sleep well at bedtime.

**– Judy Arnall, co-founder of Parenting Canada; owner of Professional Parenting Canada**

When it comes to napping, Dehn reminds parents that every child is different. "While some babies only need ten- to 20-minute cat naps, others will go down for a two- to three-hour nap. Babies under 6 months old have erratic sleep patterns that will change every day or two. After a baby is 6 months old, he should not wake from his last nap after 4 p.m. Babies who do not wake until after 4 p.m. will not be ready for bed until after 10 p.m. Parents should ensure their baby's nap is done before 4 p.m. to avoid this late bedtime."

**– Barb Dehn, RN, MS, NP**

"If a baby sleeps too much during the day, he will not sleep as well throughout the night." Heinsohn said when her children were babies, she would try to keep them awake as much as possible during the day, and if they were sleeping too long during a nap, she would lovingly wake them up.

**– Laura Heinsohn, director of Family Bureau of Investigation Parenting Workshops**

"Babies who do not have long enough naps during the day experience trouble with their nighttime sleep cycle. Overstimulation and lack of sleep begets more overstimulation and lack of sleep. Parents should make sure they known their baby's tired signs and seize the right time for a nap. Parents should make sure their baby sleeps long enough and may need to let their baby cry it out if he wakes up to soon during naptime. Parents should not let their baby sleep too long during daytime naps or too late into the afternoon or evening. A baby should not nap after 6 p.m. or too close to the baby's bedtime. Allowing a baby to sleep too long or too late will cause hardships when it comes bedtime for the baby."

**– Bette Levy Alkazian, MA, licensed marriage and family therapist**

"The better a baby sleeps during the day, the better she will sleep at night. The myth that keeping baby up during the day so that she will sleep at night is definitely not true. A well-rested baby will sleep better at night," Kerr said. Fox reminds parents that sleep begets sleep. Babies who do not sleep well during the day will be overtired and wound up, which will make bedtime harder for baby and parents. When her children got off schedule, she would often have to revert to a night of letting them cry it out. She warns that bad sleep during the day creates a cycle of bad sleep, bad eating, and more bad sleep.

**– Baby Bunching experts Linda Kerr and Cara Fox**

"How naps affect a baby's nighttime sleeping depends on the age and sleep needs of the baby. Babies who are napping twice a day are usually more rested and, thus, more likely to sleep better at night. As your child transitions from two naps a day to one nap, and then to no naps, her sleep at night might be disturbed. Parents should consider moving a baby's naptime to an earlier time or not letting their baby sleep as late during the day if nighttime sleep seems to be disturbed by naptimes."

**– Claudia Heilbrunn, parenting expert, author, and certified life coach**

"Each time a person sleeps, it relieves some of the sleep pressure (or drive to sleep) that has previously built up while the person was awake. If a sleep period like a nap occurs too close to the desired bedtime, it will be more difficult to fall asleep at that time because the person will have less drive to sleep than would otherwise have been present if the nap had not taken place. For older infants whose schedule is more regular, parents should try to avoid naps (especially long ones) too close to bedtime, as naps will take away some of the intrinsic drive to fall asleep. For younger infants, there needs to be a lot more flexibility because their days may vary more in terms of the wake times, morning naps, and level of activity, but the same general principle should be applied whenever possible. Sometimes people, young and old, may be tired because they did not get a good night sleep, so they take a nap in the afternoon. While that nap alleviates the immediate problem, it might perpetuate the issue because it can lead to a subsequent night of difficulty falling asleep. This establishes a self-perpetuating cycle of poor night sleep, daytime sleepiness, inappropriate napping, and again difficulty sleeping at night."

**– Nadav Traeger, MD, FAAP, FCCP, D, ABSM, director of pediatric sleep medicine, Maria Fareri Children's Hospital**

"This can be a difficult area for parents. Parents should not give in to the temptation that eliminating naps will increase sleep at night. The fact is that infants who sleep well at night also sleep well during the day. Parents might need to adjust nap schedule or reduce some nap durations to improve nighttime sleep, but naps should not be eliminated. He reminds parents that babies need frequent short bouts of sleep. Eliminating naps will make for a cranky baby, but not a better nighttime sleeper."

**– Dr. Brett Kuhn, CBSM, associate professor of pediatrics at the University of Nebraska Medical Center and Children's Sleep Center at Children's Hospital**

"The effect of naps on nighttime sleep depends on the baby. As a general rule, parents should not let their baby sleep past 3 p.m. As the baby gets older, they will sleep less in the day and concentrate more sleep during the night."

**– Dr. Laura Davies, diplomate, American Board of Psychiatry and Neurology**

"Some babies, if short on naptime sleep, will go to sleep easily at night. Other babies get overly tired from insufficient naps and have trouble getting to sleep at night. Toddlers and preschoolers who nap too long during the day may have trouble getting to sleep at night."

**– Helen Neville, BS, RN, author, pediatric advice nurse, health educator, specialist in inborn temperament, and researcher**

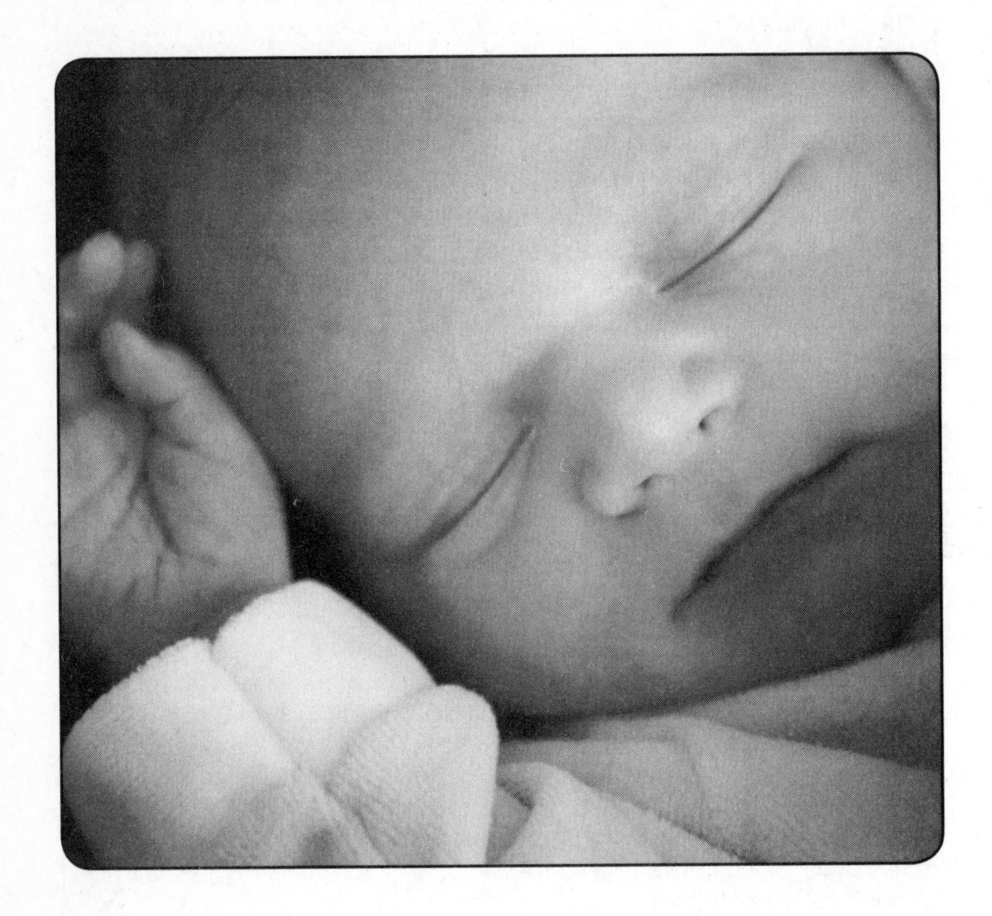

# chapter 9

## Older Siblings and Multiple Births

Getting one baby to sleep through the night can definitely be a challenge; getting more than one baby or child to sleep through the night can sometimes feel impossible. Having twins or multiple births does not just double the workload of parents – the workload will increase significantly. The same is true for having older children in the picture. If you are still trying to sleep train your older child when the new baby arrives, you will have more than twice the work ahead of you. Even if your older child is sleep trained, you might find it harder to sleep train your second baby because you have two children to care for.

### • TIP #76 •

### Pick Appropriate Bed Times for Each Child Separately

This tip applies to siblings and twins. Remember that each child is different, and even identical twins may have different internal sleep clocks. Keep separate sleep logs for your children, whether siblings or twins. Consider the drowsy signs of each of your children separately and try to determine if one child is a night owl while the other is an early bird. Your children might not be on the same sleep schedule if their natural body clocks differ.

You might find it more convenient to try to put both children to bed at the same time, but you could be suffering for the convenience. If you are trying to enforce a bedtime that is unnatural to your child, you will face additional hardship in getting her to sleep and may find she does not sleep as well as she would if you created a bedtime more appropriate to her internal system.

Consider the fact that you and your partner might not have the same sleep habits. While you might find nighttime your most energetic time of day, your partner could wake up in the morning ready to run a marathon. Your children, even if they are twins, could be just as different. Be sure you are evaluating each child separately when it comes to his or her sleep traits and internal biological clock.

## • TIP #77 •

## Do Not be Afraid of Waking Older Children

Most experts agree that this issue is more a fear of the parents than a reality. If you have an older child who is already sleep trained, he will most likely sleep through the crying of the new baby who is being sleep trained. Some experts have reported that parents are often afraid to try to sleep train a baby because of the fear of waking the older sibling. If you have an older child who is a deep sleeper, do not be afraid he will wake every time the baby cries at night.

If your older child is old enough to understand, explain to him that you are trying to teach the baby to sleep through the night and if he hears crying, he should remember the baby is just learning, and he should go back to sleep. By warning your child ahead of time, he might not suffer any lost sleep because of the baby's cries. Remind your older child that she was once a baby, too, and she had to learn to sleep well just as the new baby does.

If you are still afraid of waking your older child, move him to another room in the house until the baby is trained, or consider having him stay at a relative's house for a few nights if you plan to use a cry-it-out method with the baby. It is better to move your older child than to put off sleep training your baby because of the fear of waking an older sibling.

## • TIP #78 •

## Involve Older Children in the Process

If your older child is old enough to understand that you have a new baby who does not yet know how to sleep well, involve her in the baby's learning process. Ask her to be a good example to the baby by sleeping through the night, and have her be part of the bedtime routine by kissing the baby goodnight and playing quietly in another room in the house while you put the baby to sleep. Encourage your older child to tell the baby how to sleep through the night. Make sure your older child knows to stay in bed during the night, even if the baby wakes her up.

Some sleep experts advocate the use of a sibling bed. If your baby has been co-sleeping with you and your partner, using a sibling bed could be an easier transition than moving into a bed alone or a crib. Make sure you are adhering to good safety practices if you choose to use a sibling bed. Ask your child's pediatrician if your baby is old enough to use a sibling bed. If your baby is still at risk for SIDS, a sibling bed is not safe for your baby. Also, the older child should fully understand how a younger sibling may be injured during sleep. Many proponents of sibling beds say siblings bond more closely by sharing a bed. Usually children will end co-sleeping with their siblings on their own as they age and want to sleep alone.

# • TIP #79 •

## Ensure Healthy Sleep Habits of Older Children Before the Baby's Arrival

If you are reading this book before your baby has been born and you have another child – or if you plan to have more children – be sure you have already sleep trained the older sibling before the baby's arrival. Teaching the new baby to sleep while trying to get enough sleep yourself will be stressful, and sleep training more both children at once will only add to this stress. If the older sibling already has good sleep habits, he will also be less likely to wake during the new baby's cries in the middle of the night.

Use the tips in this book to help your older child learn to sleep throughout the night. If you have been co-sleeping with your older child, move him to his own bed before the new baby arrives. Try to make any adjustments, like this one, to your older child's sleep schedule before the new baby arrives. Your older child might experience some jealousy or other stress with the arrival of the new baby. Try to minimize the stress your older child will go through by not making too many changes all at once. If you know you will need to change the room your older child sleeps in or the time he goes to sleep once the new baby has arrived, make the change long before the arrival of the new baby.

When changing the bed of your older child, especially if he had been co-sleeping with you, make the transition gradual. If your child is old enough to understand, explain the upcoming change to him and involve him in the transition by letting him pick out his new bed or bedding. You can either slowly move your child out of your room or move him into his own room immediately with your slowly moving out of his room. If you slowly move him out of your room, start by placing a mat, sleeping bag, or mattress beside your bed, and make sure he sleeps beside the bed, not in your bed. Slowly move the mat closer to the door and then closer to his own room until your child is comfortable with falling asleep and staying asleep in his own bed. If you choose to move your child into his new room immediately, you can make his transition easier by placing a mat beside his bed for you to sleep on. Slowly move your own mat out of his room and back into your own. While your child is learning this transition, do not let him come back to sleeping in your bed. If he gets out of his own bed and comes to your room, immediately escort him back to his room and help soothe him back to sleep.

## CASE STUDY: WORD FROM THE EXPERTS: WHEN OLDER CHILDREN STILL WILL NOT SLEEP

Arnall feels the best method for getting a child between the ages of 1 and 4 to sleep through the night is by allowing co-sleeping.

– **Judy Arnall, co-founder of Parenting Canada; owner of Professional Parenting Canada**

Heinsohn suggests parents be calm and not get angry if their older child wakes in the night. "Parents should reassure their child and help them fall back asleep gently."

– **Laura Heinsohn, director of Family Bureau of Investigation Parenting Workshops**

"An older child should be able to understand that he is expected to sleep through the night and in his own bed. Identify the reason or reasons that an older child is not sleeping well, then develop a plan specific to that child and situation. In general, parents should first tell their child what is now expected of him ("From now on, you are going to be sleeping in your own bed for the whole night," for example.). An older child will need more support and may take more time transitioning into healthy sleep habits. If the child wakes up in the middle of the night, parents should address the situation right away. If he comes into your room, immediately walk him back to his room and help him fall back asleep. The transition may require a parent to sleep in bed with him at first, transition to sitting beside the bed, then right outside the door, and then checking on him every few minutes until he is used to falling asleep in his own room by himself."

– **Bette Levy Alkazian, MA, licensed marriage and family therapist**

"Consistency and routine are key for older children who still will not sleep through the night. Children need to know that bedtime is bedtime and they need to follow the rules of bedtime," Kerr said. Fox agrees: "Definitely consistency. Parents need to be loving but firm. If a child gets out of bed, parents should escort him back to his bed. Give them [children] an inch and they'll walk all over you. Parents should set up a light on a timer to signal to their child when it is time to get up in the morning."

– **Baby Bunching experts Linda Kerr and Cara Fox**

Heilbrunn believes parents need to find out why their child is having difficulty sleeping. "Parents should be aware if fears or separation anxiety, a stressful event in the child's life, or a developmental milestone could be causing regression in healthy sleep habits. Be consistent, create limits, make sure he knows what is expected of him, and realize that solutions will be different at different ages in a child's life and from one child to another."

**– Claudia Heilbrunn, parenting expert, author, and certified life coach**

While Pollak said your strategy should depend on the situation, she advises using positive reinforcement and a rewards system. "Some situations call for the use of barriers, such as a baby gate to keep your child from wandering. Parents need to pick a sleep training technique suitable for their child's temperament."

**– Karen Pollak, founder, Babies2Sleep**

Smith said she has not had issues with this because she started with good habits from day one, with the exception of when her twins are sick. She said the girls know that once they are put in their bed, they will not see her until morning. "If they really need something, they call," Smith said, and she goes to their bedside to sit with them. She ensures her girls always stay in their beds during the night.

**– Stephanie Smith, mother of twins**

"Parents should be clear and let their children know what the rules and expectations are. Children strive to know and test limits, and feel more secure with consistency than with freedom of choice. When children adhere to these rules, they should be rewarded — perhaps with a physical 'prize' such as a sticker chart, but positive one-on-one attention would be preferable by all involved. When parents act like friends instead of like parents and do not enforce limits and rules, their children will tend to act out until the parents feel forced to step in and act like parents. This is usually short-lived, inconsistent, adds more stress, and thus ultimately fails to change the child's behavior."

**– Nadav Traeger, MD, FAAP, FCCP, , D, ABSM, director of pediatric sleep medicine, Maria Fareri Children's Hospital**

Dr. Kuhn believes a sleep program for an older child must be matched to the reason for the problem. "The key is assessing the situation or problem and solving the problem that is causing the poor sleep habits. Many times, problems during bedtime are reflective of what is going on during the day. Consequently, most bedtime problems can and should be solved during daytime hours. If separation anxiety is the root problem, it should be addressed during the daytime. If a child is scared of the dark, it too should be worked on during the day. At older ages, sometimes a child becomes defiant, which affects bedtimes. This behavior should also be addressed during the daytime and not at bedtime." He teaches parents what he calls the "excuse-me drill" to help them teach older children to sleep well. He also encourages positive reinforcement of good sleep habits. Instead of parents interacting with their child when he is crying, he instructs parents to praise him when he is lying quietly in bed, displaying good sleep habits. He is currently conducting a research study on this strategy. He feels it creates an environment where parents are more comfortable with the sleep technique, as many parents are not comfortable with cry-it-out methods — and children learn they get attention when they behave well, not when they misbehave.

**– Dr. Brett Kuhn, CBSM, associate professor of pediatrics at the University of Nebraska Medical Center and Children's Sleep Center at Children's Hospital**

Dr. Davies suggests parents use star charts, with immediate rewards for behavior. "Parents also need to address any possible fears or jealousies of other children — possibly due to birth of a new baby. This issue is another reason not to have a family bed, because if an older child gets kicked out of the family bed, he or she will not know how to sleep on his or her own."

**– Dr. Laura Davies, diplomate, American Board of Psychiatry and Neurology**

When older children still will not sleep, Neville reminds parents that the goal is to maximize family sleep. "Parents should look for small steps in the right direction. If parents want their baby to sleep in his own room, parents can put sofa pillows in the child's room for a while to sleep on, so parents are nearby and can give reassurance without getting up. Once the child is sleeping better, parents can return to their own room. Many children come to the parents' bed in the middle of the night. If parents want to change that, they can put a pad or sleeping bag beside their bed, so a lonely or frightened child gets emotional closeness without the added reward of being physically side by side. Again, once the child is sleeping well beside the parent, gradually move the pad toward the child's own room".

**– Helen Neville, BS, RN, author, pediatric advice nurse, health educator, specialist in inborn temperament, and researcher**

# • TIP #80 •

## Mold Older Children in to "Heavy" Sleepers

One of the best ways to ensure the new baby will not wake her older siblings is to make the older siblings heavy sleepers. If you have raised your older children to sleep through noise, they will not be as easily roused, even when your baby is crying in the middle of the night. If you have tiptoed around the house every time your child naps or goes to sleep, you might have to do some additional training before your new bundle arrives. A white noise machine, soft music, or a ceiling fan in the child's room might make the transition easier.

Try to get your child accustomed to sleeping through noises. Do not make any effort to be quiet during your child's naptime. This does not mean you should make intentional noise or play loud music, but keep the television on and go about other business just as you would if your child were not napping. If you have been tiptoeing around, your child might need some time to adjust to the new noises. Use white noise to drown out some of the noise, and introduce new noises little by little. If your older child is old enough to understand, explain to him that you will be doing household chores while he naps and that he might hear noises during his nap. Ensure him everything is fine and that he should go back to sleep if he hears any noises.

# • TIP #81 •

## Separate Children During Bedtime if Necessary

If you have tried sleep training your baby and ended up with a crying baby and an awake toddler, you might need to separate the children. Place the older sibling in a room far enough away from your baby so the baby's cries will not disturb the older child. It is easier to move the older sibling temporarily while you teach your baby to sleep than it is to move your baby into another room once you have begun sleep training.

If you are overly concerned about waking the older sibling even before a problem has occurred, you might move your older child from the beginning. Most experts agree this issue is more of a fear than a reality. In extreme circumstances — such as when the older sibling is a very light sleeper, if you live in a small house or apartment, or you have an extremely loud baby — consider having the older child sleep at a relative's house for the first few nights of sleep training.

If your older child has established good sleep habits, it will be easier to move him to another room in the house temporarily than it will be to sleep train your baby in a room other than her own and then move her once she is trained. If your older child is old enough to understand, explain that this move is temporary until the baby is able to sleep well. Encourage your older child to continue to be a good sleeper and help his transition by offering a new blanket or stuffed animal that he can sleep with.

## CASE STUDY: WORD FROM THE EXPERTS: WAKING SIBLINGS

Arnall suggests keeping the children in separate cribs, but not worrying about making the environment too quiet for either child. Both baby and his older sibling should learn to fall asleep, stay asleep, and go back to sleep in a noisy environment. "Older children will get used to hearing a baby crying (or vice versa) and will not wake up every time the other cries."

**– Judy Arnall, co-founder of Parenting Canada; owner of Professional Parenting Canada**

When siblings are involved, "parents should establish good sleep habits for the older child before a new baby arrives in the home. It is almost impossible to train a newborn and an older child to sleep through the night at the same time. Parents can help an older child feel special by letting them choose new bedding, a special pillow, or a stuffed animal that will help them continue to sleep well with the new baby's arrival. Even if the older child wakes up when the baby cries after a few days or weeks pass, the older child will learn to sleep through the crying — and likewise other loud noises at night — which, long term, is a true blessing for parents."

**– Barb Dehn, RN, MS, NP**

Heinsohn suggests parents keep babies and toddlers/older children separate during nighttime. Her daughter has six children, and Heinsohn said, "The older children have become oblivious to crying and can sleep straight through it."

**– Laura Heinsohn, director of Family Bureau of Investigation Parenting Workshops**

Alkazian said she is asked this question over and over again by many different families. She feels that many times, parents worry more about waking older children than they should. Her advice to parents depends on the age of the sibling. "If the sibling is old enough to understand, parents should explain that the new baby is learning how to sleep and might cry for a few nights. Parents should tell the sibling that if she hears crying to just go back to sleep. Older children will be tired and should be able to fall back asleep easily. If the sibling is too young to understand or is a particularly light sleeper, parents may want to have him sleep at a relative's house for a few nights while the new baby learns to sleep. Parents can also try moving the baby to a part of the house farthest away from the sibling, so as not to disturb her sleep."

**– Bette Levy Alkazian, MA, licensed marriage and family therapist**

Kerr recalls being a mom of two children under 2 years old. Her concern for the baby waking the toddler at night made her decide to move the baby to a separate room from her toddler and to use a noise machine in the toddler's room to drown out crying. She said she may have been overly cautious considering her toddler was a heavy sleeper, but making sure the entire family slept well was important to her. She knew having two children would not allow her the luxury of sleeping when the baby slept; she knew she would need to be well rested to take care of the baby and toddler the next morning. Fox said, "Putting the baby on the opposite end of the hall or house from the toddler is a good idea." She is a big believer in making sure everyone has his or her own room or space.

**– Baby Bunching experts Linda Kerr and Cara Fox**

"Parents who choose the cry-it-out method will probably experience difficultly in keeping older children — or other members of the family — from being disturbed, unless they live in a big house or apartment. If parents are concerned with waking older children, parents might consider using a method to get their baby to sleep that does not provoke crying, such as nursing, bouncing, or rocking."

**– Claudia Heilbrunn, parenting expert, author, and certified life coach**

"Parents should create an environment where older children will not be disturbed by the baby." She suggests using white noise, earplugs, or moving the child and baby to separate areas of the house.

**– Karen Pollak, founder, Babies2Sleep**

Smith found that keeping a schedule and having her twin girls go to bed at the same time was the best option. She has kept her girls in the same room. For the first four months, she had the girls in the same bed, and they enjoyed being close to each other; it seemed to help them sleep better and longer than if they were alone. At 4 months old, they were able to stretch out, and Smith decided to put her girls in separate beds for safety reasons. Even in separate beds, she made sure they could see one another in their beds. At almost 2 years old, they still share a room and go down for bed and naps at the same time. There were times when one girl would wake the other up, but it was rare. More often that not, she had to wake the two of them at the same time for night feedings. She also went through a period of two weeks where one girl began to sleep through the night while the other still needed to get up for food. This was the time the girls tended to wake each other, and it was a great lesson for them to learn early on. Even now, Smith stills has to put them to bed at the same time because that is what they want, but they get up at different times in the morning. She advises other parents of twins that keeping a routine is so important not only for their children, but so parents can get sleep as well. The bond with twins is strong, and she feels keeping them in the same room can be very helpful. "Given that they are the same age, putting them to bed together is really the best option."

**– Stephanie Smith, mother of twins**

"Although there are no specific rules for this situation, the answer is not to somehow 'speed up' the baby's maturational process, but rather to have the older children accommodate this process. At times, it may even involve rearranging rooms and swapping beds. Hopefully, the older children have been guided well by their parents all along and already have good sleep habits so that they will easily adapt to the new situation."

**– Nadav Traeger, MD, FAAP, FCCP, D, ABSM, director of pediatric sleep medicine, Maria Fareri Children's Hospital**

Dr. Kuhn has found that many parents resist sleep training their baby because of their fear of waking the baby's older sibling. "Oftentimes, this is more of a fear than a reality. Depending on the age of the older child, there is a good chance she will be able to sleep through the baby's crying. If that is not the case, or if parents are worried about waking the older child, parents should temporarily move the older child to a different room or different part of the house until the baby is trained. If the older child is already sleep trained, this temporary move will not create a problem with her current sleep habits."

**– Dr. Brett Kuhn, CBSM, associate professor of pediatrics at the University of Nebraska Medical Center and Children's Sleep Center at Children's Hospital**

"Parents have two main choices when it comes to sleep training a baby with an older sibling present. Parents can send their older child (or children) to a sleepover for a few nights, or parents can accept the fact that everyone will be a bit cranky."

**– Dr. Laura Davies, diplomate, American Board of Psychiatry and Neurology**

"Again, this issue depends largely on individual differences. While some older children are not bothered by a baby crying during the night, other children are. To combat this issue, some parents keep the baby in their room until the baby is sleeping through the night, then move the baby into a room with a sibling."

**– Helen Neville, BS, RN, author, pediatric advice nurse, health educator, specialist in inborn temperament, and researcher**

# • TIP #82 •

## Teach Twins to Fall Asleep Separately

While some parents and experts do suggest putting twins in the same crib, twins will eventually have to learn to fall asleep by themselves. Twins cannot sleep in the same bed their whole lives and should not be kept together once they can move about freely for safety reasons. Plus, learning to sleep is a skill each one will need to learn independently. Your twins might not learn to sleep within the same time and might need two completely differently sleep strategies.

Chances are your twins will not be on the same sleep schedule. One might wake earlier than the other, and one may require an earlier bedtime. Be sure to evaluate your twins' sleep schedule and sleep training separately, and do not confine one twin to the schedule of the other twin. You might also find it easier on you to put them to bed separately, so while Dad watches one, you put the other one to bed.

Your twins will have plenty of time together and plenty of opportunities to bond. Bedtime is a time for sleep, not playing or other bonding activities. If your twins sleep better together and are on the same schedule, then feel free to let them do so. If your twins are not on the same sleep schedule and seem to be disturbed by having the other around, then sleep them separately. Just remember to evaluate each twin's needs individually.

# • TIP #83 •

## Consider Using Separate Cribs or Rooms for Twins

Although some parents insist on putting twins in the same crib during naptime and bedtime, many experts disagree with this arrangement. Your twins will need to learn to fall asleep independently and will not be able to stay in the same crib together for long, due to safety considerations. If you co-sleep your newborn twins in the same crib, they might develop an association to sleeping next to their twin that will have to be broken once you move them. Other disadvantages to co-sleeping twins are that one restless twin can wake the other; your twins will not necessarily have the same sleep schedule (one might be an earlier riser than the other, for example); and one twin may play quietly when he wakes, while the other tries to wake his twin.

Depending on the sleep habits of your twins, you might consider sleeping them in separate rooms. Just as a single baby can wake an older sibling at night, so can a twin wake the other. It might be easier to sleep train your twins if you sleep them in separate rooms. Remember that just because your babies are twins does not mean they will have the same sleep needs. Accurately evaluate your twins as individuals and decide the best sleep times and strategies accordingly. Your twins will have plenty of bonding time together and do not need to sleep together to have a close relationship.

*Photo courtesy of Sivan Grosman, founder of Sivan Photography (**http://sivanphotography.com**)*

# chapter 10

## Changes in Routine

Once you have selected and implemented a sleep schedule and have created an environment where you and your baby are sleeping well, you might think sleep training is over. That is not the case. As your baby grows, other factors will affect her sleep, and other obstacles will present themselves as barriers to your child's sleep. Planning ahead for such changes will help you better understand and cope with the disruptions to your child's sleep schedule. Many of these disruptions will be impossible to avoid altogether, but being prepared for them can make the difference between having a minor, temporary change in sleep and a major setback during the night.

### • TIP #84 •

### Milestones will Impact Your Child's Sleep Schedule

Your child is a unique human being with a distinctive personality and characteristics. Your child will also experience constant change. Remember that he is growing rapidly and undergoing changes constantly. These changes will impact his sleep schedule at different times and to varying degrees. Do not believe that once your baby has started sleeping through the night, he always will do so. Be understanding of your child's changes and adjust your bedtime routine or sleep schedules as appropriate at different stages of his life.

As your child goes through developmental milestones, his sleep patterns will often vary. If you are potty training him, you might notice he starts resisting bedtime more than usual. This change might be due to the stress of trying to learn another new task, which in this case is using the potty. Some experts suggest the most impactful milestone to your child's sleep schedule is when he learns to walk. Be aware of possible upcoming milestones, and try to be patient if he shows some sleep training regression during or right before a major milestone is reached. During these times, try hard to keep your sleep training on schedule and consistent. Once your child gets past the milestone, his sleep should return to the normal schedule.

# • TIP #85 •

## Stress Can Impact Your Baby's Sleep

When the world around your family changes, this adds stress to you and your baby. If Mom or Dad returns to work or you move into a new house, your baby will be impacted by the change. To keep everyone sleeping well through these changes, remember to maintain consistency in bedtime and daytime routines as much as possible. If you will have to change the bedtime routine to accommodate Mom or Dad's returning to work, make the schedule change before the parent is back at work. This allows your baby to get used to the schedule change before another change is present.

## • TIP #86 •

## After a Temporary Routine Change or Illness, Resume the Normal Schedule ASAP

During an illness, sleep training could fly right out the window. If your child is sick, you do not want to let her cry at night. She might be crying because she has a fever or has thrown up, not because she is just resistant to sleep. If she has a cold, she might also have a difficult time going to bed due to a stuffy nose. During these times, comfort your baby and allow her to fall asleep any way she can. You might resort to rocking your baby to bed while she is ill or letting her fall asleep at the bottle or while nursing. Try not to overreact by allowing too much regression of sleep training for a slight sniffle. Use your parenting instincts to know how much your child needs you. If she is ill but is still sleeping well, do not rock her to bed just because you want to. Make sure you are doing whatever you need to do to comfort your child during her illness without overreacting to the situation.

If your child is on medication (over-the-counter or doctor-prescribed), make sure to ask your child's pediatrician how the medication might affect her sleep. You might need to adjust the time of day you give your child the medication. You may need to be extra patient and sympathetic during an illness if the medication is keeping your baby up at night.

Ear infections can also impact your baby's sleep. Many babies will be most uncomfortable during sleep when they have an ear infection. You might even first notice that your child has an ear infection due to sudden disturbed sleep. Be extra considerate to your baby's situation. Chances are she longs to go to sleep just as much as you are longing for her to fall asleep.

Once your child is over the illness, resume sleep training or your old sleep strategies immediately. Try not to "ease" back into the training by tapering off your illness-comforting habits. Instead, resume your normal sleep training schedule just as you were doing before the illness hit. Your baby might resist the switch, but do not drag out the process and trick your baby into thinking the illness-comforting techniques will be the new sleep method.

# • TIP #87 •

## Do Not Disrupt Your Baby's Sleep Schedule to Accommodate Visiting Family or Friends

When grandparents or friends come to visit, you might be tempted to keep your baby awake longer than usual or wake him from a nap sooner than you should. But resist the temptation to change your baby's sleep schedule, especially if you are still sleep training, to accommodate visitors. Keeping your baby up later at night will only create a fussy child for visitors and a more difficult time getting your baby to sleep that night.

Explain to your family that your child is in sleep training and that she needs to be in bed at a specific time. Try to schedule visiting with relatives around the baby's bedtime and naptimes. Ask them to come at times when the baby is awake normally, and ask them to make plans to do other activities while the baby is napping or down for bedtime. Your guests should understand, and if not, explain to them that you are in the middle of sleep training and that you cannot break your baby's schedule.

The hazard of disrupting your baby's schedule is twofold. First, you may experience a relapse of old habits and have to retrain good behaviors, creating a longer process of sleep training for you and your baby. Second, if you keep your baby up longer than usual or wake him earlier than you should, you will have a tired, cranky baby on your hands. This will make visiting less pleasant for you, your baby, and your guests.

# • TIP #88 •

## Do Not be Discouraged if Old Techniques Stop Working

Just as your baby's circadian rhythm will change, so will his reaction to certain stimuli or rewards. You will need to make appropriate changes to your child's bedtime routine as he grows and ages. While a 6-month-old baby will have a very simple routine, a 2-year-old child will have a longer, more complicated bedtime routine. Be sure you are changing routines and tactics as your child grows and changes. If you find an old technique does not work, try to identify why the routine is not successful. If your child seems to have outgrown the technique or process, find one more age-appropriate. An older child might respond well to a sleep chart that rewards a good night's sleep with stars. Find a reward system your child will respond to or a technique that best suits your child's personality.

If an old technique stops working due to an illness, developmental milestone, vacation, or other temporary affect, try to continue the old method or revert back to retraining that method. Your child might just be experiencing a temporary regression that will pass quickly if you consistently maintain the routine.

## • TIP #89 •

## Be Patient and Know that Temporary Periods of Disrupted Sleep are Normal

Sometimes your baby will experience sleep disruptions for no known reason. You might have a well-trained baby suddenly begin waking at 3 a.m. and crying for no apparent reason. Be patient when these sudden changes occur. Do not worry if your child experiences temporary disruptions or setbacks in her normal sleep routine. Try to identify if there are other factors affecting your child's sleep to determine if you can help resolve the issue. If no factors are present, wait a few nights or a week to see if the problem resolves by itself. You might need to change certain sleep tactics or instill a retraining program if sleep issues persist for longer periods. Otherwise, try to ride out the issue and remember that even as adults, we suffer unexplained sleeplessness at times.

If a child is having difficulty during the day, such as resistance to authority, these issues will also show up at night. Be sure to solve these issues during the day. It is much easier to deal with a behavioral issue during the daytime when everyone is well rested.

During the night, all issues will be more difficult to cope with because you and your child will be tired and possibly grumpy.

## CASE STUDY: WORD FROM THE EXPERTS: WHEN OLD TECHNIQUES STOP WORKING

Arnall said, "That's parenting!" She suggests parents think about their choices when they are faced with this issue. "Sometimes, parents should just accept the present situation. Waiting out the situation can sometimes be the best solution. Parents should not feel compelled to make a change just because an old technique temporarily stops working."

**– Judy Arnall, co-founder of Parenting Canada; owner of Professional Parenting Canada**

Dehn tells parents that it is "absolutely, perfectly normal" for old techniques to stop working. "As babies age and develop, their sleep patterns will change. Parents should expect these changes and plan accordingly. Once babies become toddlers, parents will most likely have to employ new tactics to get their toddler to sleep through the night."

**– Barb Dehn, RN, MS, NP**

"Parents in this situation should try the old technique again or get help from an expert or friend. The flaw often lies in the execution of the technique and not in the technique itself. Oftentimes, a baby can start to outsmart the system, which means bedtime is a test of wills. Parents must be stronger and smarter than their baby and teach him that he needs a good night's sleep."

**– Bette Levy Alkazian, MA, licensed marriage and family therapist**

"Since babies change all the time, parents should realize that a technique that worked last week might not work the following week. Parents should be open to new things and consider that when one plan stops working, it might be time to make a change of plans," Kerr said. Fox also reminds parents to be flexible: "If an old plan does not work for several nights in a row, chances are it will never work again. Early in a baby's life, she is constantly growing and outgrowing schedules, feedings, swaddling, and other techniques that might have once worked well."

**– Baby Bunching experts Linda Kerr and Cara Fox**

Heilbrunn reminds parents that everything a child does is temporary. "Methods stop working because babies are not machines; many factors — such as developmental stage, stress level, and current achievements — play a role in how well babies sleep." If a method stops working, parents should evaluate their child's physiological and emotional states to determine what method will work best. Remember that your method may have to change, Heilbrunn advises. "If your child is sick, continuing the cry-it-out method during his sickness would be inappropriate."

**– Claudia Heilbrunn, parenting expert, author, and certified life coach**

"Parents should consider timing when an old technique stops working. Parents should ask themselves if their child is facing a milestone, illness, or other significant change. Once parents understand why the technique may have stopped working, they should modify it to their baby's current age or situation."

**– Karen Pollak, founder, Babies2Sleep**

Smith reminds parents they need to be flexible and willing to try new things. "Babies grow and change, and so do their actions and habits. Do not be afraid to try something new."

**– Stephanie Smith, mother of twins**

According to Dr. Traeger, as a child grows and matures, parents will face many changes and challenges. "Some of the issues will be transient, such as crying and poor sleep due to teething or an illness, while other changes will be more gradual and will occur in parallel to the acquisition of new physical and cognitive abilities. Once good sleep habits are established both of these types of changes can be overcome much more easily. Parents do not need to start from scratch, but just adapt and make modifications."

**– Nadav Traeger, MD, FAAP, FCCP, D, ABSM, director of pediatric sleep medicine, Maria Fareri Children's Hospital**

Dr. Kuhn spends time evaluating why the old technique stopped working before creating a treatment to match the reason for the problem. "Sometimes a child gets tired of a certain reward and will stop behaving, and sometimes an environmental change will create an issue with sleep behavior. Parents who are not monitoring their child's sleep schedule might not realize that naps are lasting too long or are too late into the day, which ends up affecting bedtime routines. The key is to find the cause of the problem before trying to create a solution to it."

**– Dr. Brett Kuhn, CBSM, associate professor of pediatrics at the University of Nebraska Medical Center and Children's Sleep Center at Children's Hospital**

"Parents should check to see if their baby is sick or teething when old techniques stop working."

**– Dr. Laura Davies, diplomate, American Board of Psychiatry and Neurology**

"Most likely, a baby is now in a growth spurt or a new stage of development, which is causing the old techniques to stop working. If this is the case, parents should do something different — feed more often to get through a growth spurt or simply change plans if it is a change in development."

**– Helen Neville, BS, RN, author, pediatric advice nurse, health educator, specialist in inborn temperament, and researcher**

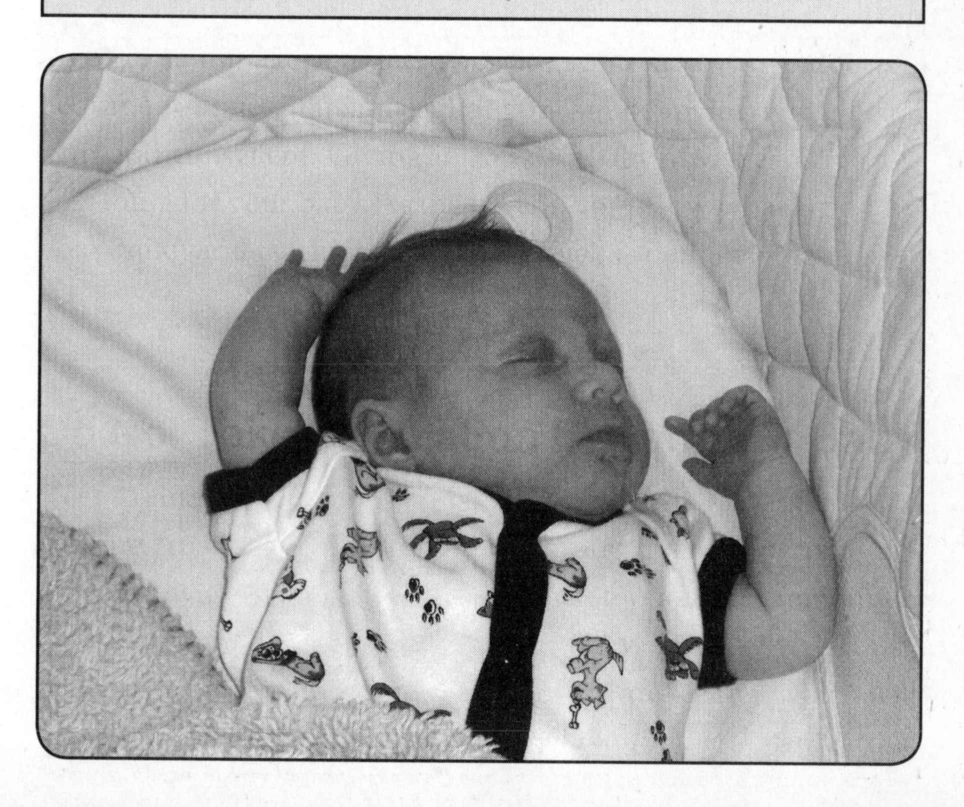

*Photo courtesy of Sivan Grosman, founder of Sivan Photography (**http://sivanphotography.com**)*

# chapter 11

## Sleepless Parents

When you finally get your new bundle of joy to peacefully sleep through the night, you might expect to enjoy the same peaceful slumber he is. Many parents find this is not the case at all. Once the baby is sleeping through the night, you could find yourself tossing and turning the whole night and end up just as tired the next morning as you were before your baby was sleep trained. Realize this occurrence is not uncommon. You have trained your body to stay up with your baby or wake up during the night to care for him. Now that he no longer needs your help during the night, you have to retrain your body to fall asleep and stay asleep throughout the night. Be patient with yourself just as you were with your baby while he was in sleep training.

### • TIP #90 •

### Identify Root Causes of Sleepless Nights

The first step to getting back to a restful night's sleep is to identify the root cause or causes of your sleeplessness. Ask yourself why you are having trouble falling or staying asleep. You might find yourself listening for cries or worried your baby is awake and checking on him needlessly throughout the night. You might find yourself lying in bed worried about the next day's events, when and how you will return to work, or other personal issues. Or, you might just find your body has trained itself to sleep lighter, and you are easily woken by the slightest creak or pitter-patter during the night.

Once you have identified the cause of your sleeplessness, take specific measures to address that issue. If you are keeping yourself awake worried about your baby, make a schedule for checking on your child. Once he is down for the night, check on him once more before you go to bed and then not again until morning. Remind yourself that he is all right, and try to resist the urge to continually check on him during the night. You might taper off these frequent check-ins slowly, if you find it too much to stop checking on your baby altogether. Remember that these check-ins will keep you from falling asleep, will wake you up more, and could possibly disturb the sleep of your baby. Remind yourself that your baby is sleeping, just as you have trained him to do, and rest assured that he will be fine until morning.

If you find yourself worrying about the next day's events or other issues in your life, try writing them down, then forget about them until the morning. Keep a pen and pad of paper by your bed. Before you turn in for the night, write down any worries or concerns you have. If you wake up in the middle of the night worried about something, quickly jot it down and go back to sleep. Tell yourself you will deal with these issues in the morning after a good night's rest.

If you find yourself programmed to be a light sleeper, you might consider a white-noise device or machine for your own bedroom. You do not want to drown out the cries of your baby, but you do want to get past waking up alarmed by other noises. If you do not own a white noise machine or do not want to purchase one, consider turning on a ceiling fan, air purifier, or using an alarm clock that has a soothing ocean or similar sound.

Whatever the reason for your sleeping difficulties, you will not be able to solve them until they are clearly identified. While it might just take some time to get used to the new routine of your baby, there are some things you can do to help speed up the process. If your sleeplessness lasts longer than a few weeks, consider seeking medical help. Talking to someone about your issue might also help shed some light on why you are not sleeping well. Consider speaking with a counselor, psychologist, psychiatrist, or a trusted friend or relative.

## • TIP #91 •

## Create Order and Structure in Your Own Life

Your circadian rhythm thrives on schedules and regularity, just as your baby's does. Set your own schedule during the day so you wake, eat, exercise, work, play, and sleep at the same times each day. Keep this routine as much as possible every day of the week, including weekends. Varying your routine during the weekend can wreak havoc on your body and set you up for a week of irregular sleep, drowsiness, and not-so-optimal daytime functioning. If you are your baby's primary caregiver, set your own schedule based on your baby's. If you feed your baby four times a day, set your own meal times to start after your baby is done. Get a calendar, day planner, or create your own sleep, eat, and play logs. The sooner you get your timing system adjusted to a regular schedule, the sooner you will be enjoying restful nights.

## • TIP #92 •

## De-stress Before Your Bedtime and Create a Bedtime Routine for Yourself

Just as counselors suggest you should not go to bed angry, you also should not go to bed stressed. Trying to fall asleep when you are overly stressed will be next to impossible. Find a way to de-stress before you go to bed. You might be able to accomplish this by simply creating a calming bedtime routine. You might find you need additional help de-stressing. If you are worried about forgetting things or having a busy schedule, plan ahead. Use calendars or day planners and lists to keep track of daily routines and other important items. If you cannot seem to find the time to pay bills, try setting up automatic bill pay so you no longer need to worry about this. You might also need to ask your partner for additional help. If you feel you are being overworked day after day, you might be carrying too many responsibilities. Do not be afraid to ask for help and to ask your partner to take on a few extra chores or tasks around the house.

Being a parent is a full-time job. You might find yourself running around all day long and then scrambling off to bed in a hurry. This pattern can make a restful night's sleep challenging. You need to give yourself time to unwind and relax before your head hits the pillow. Just as you created a relaxing and calming bedtime routine for your baby, you need to have a similarly relaxing plan for yourself. You might not need a bedtime feeding or diaper change, but you do need time to relax and let yourself know bedtime is coming soon. Find a routine that allows you to de-stress and prepare for bed. You might have the time and luxury to soak in a warm bath before bed. If not, try washing your face with a warm cloth as a quicker substitute. Put on your pajamas and find a soothing activity (preferably not television) to engage in right before you fall asleep, such as reading, listening to calm and quiet music, or writing in a journal. You might write down the next day's plans and say a prayer or meditate. Whatever you choose, make sure it is something you will be able to continue each night, and something you find calming and soothing.

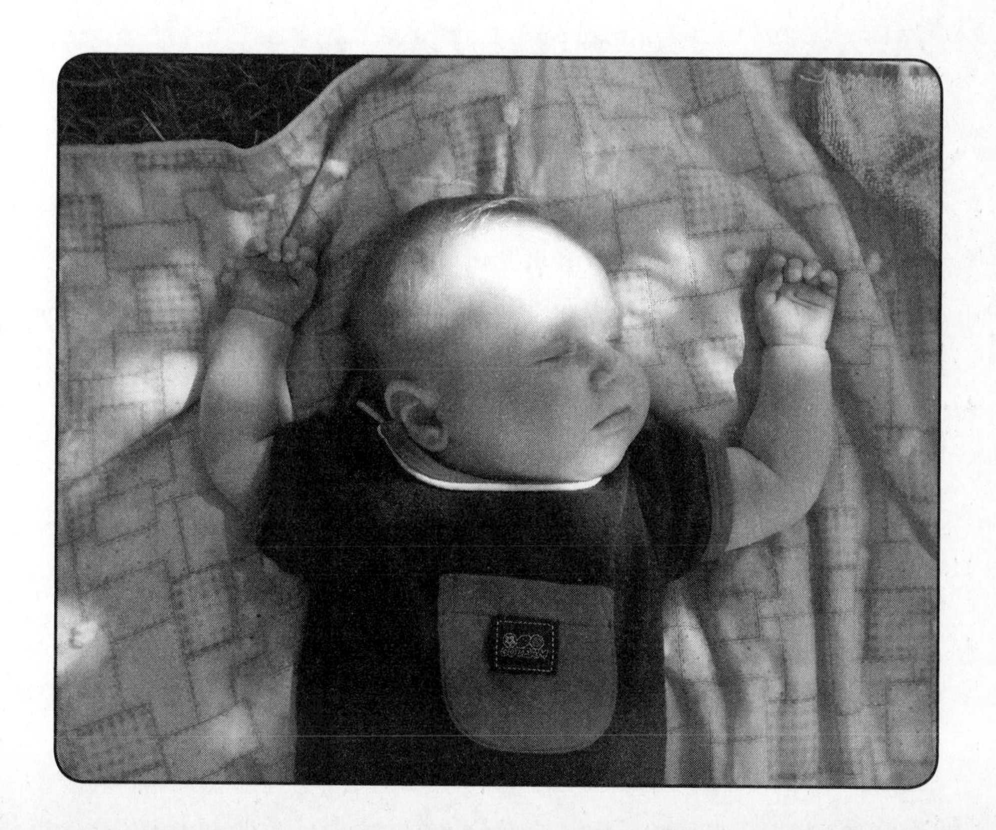

Part of your own routine, just as with your child, should be an appropriate and consistent bedtime and wake time. Your sleep schedule should be regular so your body's timing can adjust to the routine. If your sleep schedule is inconsistent, your body will never learn when it should be asleep and when it should be awake. And, just as you did with your baby, you need to set an appropriate bedtime for yourself. If you stay up later than your body wants to, you will find yourself with a second wind of energy. While this might help get all the laundry done in one night, it will not help your body get back to a normal and healthy sleep schedule. Remember that crashing is not a healthy sleep habit for you or your baby. Read your own drowsy signs and set a bedtime that you can maintain consistently and that is appropriate for your individual body's timing system.

## • TIP #93 •

## Give Yourself Time to Relearn How to Sleep Through the Night

Once you are in the habit of waking up in the middle of the night to take care of your baby, whether for a nighttime feeding or to help him fall back asleep on his own, you will have to retrain your body to sleep through the night. Be patient and remember that sleep training (even for adults) takes time. Some experts say it can take one to three months for parents' sleep schedules to return to "normal" after their baby has started sleeping soundly through the night.

Remind yourself you need to relearn to sleep through the night. Find a saying, prayer, or poem you can read or say to yourself each night before bed to remind yourself you can get a good night's sleep. Many parents find themselves so worried about not sleeping well that they cannot sleep well. Do not get caught up in the cycle of not sleeping. Be patient as you relearn to sleep well. You might find it helpful to keep sleep logs for yourself while you are trying to get back to a normal sleep schedule. Your logs will help you see the small progress you are making, which might cause you to worry less and, thus, get more sleep.

• TIP #94 •

## Exercise Daily

Although this tip might at first seem impossible, it does not have to be. You might not have the time to go to the gym for an hour every day or even jump on the treadmill at home for 30 minutes. You should, however, be able to incorporate some form of exercise into your daily life. Vacuuming the house can be considered exercise, as can other household chores and cleaning. Laundry and unloading the dishwasher can also be turned into an exercise routine. The American Academy of Physical Medicine and Rehabilitation offers a list of household chore exercise on their Web site at **www.aapmr.org/condtreat/pain/hsehold.htm**. You might be able to get outside and pick up leaves while your baby plays in the grass or an outdoor crib. You could buckle your baby into the stroller and take a brisk walk around the block.

Try to schedule more formal exercise routines three times a week for approximately 30 minutes per session. Find a few other neighborhood mothers to schedule exercise dates with. You can find activities that are baby-friendly or plan these exercise dates at times when your partner or a sitter is available. Make exercise a priority in your life. It will not only help you sleep better, but help you to be healthier and feel better overall.

Plan your exercise for early in the day if possible. Working out within one or two hours of bedtime will make falling asleep more difficult. Try to schedule your workouts or household chores early in the day, before dinner.

# • TIP #95 •

## Avoid Caffeine or Other Stimulants Late in the Day

Most experts recommend staying away from coffee or other stimulants six to eight hours before your bedtime. Caffeine does more than temporarily wake you up; it has long-lasting affects on your body. Caffeine stays in your body for up to eight hours, much longer than we physically feel the effect of it. Once caffeine enters our body, it starts affecting certain hormones. Caffeine inhibits the body's absorption of the hormone that calms the body, adenosine. This effect causes you to feel more awake temporarily but can be harmful to your sleep. Caffeine also raises your adrenaline and dopamine levels, which contributes to temporary alertness but can cause a "crash" effect later, leaving you feeling tired. The stress hormone, or cortisol, is also increased with the consumption of caffeine. The side effects of an increase in cortisol include weight gain, moodiness, heart disease, and diabetes.

Caffeine in small to moderate amounts can be helpful to get you through the day. By limiting your intake and not consuming caffeinated products after 2 p.m., you can experience the positive effects of caffeine without the negative side effects. Studies have shown that caffeine consumed before a workout can boost your energy during exercise and may assist in burning more calories while you work out.

Products that include caffeine are coffee, soda pop, tea, energy drinks, and chocolate. For a more complete list of foods containing caffeine, check out **www.nutritiondata.com** and search for "caffeine."

Stimulants can be found in some medications, including over-the-counter cold remedies and migraine relievers and cigarettes. If you are a smoker, consider quitting for sleep's sake — not to mention your overall health and the health of your family.

# • TIP #96 •

## Eat Healthy During the Day and Avoid Big Meals Before Bedtime

Healthy eating is important for good sleep and overall health. Avoid junk food or foods high in sugar that will cause an energy boost followed by a crash. Start your day by eating breakfast at home each morning, and not by driving to a fast-food restaurant. Find breakfast foods that pack long-lasting energy, ones that have complex carbohydrates and proteins. Before grocery shopping, make a list and only buy the items on the list. This method of shopping will prevent impulsively buying cookies or other junk food. If you do not have these items in your house, you will be much less likely to eat them. Stock up on healthy snacks like fruit, low-fat yogurt, and whole-grain crackers. Commit to eating healthy and teaching your children the same. You will feel better and have more energy throughout the day.

You should avoid eating food, especially big meals with a lot of carbohydrates, three hours before bedtime. While certain foods can make you sleepy, they will not help you sleep better throughout the night. Even foods with a high tryptophan content have only been proved to help you fall asleep, not stay asleep, and will not help you get the restful sleep you need to feel rejuvenated the next day. Eating a big meal also creates more work for your body as your system breaks down and digests the meal. This process will keep you awake — not make you sleepy. And digestion is best done in the standing up position, not lying down. If you find yourself hungry an hour before bedtime because you have not had time to eat, resist the urge to gorge on a big meal. Eat a small, nutritious snack so you will not go to bed hungry but also will not be working overtime to digest a large meal.

Watch your alcohol intake as well. While one glass of wine at night might help you relax and fall asleep more easily, too much alcohol leads to restless sleep and waking earlier than usual. If you are breastfeeding, your alcohol intake should be minimal. Do drink plenty of water during the day without guzzling large glasses right before bed, which would cause nighttime bathroom breaks to disturb your sleep.

# • TIP #97 •

## Create a Relaxing Environment Conducive to Sleep

Your bedroom should be your safe haven; it should be your escape from the world. Create an environment that is relaxing and a place you look forward to going to every evening. If your bedroom is in disarray, needs painting, and is a constant reminder of more things you need to do but do not have time for, fix it. Make your bedroom top on the list of things to do and create a place you will feel safe and at ease in. Make sure you are sleeping on a comfortable mattress with comfortable sheets and pillows, too. If you and your partner disagree on temperature, be sure to work out a compromise before bedtime so you are not having a thermostat battle each night.

Many experts recommend leaving the television out of the bedroom. The bedroom should be a place for sleep and intimate relations between you and your partner. Watching television can detract from both of those intentions. Consider removing the television altogether from your bedroom or set a limit on when the television will be turned off for the evening.

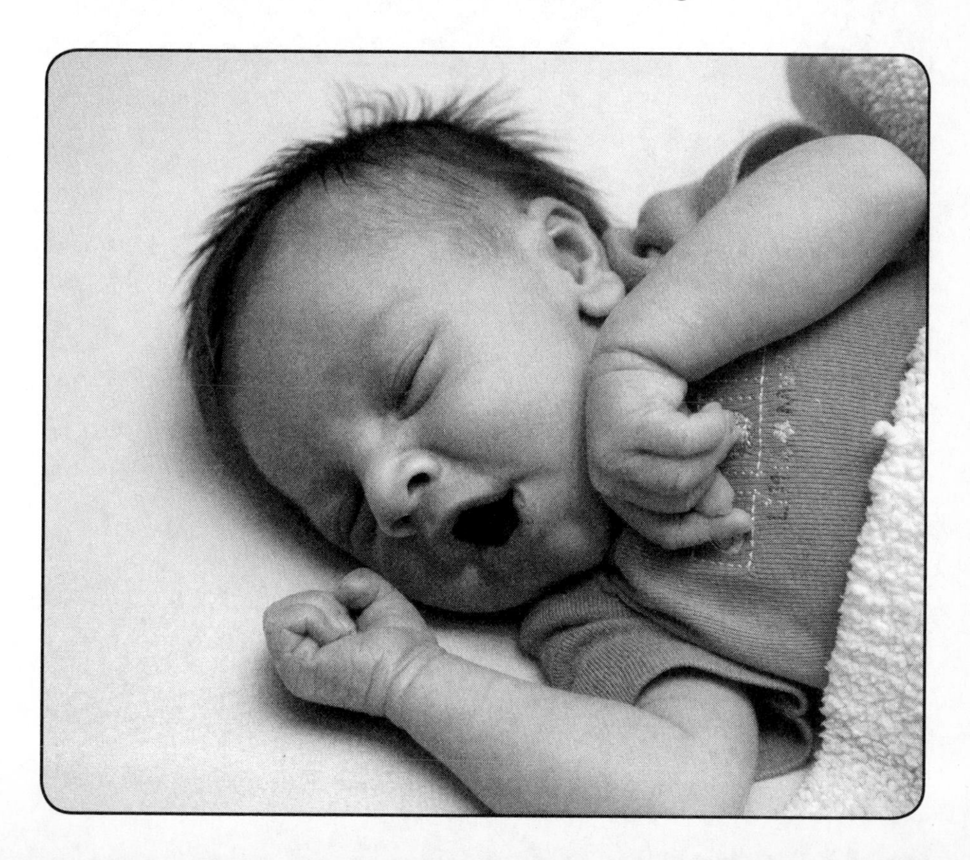

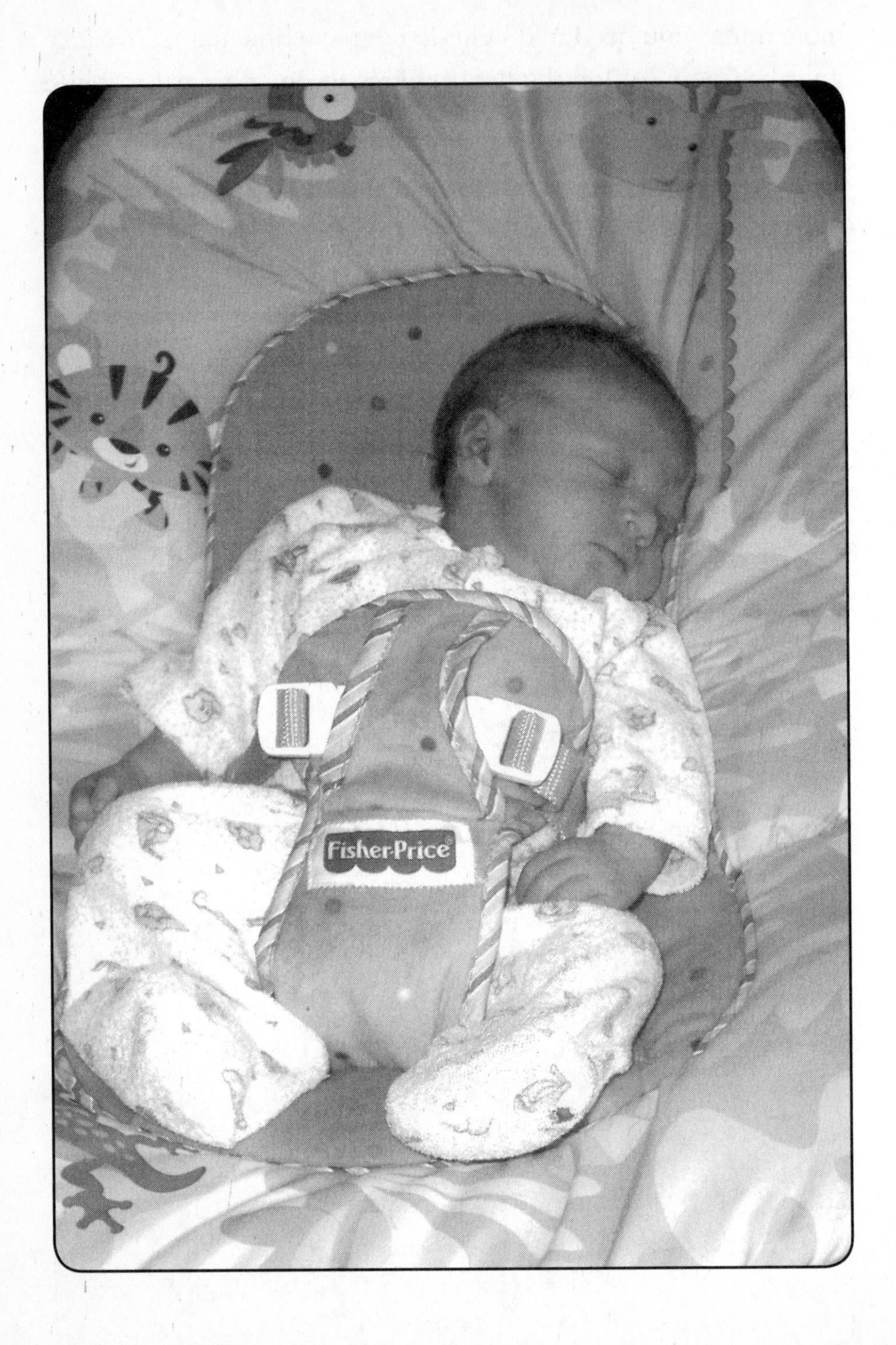
Fisher-Price

# chapter 12

## When All Else Fails

Sleep training your baby or child can feel like a never-ending nightmare. Sometimes nothing seems to work. Other times, certain strategies work for a night or two, but your baby soon reverts to screaming throughout the night. While you are trying to be patient and understanding, sometime sleep training can seem to be more than you can take. This chapter will give you some final tips to get you through those rough times during training.

### • TIP #98 •

### Take a Break

When your frustration level rises and your sleep deprivation has you falling asleep at your desk or while drinking coffee driving to work, stop training and get some rest. You are not giving up on training; you are just taking a well-needed break.

You might decide to let your baby sleep in your bed for a night or two until you can catch up on sleep. You might decide to take a night off, put your baby in her crib, and wear earplugs while your partner continues training your baby.

When you feel you are at your wits' end, do not continue to push yourself past your limits. If your baby has not been sleeping well for weeks or months, another night or another few nights will not dramatically affect her sleep training long term. Take care of yourself and your own well-being so that you can approach sleep training with a clear head and a positive attitude.

# • TIP #99 •

## Do Not Play the Blame Game

If you have tried everything and nothing seems to be working, avoid the temptation to blame someone. Do not point the finger at your partner for being inconsistent with training, or at your mother for not maintaining your training schedule when she babysits.

Do not blame your baby for being a "bad" child or "bad" sleeper. Pointing the finger will only serve to add to current tensions, which will make sleep training even harder. Remember to create a united front with your partner, and be sure you are both working together to train your baby to sleep well.

Do not blame yourself, either. If you are having difficulty getting your baby to sleep through the night, it does not mean you are a bad parent. In fact, you could do everything right and try every tip in this book and still experience issues with getting your baby to sleep. Take heart in knowing it is not your fault.

# • TIP #100 •

## Remind Yourself that Sleep Training is Worth the Effort

Imagine the day when your whole family is sleeping well throughout the night, bedtime is a peaceful time of sharing stories and cuddle time, and naps are a breeze. Your baby is happy throughout the day and enjoys playtime, naptime, and bedtime equally.

That day is not far away and is attainable. While the training can be hard, the reward will be worth it.

# • TIP #101 •

## Get More Help

If you have tried the last 100 tips consistently and nothing has worked, then it might be time to look elsewhere for answers. Although this book has offered many different tips from experts across the field, not all answers will work for all babies or families. If you just cannot seem to find the answer to your baby's sleep issues, it is time to seek the advice of another. Sometimes the answers are just too hard to see when you are faced with the issue each day. Outside assistance might be needed to shed light on the best methods to solve those issues.

Remember that all babies cry. All babies face challenges with learning new skills, and sleeping well is a skill babies must learn. Find hope in knowing there are countless experts, Web sites, doctors, psychologists, and organizations to help you. If knowing that does not offer hope, remember this: Everything your child does is temporary. Once your child grows up, you will most likely be dragging him out of bed to go to school in the morning. While it might seem like you have not slept in weeks – and perhaps you really have not– you soon will be sleeping well, and this phase will only be a faint memory.

Do not give up on your child or doom yourself and them by saying your baby is just a "bad" sleeper. Find help from someone who can evaluate your baby and your family's individual needs and issues, and can work with you to help solve them.

Remember that healthy sleep is vital to a happy and healthy life for you and your child. Make good sleep a priority for your family, and work to solve any outstanding sleep issues you or your child still has.

When you need to find more help for sleep training your baby, first be sure you are well rested enough to find it. If you have been solely in charge of sleep training your baby, ask your partner to take over for a night or two while you get some rest. You might be able to ask a trusted friend or relative to take over nighttime duties while both you and your partner get some well-deserved sleep. Make sure you are taking care of yourself and are ready to receive help before you ask for it.

Ask your child's pediatrician if he or she has advice or can refer you to a sleep specialist. Check out area sleep coaches. Many of these coaches will come to your house to evaluate your individual situation. Some offer phone consultations to help answer questions regarding your child's sleep. Other coaches will spend one to several nights at your house, guiding you step by step through your sleep program.

Interview these sleep coaches before you hire one to be sure their philosophies on sleep training are consistent with your parenting philosophies. Some coaches design individual programs based on each family's issues and goals for sleep.

Join a parent group that might be able to offer advice or even just sympathy while you are trying to sleep train your baby. Your frustration might be built up because you have not had a sounding board to let off your steam. A group of other parents might be just what your need to get through this rough patch, regroup, and continue a sleep training program for your baby.

Helpful resources are everywhere. Be sure to use the resources you have most readily at your side, such as your partner, other family members, or close friends.

*Appendix B lists biographies and contact information for the experts whose responses were listed in this book. If a particular expert matches your beliefs, contact him or her with more specific questions or referrals to sleep experts in your area. See Appendix C for a list of additional resources, including helpful Web sites and organizations.*

## CASE STUDY: WORD FROM THE EXPERTS: TIRED, FRUSTRATED PARENTS WHO NEED HELP FAST

"Parents should either accept their situation or ask for help. Some organizations will offer nighttime assistance to parents who are at their wits end and need a good night's sleep. This period does not last forever. Sleeplessness is an occupational hazard of parenting."

**– Judy Arnall, co-founder of Parenting Canada; owner of Professional Parenting Canada**

Dehn tells parents any quick fix strategies should be decided on during the day with both parents thinking coherently and rationally. "Parents must be committed to sticking to the plan, and most plans — if followed religiously — will only take a week to start being effective."

**– Barb Dehn, RN, MS, NP**

"The quickest method for getting a baby to sleep through the night is to let him cry it out. This method is also the most uncomfortable for the parents. Most importantly, parents must be proactive and have a plan ahead of time. It is also important that both parents are comfortable with their decision and in agreement so that the strategy they employ does not cause stress to their marriage."

**– Bette Levy Alkazian, MA, licensed marriage and family therapist**

Kerr recommends frustrated parents read Healthy Sleep Habits, Happy Child by Marc Weissbluth. Fox agrees with the book's recommendations and suggests another tip: "If worse comes to worst, the tougher parent should enforce the cry-it-out method while the other parent wears earplugs.

**– Baby Bunching experts Linda Kerr and Cara Fox**

Pollak advises parents to pay attention to their baby's sleep cues, learn to anticipate their baby's sleep needs and issues (instead of merely reacting to them), be purposeful about the sleep process, establish quality sleep routines and, of course, be consistent.

**– Karen Pollak, founder, Babies2Sleep**

"If parents want to get more sleep without the baby crying, they should bring him into their bed. If your goal is to teach your baby to learn to fall asleep on his own, you should pick a sleep method and be consistent. The reason parents have trouble getting a baby to sleep is often because the parents are not following through with their chosen method. If parents have chosen the crying-it-out method, they must stick to it every night. If parents pat their baby to get him to fall asleep, they must refrain from picking him up on occasion. Consistency is the key. If parents' only concern is a good night's sleep, bringing their baby into the bed with them is the easiest and quickest way."

**– Claudia Heilbrunn, parenting expert, author, and certified life coach**

"When desperation and frustration have reached a boiling point, sometimes parents are advised to just give in to the child's needs or demands for a few nights. This allows the parents to rejuvenate and then be able to better withstand the transient sleep deprivation that will occur with enforcing bedtime rules."

**– Nadav Traeger, MD, FAAP, FCCP, D, ABSM, director of pediatric sleep medicine, Maria Fareri Children's Hospital**

Dr. Kuhn said it depends on what habits a parent is trying to correct, but he suggests that the quickest method to get a baby to sleep through the night is the crying-it-out method. "Changing the dynamic by switching parents can sometimes be enough to get a child broken from a bad habit quickly."

**– Dr. Brett Kuhn, CBSM, associate professor of pediatrics at the University of Nebraska Medical Center and Children's Sleep Center at Children's Hospital**

"Parents should know ahead of time that it will take a week or two to change bad sleep habits of their baby. Sleep is primarily an aspect of temperament and is not likely a disorder, just a part of who your baby is."

**– Dr. Laura Davies, diplomate, American Board of Psychiatry and Neurology**

"Unless the baby has reached a new stage of development or the baby has an easy, adaptable temperament, there is nothing parents can do. Parents can spell each other off, whereby Dad takes one feeding and Mom another. The best thing for tired moms is for them to nap during the day as needed."

**– Helen Neville, BS, RN, author, pediatric advice nurse, health educator, specialist in inborn temperament, and researcher**

*Photo courtesy of Sivan Grosman, founder of Sivan Photography (**http://sivanphotography.com**)*

# conclusion

When trying to function on a few hours of sleep, issues can seem more catastrophic than they really are. Parents need an adequate amount of sleep in order to handle even the most basic of tasks during the day. The stress of returning to work, handling family finances, or managing the schedules of older children can be compounded when your head is blurry from exhaustion. Getting a full night of sleep is not only necessary for your baby to function well throughout the day, but it is necessary for you, your partner, and other children as well.

If you have diligently tried to implement the strategies listed in this book and have yet to get a full night of sleep, give in to your child's requests long enough to sleep well and then try the strategies over again. Take a break. Perhaps your baby is not ready for a regimented sleep routine. Take a few weeks off sleep training and start again next month. If you are trying to sleep train during an already stressful time, such as during a move, over the holidays, or when you are sending other children back to school, consider delaying the training until your life has calmed down a bit. Handling sleep training during an already-stressful time will likely not work. You will likely be unable to consistently implement your strategies, and your efforts will be for nothing.

When you feel as if you might never sleep well again, remember: Children are constantly changing. What did not work this month might work well next month. This will not last forever; give it time. Soon, your baby will be a teenager, and you will miss the time you spent rocking her to sleep each night and long for the situation you are currently in.

## CASE STUDY: WORD FROM THE EXPERTS: LAST RESORT

When parents have tried everything and nothing has worked, Arnall said, "Parents should scream, yell, and express their feelings fully — not in front of children, of course. Once all those emotions are out, parents should focus on problem solving to find a solution that will help the baby, and them, sleep through the night."

**– Judy Arnall, co-founder of Parenting Canada; owner of Professional Parenting Canada**

"Parents should seek help from a sleep consultant, pediatrician, or parent coach when they feel they are at their wits' end. An expert may be able to examine their baby's current sleep routine and make suggestions for improving it. Sometimes, holding a baby or deciding to let the baby cry it out are the only ways to get a baby back to sleep. If a child's behavior is not normal, parents should realize that he may be coming down with a cold or ear infection that will not be noticeable for a day or two after the fussiness starts. A little love can go a long way. There should be intention and commitment commitment in the strategies parents choose to get their baby to sleep through the night." She advises against techniques of desperation. She believes that desperation techniques can lead to bad habits being developed. She also cautions against parents changing strategies during a desperate moment.

**– Bette Levy Alkazian, MA, licensed marriage and family therapist**

"Parents should put themselves in their baby's shoes and try to understand what is causing the problem. Parents who really understand their baby's developmental stage, temperament, stress level, and sensitivity level will probably find the key to help their baby fall asleep."

**– Claudia Heilbrunn, parenting expert, author, and certified life coach**

Smith feels that something is out there that will work for every child. "It just depends on if parents give it time and truly stick to it."

**– Stephanie Smith, mother of twins**

"When parents have read 'every book' and 'done everything,' they usually are missing some simple key step in the process." Traeger's best advice to parents is for them to go back to the basics. He also advises parents speak to their physician to ensure that the problem is just behavioral and not due to a medical condition."

**– Nadav Traeger, MD, FAAP, FCCP, D, ABSM, director of pediatric sleep medicine, Maria Fareri Children's Hospital**

"If parents feel they have tried everything and nothing is working, they should get help. Consistent, effective intervention usually produces results within three days to one week. The younger the age of the child, the more effective interventions seem to be. Parents should enlist the help of a pediatric sleep specialist with years of experience dealing with multiple children. These specialists have a large 'toolbox' to work with and can match treatments to a specific family and specific child."

**– Dr. Brett Kuhn, CBSM, associate professor of pediatrics at the University of Nebraska Medical Center and Children's Sleep Center at Children's Hospital**

When all else seems to fail, Neville advises parents call on relatives and friends so parents can get some time off to sleep. "If needed, parents can even hire a sitter so that they can catch up on some sleep on the weekend."

**– Helen Neville, BS, RN, author, pediatric advice nurse, health educator, specialist in inborn temperament, and researcher**

*Photo courtesy of Sivan Grosman, founder of Sivan Photography (**http://sivanphotography.com**)*

# appendix a

## Checklists, Sleep Logs, and Charts

## Average Sleep Needs of Babies and Toddlers

| AGE | TOTAL HOURS OF SLEEP | HOURS OF DAYTIME SLEEP | NUMBER OF NAPS | HOURS OF NIGHTTIME SLEEP |
|---|---|---|---|---|
| Newborn | 16 | No distinct pattern | 7 periods of sleep within 24 hours | No distinct pattern |
| 1 month | 15-16 | 8.5-10 | 3 | 6-7 |
| 3 months | 13-15 | 5-6 | 3 | 10-11 |
| 6 months | 11-15 | 2-4 | 2-3 | 9.25-12 |
| 9 months | 13-15 | 2-4 | 2 | 11-12 |
| 1 year | 12-15 | 1.5-3 | 1-2 | 9-12 |
| 1 year, 6 months | 12.5-14 | 1.5-3 | 1 | 11-11.25 |
| 2 years | 11-14 | 1-3 | 1 | 11-12 |
| 3 years | 11-14 | 0-2 | 0-2 | 10.5-12 |
| 4 years | 11-12 | 0-2 | 0-1 | 11-12 |
| 5 years | 11-12 | 0 | 0 | 11-12 |

***This chart was compiled from various sources. See the Bibliography for a complete list of sources.*

## Weekly Sleep Log

| DAY/DATE | BEDTIME ROUTINE (TIME, LENGTH, SEQUENCE) | WHERE, HOW, WHEN TO BED | NUMBER/ DURATION OF NIGHTTIME WAKINGS | NUMBER/ AMOUNT (OUNCES/ TIME) OF NIGHTTIME FEEDINGS | TOTAL NIGHT-TIME SLEEP (SUBTRACT TIME AWAKE DURING NIGHT) | OTHER NOTES |
|---|---|---|---|---|---|---|
| Monday ___/___/___ | | | | | | |
| Tuesday ___/___/___ | | | | | | |
| Wednesday ___/___/___ | | | | | | |
| Thursday ___/___/___ | | | | | | |
| Friday ___/___/___ | | | | | | |
| Saturday ___/___/___ | | | | | | |
| Sunday ___/___/___ | | | | | | |

# Weekly Daytime Sleep Log

| DAY/DATE | WAKE-UP TIME | FIRST NAPTIME, WHERE, HOW, WHEN, HOW | SECOND NAPTIME, WHERE, HOW, WHEN, HOW | THIRD NAPTIME, WHERE, HOW, WHEN, HOW | DAYTIME ACTIVITY LEVEL | TOTAL DAYTIME SLEEP (SUBTRACT TIME AWAKE DURING NIGHT) |
|---|---|---|---|---|---|---|
| Monday ___/____/____ | | | | | | |
| Tuesday ___/____/____ | | | | | | |
| Wednesday ___/____/____ | | | | | | |
| Thursday ___/____/____ | | | | | | |
| Friday ___/____/____ | | | | | | |
| Saturday ___/____/____ | | | | | | |
| Sunday ___/____/____ | | | | | | |

## Weekly Daytime Feeding Log

| DAY/DATE | WAKE-UP TIME | FIRST FEEDING TIME, WHERE, HOW, WHEN, HOW | SECOND FEEDING TIME, WHERE, HOW, WHEN, HOW | THIRD FEEDING TIME, WHERE, HOW, WHEN, HOW | FOURTH FEEDING TIME, WHERE, HOW, WHEN, HOW | TOTAL FEEDING AMOUNT IN 24-HOUR PERIOD (INCLUDE NIGHT FEEDINGS |
|---|---|---|---|---|---|---|
| Monday ___/___/___ | | | | | | |
| Tuesday ___/___/___ | | | | | | |
| Wednesday ___/___/___ | | | | | | |
| Thursday ___/___/___ | | | | | | |
| Friday ___/___/___ | | | | | | |
| Saturday ___/___/___ | | | | | | |
| Sunday ___/___/___ | | | | | | |

# Weekly Diaper Log

| DAY/DATE | FIRST CHANGING TIME, WHERE, HOW, WHEN, AMOUNT | SECOND CHANGING TIME, WHERE, HOW, WHEN, AMOUNT | THIRD CHANGING TIME, WHERE, HOW, WHEN, AMOUNT | FOURTH CHANGING TIME, WHERE, HOW, WHEN, AMOUNT | FIFTH CHANGING TIME, WHERE, HOW, WHEN, AMOUNT | SIXTH CHANGING TIME, WHERE, HOW, WHEN, AMOUNT |
|---|---|---|---|---|---|---|
| Monday ___/___/___ | | | | | | |
| Tuesday ___/___/___ | | | | | | |
| Wednesday ___/___/___ | | | | | | |
| Thursday ___/___/___ | | | | | | |
| Friday ___/___/___ | | | | | | |
| Saturday ___/___/___ | | | | | | |
| Sunday ___/___/___ | | | | | | |

# Setting the Mood Checklist

## Distracting environment

- ☐ Remove loud colors from walls, posters, mobiles, etc.
- ☐ Remove scary objects (large stuffed animals, etc.)
- ☐ Remove interesting items (aquariums, toys, other objects hanging above crib)

## Room/furniture

- ☐ Make sure room is not too noisy
- ☐ Make sure room and crib are safety-approved

## Bed/bedding

- ☐ SIDS-proof crib, mattress, and bedding
- ☐ Get rid of toys, pillows, or blankets in the crib

## Sound

- ☐ Remove all disrupting sounds, like mobiles or toys
- ☐ Do not place baby in noisiest room of the house
- ☐ Consider white-noise machine
- ☐ Consider playing soft, calming music or soothing sounds

## Sleepwear

- ☐ Ensure sleepwear keeps baby warm but not hot
- ☐ Avoid loose sleepwear baby could get tangled in or suffocate on
- ☐ Ensure sleepwear is safety-approved and flame-resistant
- ☐ Never put hat on baby when in bed

## Pacifiers

- ☐ If breastfeeding, wait one month to introduce pacifiers
- ☐ Consider pacifier use to help prevent SIDS (only when baby is falling asleep)
- ☐ Do not attach pacifiers to baby or crib
- ☐ Sprinkle pacifiers around crib so baby can find one at night
- ☐ Do not reinsert pacifiers during the night

## Bedtime story

- ☐ Pick stories that are quiet and soothing
- ☐ Limit stories to a predetermined amount as part of a bedtime routine

## Lighting

- ☐ Keep room dark (an eight or nine on a scale of one to ten)
- ☐ Babies do not need nightlights, but toddlers might (if scared of the dark)

## Temperature

- ☐ Keep the room between 68 and 72 degrees Fahrenheit
- ☐ Do not place space heaters in your baby's room
- ☐ Check baby's temperature during the night by placing hand behind baby's neck or on tummy; overheating is linked to SIDS

## Smell

- ☐ Consider smell of room (should be fresh, not musty)
- ☐ Ensure there is good ventilation and air circulation

- ☐ Consider aromatherapy as a soothing sleep association
- ☐ Remember that your baby's sense of smell is more sensitive than yours

## Position

- ☐ Always place your baby on back to sleep, even for naps

*Photo courtesy of Sivan Grosman, founder of Sivan Photography (**http://sivanphotography.com**)*

# appendix b

Expert Biographies and Contact Information

## Bette Levy Alkazian, MA

**Licensed Marriage and Family Therapist, Parent Educator, Parenting Coach**
**805-230-2464**
**bette@balancedparenting.com**
**www.balancedparenting.com**

Bette Levy Alkazian, a licensed marriage and family therapist and parent and family coach, works with families to ease the challenges of raising children. Alkazian has also worked for many years as a parent educator and lecturer. Through her private coaching practice — Balanced Parenting — Alkazian provides tools and insights to help families achieve, restore, and maintain balance at home. Alkazian has been married to her husband Jeff for 23 years, and they are the parents of three daughters, ages 8 to 17.

## Judy Arnall, BA

**Speaker, Author, Parent Educator and Curriculum Developer**
**Co-Founder, Attachment Parenting Canada**
**Owner, Professional Parenting Canada**
**403-714-6766**
**jarnall@shaw.ca**
**www.judyarnall.wordpress.com**

Judy Arnall is an award-winning international speaker and a presenter of seminars on various parenting topics. She is a professional member of The Canadian Association of Professional Speakers. A well-known Canadian expert on parenting, she has given advice for television interviews on Global TV, Shaw TV, CTV, and national magazines such as *Chatelaine, Today's Parent, Canadian Living, Globe and Mail Newspaper, Natural Parenting, ParentsCanada,* and *Canadian Family Magazine*. She is a regular contributor to Calgary's *Child Magazine* for the past 12 years and a regular guest on Global TV for the past five years.

Her background includes a Bachelor of Arts degree and an Advanced Toastmaster Silver Speaker Award. She has been employed by Calgary Health Region, Perinatal Education for the past eight years and Families Matter Society for the past ten years. Judy has delivered hundreds of quality parent education sessions to thousands of parents in schools, libraries, corporate workplaces, and social agencies. She teaches parent effectiveness training (PET) at The University of Calgary, Continuing Education and speaks for

LifeSpeak Inc. as well as Women's Health Resources and Southern Alberta Child and Youth Health Network. An authorized facilitator of the PET series, Arnall has helped develop and present the Alberta-wide Terrific Toddlers five-week course curriculum with Families Matter and Calgary Health Region's Three Cheers for the Early Years Program.

Arnall is author of *Discipline Without Distress: 135 Tools for Raising Caring, Responsible Children Without Time-Out, Spanking, Punishment or Bribery*. She has also written many articles on parenting, published in various newspapers, magazines, and periodicals. She is a discipline and behavior expert at *Mothering Magazine Online*. Having read 356 parenting books to date, and combined with her experience volunteering on the city-wide crisis telephone lines for 13 years, Arnall has a broad understanding of the issues facing parents, families, and relationships in the new millennium. She is a believer in helping parents make informed decisions based on valid, evidence-based parenting information. She lives in Calgary, Alberta, Canada, with her husband and five children.

## Laura Davies, MD

**Diplomate, American Board of Psychiatry and Neurology, with Subspecialty Certification in Child and Adolescent Psychiatry**
**415-425-6156**
**2266 Union Street**
**San Francisco, CA 94123**

Dr. Davies attended Princeton University in 1992 and University of Southern California in 1997. She conducted her residency and fellowship at University of California, San Francisco. She is bilingual in Spanish. She is also the mother of a 9-year-old who still occasionally has trouble falling asleep.

## Barbara Dehn, RN, MS, NP

**Blue Orchid Press, LLC**
**1780 Austin Avenue**
**Los Altos, CA 94024**
**650-823-3764**
**Barb@NurseBarb.com**
**www.NurseBarb.com**

Blue Orchid Press®

Barbara Dehn graduated from the University of California, San Francisco with a Master of Science degree and as a women's health nurse practitioner. She earned her Bachelor of Science in Nursing from Boston College in Chestnut Hill, Massachusetts. Currently a nurse practitioner at the Women Physicians OB/GYN Medical group in Mount View, California, Barb is also the founder and CEO of Blue Orchid Press, a provider of innovative women's health guides. These were developed to help women navigate important transitions in their lives. Her personal guides to health are used by over 3 million women in the United States and include subjects such as pregnancy, breastfeeding, fertility, and menopause. Dehn is a national speaker and serves as a consultant and on advisory boards for several pharmaceutical and biomedical companies. She is a popular lecturer at Stanford and San Jose State.

An accomplished and in-demand national speaker for consumers and professional groups on the complete range of women's health topics, she has made numerous appearances on local and national television, including NBC's *In the Loop* and ABC's *Good Morning America Now.* Dehn is a regular contributing health expert on ABC's *View from the Bay* in San Francisco. Her online blog, Barb's Daily Dose (**www.NurseBarb.com**), contains up-to-date health information. She writes a regular column for The Cradle.com and contributes to various magazines and newspapers. Dehn is a member of the American Academy of Nurse Practitioners, the California Association of Nurse Practitioners, and the North American Menopause Society. Barb received the Nurse Practitioner of Distinction award for California in March 2008. She also received an Inspiration in Women's Health Award and the Golden Lamp award for her positive portrayal of nurses in the media. Dehn lives in Northern California with her husband and son.

## Laura Lee Heinsohn

**Director of Family Bureau of Investigation Parenting Workshops (FBI Parent Workshops); One-on-One Parent Coach**
**www.familybureauofinvestigation.com**
**503-975-8179**
**lauraheinsohn@yahoo.com**

Laura Heinsohn, author of *Cracking the Parenting Code,* is the founder of Family Bureau of Investigation™ relationship workshops and is a one-on-one parenting coach. She has been married to her husband, Randy, for 29 years. They have two children, eight grandchildren, and have parented eight Brazilian exchange students. Heinsohn and her family call Oregon home.

## Claudia Heilbrunn

**Owner, Significant Self**
**212-222-4394**
**claudia@significantself.com**

Claudia Heilbrunn is a parenting expert, writer, and certified life coach for first-time mothers. She helps mothers who feel overwhelmed, frazzled, and confused become calm and confident mothers who make the right choices for both themselves and their child. Heilbrunn offers insights, tips, strategies, and consistent support to new mothers to increase their satisfaction, joy, and well-being day to day. She is the author of *My Significant Self,* a biweekly e-zine for first-time mothers, and the owner of Significant Self, a life coaching company that helps new mothers to hold on to themselves without shortchanging their children.

## Linda Kerr

**703-476-3953**
**www.babybunching.com**
**babybunching@gmail.com**

Linda Kerr, 33, has returned to the United States with her family after three years abroad (in Sweden and Qatar). She lives in northern Virginia with her husband and son and daughter, who were born 16 months apart. Kerr has a degree in journalism and worked in public relations for nine years, but took several years off while she followed her husband around the world as the wife of a former undercover CIA officer, now turned Senate adviser. Kerr has written for *Washington Parent* magazine. She has been part of playgroups with friends from Sweden, Norway, Brazil,

Scotland, Australia, England, Germany, Finland, and America, which has given her an interesting perspective on parenting. In her spare time, she blogs on her site, Monkey Business, as well as on DC Metro Moms.

## Cara Fox

**678-842-0052**
**www.babybunching.com**
**babybunching@gmail.com**

Cara Fox, 32, lives in Atlanta, Georgia, with her husband and three sons under the age of 4. In her former life, Cara saved the world as the administrator of a non-profit foster care organization. She now puts her degrees in social work and public administration to work on a daily basis as she navigates her baby bunch through the formative years. Fox blogs on her site The Fox Factor, on Deep South Moms, and on "Two Kids Two Close" for *Atlanta Parent Magazine*. In her "free" time, she has an active social calendar centered mostly around other mothers met through playgroups and play dates, and she nurses an addiction to volunteering. She claims that "this baby bunching thing" may be easier for her sometimes because she has a significant hearing loss, and without her hearing aids, she cannot hear the whining, fighting, and loud toys that drive most mothers to insanity.

## Brett R. Kuhn, Ph.D., CBSM

**Licensed Psychologist**

**Associate Professor, Pediatrics**

**University of Nebraska Medical Center**

**402-559-6408**

**brkuhn@unmc.edu**

Dr. Brett Kuhn is a licensed psychologist and associate professor of pediatrics at the University of Nebraska Medical Center (UNMC). He is certified in behavioral sleep medicine by the American Academy of Sleep Medicine, and recently joined the Children's Sleep Center at Children's Hospital in Omaha. He has published over 30 professional journal articles and book chapters on children's behavioral health issues, including sleep problems, elimination disorders, and child behavior problems. Dr. Kuhn co-authored *The Toddler Owner's Manual: Operating Instructions, Troubleshooting Tips, and Advice on System Maintenance*. Brett and his wife, Tami, have three children. And yes, he says, they all sleep just fine.

Sleep Disorders Center
IN AFFILIATION WITH UNIVERSITY OF
NEBRASKA MEDICAL CENTER

## Helen Neville, BS, RN

**Author, Pediatric Advice Nurse, Health Educator, Specialist in Inborn Temperament, and Researcher**

**510-654-2018**

**helenwork@sbcglobal.net**

Helen Neville is the parent of two adult children and grandparent of one child. She has worked at a large HMO in northern California for over 30 years as a pediatric advice nurse, health educator, specialist in inborn temperament, and researcher. She has authored numerous books and publications, including: *Is This a Phase? Child Development and Parent Strategies, Birth to 6 Years; ; Temperament Tools: Working with your Child's Inborn Traits;* and "No-Fault Parenting: 5-step problem-solving process and array of practical solutions to hundreds of daily issues with children under 6."

## Karen Pollak

**Founder, Babies2Sleep**
**P.O. Box 321, Danville, CA 94526**
**925-330-5660**
**www.babies2sleep.com**

babies2sleep®
Helping parents help their babies

Karen Pollak is a perinatal and parent educator and subject matter expert on infant and toddler sleep. For over ten years, she has mentored thousands of new and expectant parents and helped them thrive during this joyful but demanding time in their lives. Pollak's practical and effective solutions to day-to-day challenges have helped new mothers and fathers enhance the quality of their family life and establish positive relationships with their young children. In addition to operating Babies2Sleep, Pollak is the founder of DoubleTalk, which offers highly acclaimed education and support programs for new parents of twins. DoubleTalk has achieved the highly coveted five-star rating by the Lila Guide and Babies by the Bay. Pollak and her family live in the San Francisco Bay area. She is the mother of three sons, including fraternal twins.

## Stephanie Smith

**Mother of twins**

**ssmith@fortosage.net**

Stephanie Smith is a full-time working mother of 2-year-old twin girls who have successfully slept through the night since 3 months old. She and her husband, Stacey, have been married five years.

## Nadav Traeger, MD, FAAP, FCCP, D, ABSM

**Director, Pediatric Sleep Medicine at the Maria Fareri Children's Hospital at Westchester Medical Center and New York Medical College**

**Board-certified by the American Board of Sleep Medicine and by the American Academy of Pediatrics, Subboard of Sleep Medicine.**

**Children's and Women's Physicians of Westchester, LLP**

**New York Medical College**
**Munger Pavilion, Room 106**
**Valhalla, NY 10595**
**914-493-7585**

Dr. Traeger is 36 years old and married with two children. Currently living in New York, he attended the Albert Einstein College of Medicine. Dr. Traeger trained in Pediatrics at Montefiore Medical Center and in Pediatric Pulmonology and Sleep Medicine at the Children's Hospital of Philadelphia. He has been working in Westchester, New York, since 2004.

# appendix c

## Additional Resources

## Books on Babies

*The Baby Book*, by William Sears, M.D. and Martha Sears, R.N.

*Attachment Parenting*, by Katie Allison Granju, William Sears, and Betsy Kennedy

*Your Baby and Child: From Birth to Age Five*, by Penelope Leach

*What to Expect the First Year*, by Heidi Murkoff, Sandee Hathawayand, B.S.N., Arlene Esenberg, and Sharon Mazel

*Secrets of the Baby Whisperer: How to Calm, Connect, and Communicate with Your Baby* by Tracy Hogg and Melinda Blau

*Baby's Eat, Sleep & Poop Journal, Log Book* by Sandra Kosak

*Itsy Bitsy Yoga: Poses to Help Your Baby Sleep Longer, Digest Better, and Grow Stronger* by Helen Garabedian

*Baby Om: Yoga for Mothers and Babies* by Laura Staton and Sarah Perron

*Yoga Baby : Exercises to Help You Bond With Your Baby Physically, Emotionally and Spiritually* by DeAnsin Goodson Parker, Ph.D., and Karen W. Bressler

*The Baby Owner's Manual: Operating Instructions, Trouble-Shooting Tips, and Advice on First-Year Maintenance* by Louis Borgenicht, Joe Borgenicht, Paul Kepple, and Jude Buffum

*The Postnatal Exercise Book: A Six Month Fitness Programme for Mother and Baby* by Barbara Whiteford and Margie Polden

## Books on Adult Sleep

*The Promise of Sleep: A Pioneer in Sleep Medicine Explores the Vital Connection Between Health, Happiness, and a Good Night's Sleep* by Dr. William Dement and Christopher Vaughan

*The Harvard Medical School Guide to a Good Night's Sleep* by Lawrence Epstein and Steven Mardon

*Say Good Night to Insomnia: The Six-Week, Drug-Free Program Developed at Harvard Medical School* by Gregg D. Jacobs and Herbert Benson

*Power Sleep: The Revolutionary Program That Prepares Your Mind for Peak Performance* by James B. Maas, Megan L. Wherry, David J. Axelrod, and Barbara R. Hogan

## Books on Baby/Toddler Sleep

*(See also Bibliography)*

*The Baby Sleep Book : The Complete Guide to a Good Night's Rest for the Whole Family* by William Sears, M.D., Martha Sears, R.N., Robert W. Sears, M.D.

*The 90-Minute Baby Sleep Program: Follow Your Child's Natural Sleep Rhythms for Better Nights and Naps* by Polly Moore

*The Happiest Baby on the Block: The New Way to Calm Crying and Help Your Newborn Baby Sleep Longer* by Harvey Karp

*On Becoming Baby Wise: Giving Your Infant the Gift of Nighttime Sleep* by Gary Ezzo and Robert Bucknam

*The Complete Idiot's Guide to Sleep Training your Child* by Ph.D., Melissa Burnham and Jennifer Lawler

*The No-Cry Sleep Solution for Toddlers and Preschoolers: Gentle Ways to Stop Bedtime Battles and Improve Your Child's Sleep* by Elizabeth Pantley

*Sleeping Through the Night, Revised Edition: How Infants, Toddlers, and Their Parents Can Get a Good Night's Sleep* by Jodi A. Mindell

*The Lull-A-Baby Sleep Plan: The Soothing, Superfast Way to Help Your New Baby Sleep Through the Night...and Prevent Sleep Problems Before They Develop* by Cathryn Tobin

*52 Sleep Secrets for Babies* by Kim West

## Books on Co-Sleeping

*Sleeping with Your Baby: A Parent's Guide to Cosleeping* by James J. McKenna

*Break the Co-Sleeping Habit: How to Set Bedtime Boundaries - and Raise a Secure, Happy, Well-Adjusted Child* by Valerie Levine

*Good Nights: The Happy Parents' Guide to the Family Bed (and a Peaceful Night's Sleep!)* by Maria Goodavage and Jay Gordon

*The Attachment Parenting Book: A Commonsense Guide to Understanding and Nurturing Your Baby* by William Sears and Martha Sears

*It's Time to Sleep in Your Own Bed (Transition Times)* by Lawrence E. Shapiro and Hideko Takahashi

## Web Sites

### Crib safety tips

**www.cpsc.gov/CPSCPUB/PUBS/5030.html**

**http://www.healthychildren.org/english/search/pages/results.aspx?Type=Keyword&Keyword=Crib+safetywww.drspock.com/article/0,1510,5226,00.html**

**www.babycenter.com/0_how-to-buy-a-crib_432.bc**

**www.consumerreports.org/cro/babies-kids/resource-center/guide-to-childproofing-and-safety/crib-safety-tips/crib-safety-tips.htm**

**http://babyparenting.about.com/cs/preparinghome/a/safecrib.htm**

## Baby sleep tips

www.babycenter.com/baby-sleep-basics

www.askdrsears.com/html/7/T070100.asp

www.mayoclinic.com/health/baby-sleep/FL00118

www.time.com/time/health/article/0,8599,1728755,00.html

www.helpingyourbabysleep.com

www.theparentreport.com/resources/ages/infant/sleep/76.html

http://kidshealth.org/parent/growth/sleep/sleepnewborn.html

## Baby exercise tips

www.baby-place.com/services/fitness.htm

www.self.com/fitness/blogs/freshfitnesstips/2008/11/baby-and-me-workout.html

www.bellaonline.com/articles/art9571.asp

## Adult sleep tips

www.sleepnet.com/proff.htm

www.nlm.nih.gov/medlineplus/sleepdisorders.html

www.talkaboutsleep.com

## Sleep logs *(Free or available to purchase)*

www.forgetmenottots.com (available to purchase)

www.babycenter.com/0_how-to-track-your-babys-sleeping-patterns_7643.bc

## Mommy and baby exercise

www.dswfitness.com/docs/Mom&BabyExercise.pdf

www.babycenter.com/404_are-baby-exercise-classes-a-good-way-to-help-my-child-develo_6870.bc

www.babycenter.com/0_how-to-exercise-with-a-baby-in-tow-products-that-help_1453205.bc

www.babycenter.com/0_how-to-exercise-with-a-baby-in-tow-products-that-help_1453205.bc

## Aromatherapy for babies

www.aromababy.com

www.aromathyme.com/kids.html

www.babyaromatherapy.com

www.babyblossoms.com

## Baby massage and safe lotions

http://parenting.ivillage.com/newborn/ncare/0,,lz_76tp,00.html

www.infantmassageusa.org

www.babymassage.com

www.lovingtouch.com

www.thedailygreen.com/living-green/blogs/organic-parenting/safe-baby-lotion-alternatives-55030601

## Co-sleeping

www.cosleeping.org

http://kidshealth.org/parent/general/sleep/cosleeping.html

**www.breastfeeding.com/reading_room/co_slepping.html**

**http://babyreference.com/Cosleeping&SIDSFactSheet.htm**

### Breastfeeding

**www.breastfeeding.com**

**www.womenshealth.gov/breastfeeding**

**www.cdc.gov/breastfeeding**

**www.llli.org**

## Helpful Organizations

American Academy of Pediatrics: **www.aap.org**

American Academy of Sleep Medicine: **www.aasmnet.org**

American Association of Sleep Technologists: **www.aastweb.org**

Better Sleep Council: **www.bettersleep.org**

National Center of Sleep Disorders Research (NCSDR): **www.nhlbi.nih.gov/about/ncsdr/index.htm**

National Institute of Child Health and Human Development: **www.nichd.nih.gov**

National Sleep Foundation: **www.sleepfoundation.org**

Sleep Research Society: **www.sleepresearchsociety.org**

### Disorders

American Sleep Apnea Association: **www.sleepapnea.org**

Narcolepsy Network, Inc.: **www.narcolepsynetwork.org**

### Baby sleep organizations

First Candle/SIDS Alliance: **www.sidsalliance.org**

National Sudden and Unexpected Infant/Child Death and Pregnancy Loss Resource Center: **www.sidscenter.org**

American SIDS Institute: **www.sids.org**

SIDS Mid-Atlantic: **www.sidsma.org**

## Other SIDS Web Sites/Articles

SIDS Network: **http://sids-network.org**

KidsHealth's site on SIDS: **http://kidshealth.org/parent/general/sleep/sids.html**

BabyCenter's site on reducing the risk of SIDS: **www.babycenter.com/0_reducing-the-risk-of-sids_419.bc**

National Institute of Child Health and Human Development's site on their "Back to Sleep" Campaign: **www.nichd.nih.gov/sids/sids.cfm**

SIDS Families: A site dedicated to families who have lost children due to SIDS: **www.sidsfamilies.com**

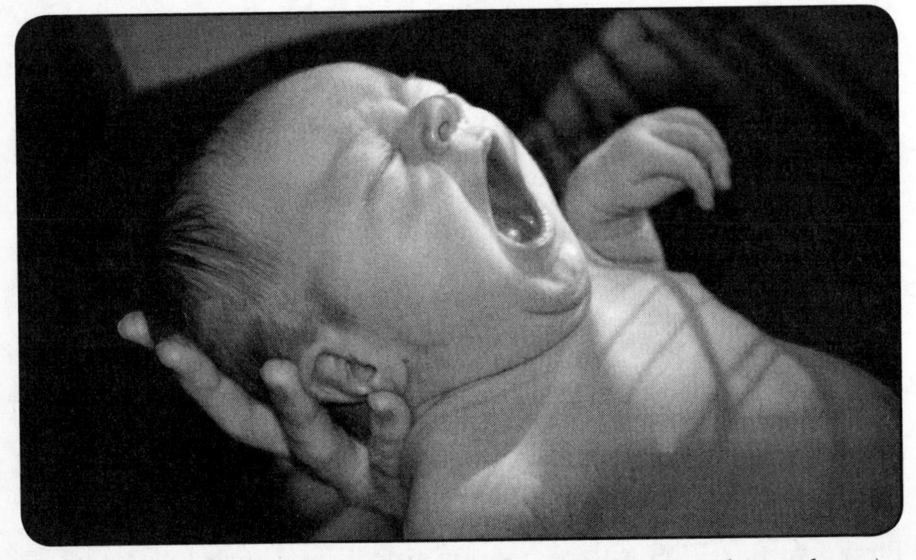

*Photo courtesy of Sivan Grosman, founder of Sivan Photography (**http://sivanphotography.com**)*

# bibliography

## Books

Douglas, Ann, *Sleep Solutions for Your Baby, Toddler, and Preschooler*, Wiley, Mississauga, Ontario, 2006.

Ferber M.D., Richard, *Solve Your Child's Sleep Problems*, Simon & Schuster, New York, NY, 2006.

Giordano, Suzy and Lisa Abidin, *The Baby Sleep Solution: A Proven Program to Teach Your Baby to Sleep Twelve House a Night*, The Penguin Group, New York, NY, 2006.

Pantley, Elizabeth, *The No-cry Sleep Solution: Gentle Ways to Help Your Baby Sleep Through the Night*, McGraw-Hill, New York, NY, 2002.

Waldburger LCSW, Jennifer and Jill Spivack, LMSW, *The Sleepeasy Solution: The Exhausted Parent's Guide to Getting Your Child to Sleep – from Birth to Age 5*, Health Communications, Inc., 2007.

Weissbluth M.D., Marc, *Healthy Sleep Habits, Happy Child*, Ballantine Books, New York, 2003.

West, Kim and Joanne Kenen, *Good Night, Sleep Tight: The Sleep Lady®'s Gentle Guide to Helping Your Child Go to Sleep*, Stay Asleep, and Wake up Happy, Vanguard Press, New York, NY, 2006.

## Articles

Spencer, Paula, "And to All a Good Night!," *Parenting*, September 2008.

## Web sites

**www.parents.com/sleep/issues**

**www.mayoclinic.com/healthy/baby-sleep/FL00118**

**www.babycenter.com/au/baby/sleep/sleepallnight**

**www.mindspring.com/~drwarren/sleep.htm**

**www.babycenter.com/0_how-much-sleep-does-your-child-need_7645.bc**

**http://stress.about.com/od/stresshealth/a/caffeine.htm**

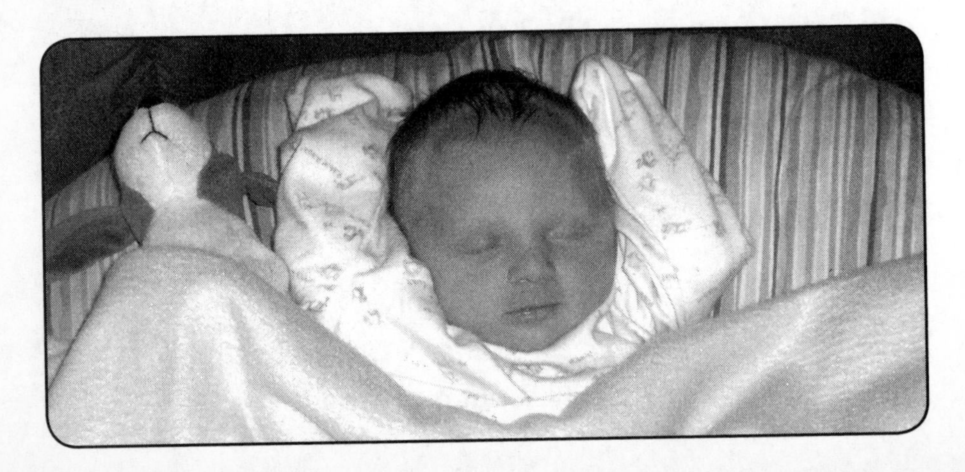

# biography

Jessica Linnell

Author Jessica Linnell is writer and editor living in the metro Atlanta area with her lab mix, Monte. Her first book, *Off to College: Now What? A Practical Guide to Surviving and Succeeding Your First Year of College,* also published by Atlantic Publishing Group, Inc., was released in early 2009. Her previous works have been published in *Atlanta* magazine, *Cherokee Living,* and other local and international trade publications. Throughout her career, Linnell has worked for newspapers, magazines, and corporations as a proposal writer and technical editor. She served ten years as a public health technician with the Air Force as active duty and in the National Guard. She earned a bachelor's degree in communications with a minor in English from Reinhardt College in Waleska, Georgia. When she is not writing or editing, she keeps busy with hiking, backpacking, skydiving, caving, and other adventures.

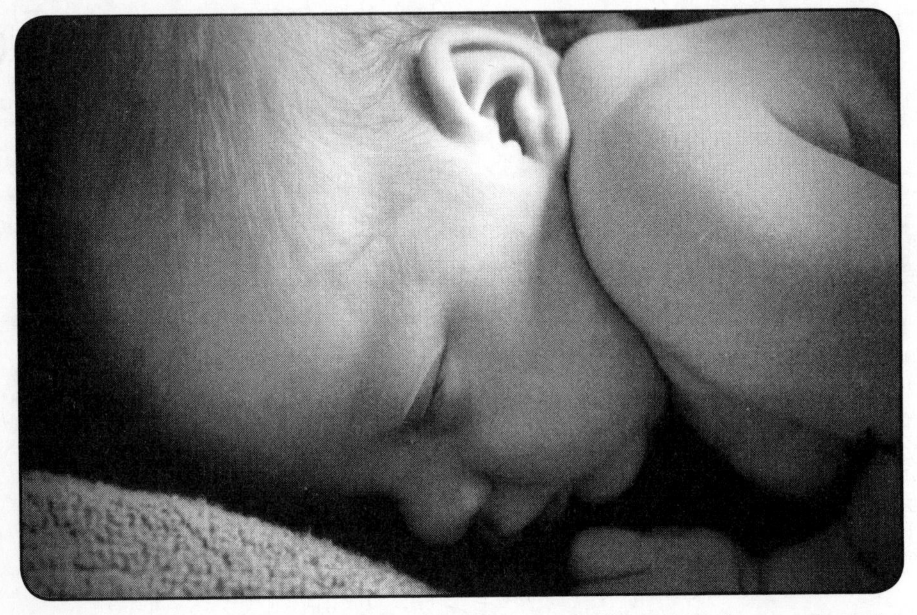

*Photo courtesy of Sivan Grosman, founder of Sivan Photography (**http://sivanphotography.com**)*

# index

## A

AAP, 279, 47-50, 75, 111, 136-137, 143

Allergies, 64-66, 156-157

American Academy of Pediatrics, 272, 279, 47

American Academy of Physical Medicine and Rehabilitation, 237

Aromatherapy, 262, 278, 142-143

## B

Bad habits, 40, 51, 63, 66-67, 74, 80, 118, 171, 178, 181, 183-185, 192, 253, 22

Bath, 40, 235, 52, 74, 103, 118, 152, 154, 156-159, 167-168

Bedding, 260, 48-49, 130, 132, 207, 215

Bedtime story, 261, 121, 139

Body rocking, 78

Bottle, 40, 223, 54, 64-65, 71, 74, 100, 131-132, 157-158, 183, 185

Breastfed, 32

Breastfeeding, 261, 266, 279, 32, 49, 240, 75, 98, 107, 110, 137, 146, 167, 172, 175, 177, 184

## C

Caffeine, 282, 238-239

Circadian rhythm, 26-27, 33, 36, 225, 233, 144, 165

Circadian rhythm, 26-27, 33, 36, 225, 233, 144, 165

Co-sleeping, 276, 278, 48-49, 101, 107-114, 157-158, 206-208, 219

Colic, 43, 64-65, 97, 161

Consumer Product Safety Commission, 130

CPSC, 276, 130

## D

Drowsy signs, 236, 100, 105, 160, 165, 194, 198, 204

## E

Environmental factors, 26, 36

Exercise, 274, 277-278, 233, 237-239, 182

Extinction method, 86

## F

Family bed, 276, 52, 107-114, 133, 210

Ferber method, 40, 86, 90-94, 96, 101-102, 104, 118, 177, 192

## G

Gastroesophageal reflux disorder, 65

## H

Head rolling, 78

Heavy sleeper, 216

## I

Illness, 36, 43, 223-224, 226, 228, 66, 80, 116

Inconsistency, 76, 118-119

## M

Mattress, 260, 48-49, 241, 65, 108, 110, 130, 132-133, 207

Mood, 260, 66, 127-128, 139, 147, 183

Multiple births, 203

## N

Naptime, 257, 41, 245, 92, 134, 141, 147, 162-166, 187-189, 191-198, 200-201, 212, 219

Narcolepsy, 280, 64, 66

National Sleep Foundation, 279, 38, 21

Newborn, 255, 275, 278, 26-28, 32, 37, 42, 56, 74-75, 100, 115, 143, 146, 176, 184, 215, 219

Nightlights, 261, 141, 148

Nighttime feedings, 256, 36-37, 41-42, 52, 98, 108, 110, 131, 146, 175-177, 183, 185

No-cry method, 118, 195

Non-REM sleep, 27

## O

Older siblings, 203, 212

## P

Pacifier, 261, 49, 64, 72, 81, 136-137, 159, 175, 183

Pajamas, 40, 235, 135-136, 152, 157-158, 168

Parent group, 247

Patient environment, 45

Potty training, 36, 222

Psychological disorders, 67

## R

REM sleep, 27

Rest time, 165, 198

Rhythmic behaviors, 78-79

Richard Ferber, 90

## S

Separation anxiety, 36, 44, 70-71, 89, 209-210

Separation anxiety, 36, 44, 70-71, 89, 209-210

Sibling bed, 206

Sickness, 228, 64

SIDS, 261, 280, 47-50, 65, 108, 111-112, 129, 132-133, 135-136, 142-144, 149, 206

Sleep associations, 57, 71, 90, 135, 172-173, 175-176, 189, 22

Sleep coach, 25, 102, 119, 146, 165

Sleep log, 256-257, 51-53, 56-58, 72, 90, 106, 116-117, 196

Sleep problems, 270, 275, 281, 63-64, 76, 90, 104, 23

Sleep sack, 135

Sleep tactics, 37, 39-40, 226, 176

Sleepless parents, 231

Sleepwear, 260, 49, 133, 135

Smell, 261-262, 83, 141-143

Snoring, 64-66

Space heaters, 261, 135, 142

Stalling tactics, 121, 169

Stimulation, 139, 147, 182

Stress, 282, 36, 43, 222, 228, 238, 248, 73, 78, 87, 93, 123-125, 137, 162, 206-207, 209, 251, 253

Sudden Infant Death Syndrome, 47

## T

Teething, 36, 44, 228-229, 59

Temperature, 261, 49, 241, 116, 132, 135-136, 141-142, 148-149, 183

Toddler, 270-271, 275, 281, 227, 102, 112, 147, 214, 216, 23

Tummy time, 49, 182

Twins, 271-272, 34, 40, 228, 60, 89, 113, 148, 159, 166, 184, 203-204, 209, 217-220, 253

## W

Wake-up time, 257-258, 161-162

Waking siblings, 215

White noise, 40, 233, 82-83, 102, 134-135, 141, 147, 159, 212, 216